The Vanguard Guide To

Investing During Retirement

The Vanguard Guide To

INVESTING DURING RETIREMENT

Managing Your Assets In Retirement

Second Edition

McGraw-Hill
New York San Francisco Washington, D.C. Auckland Bogotá
Caracas Lisbon London Madrid Mexico City Milan
Montreal New Delhi San Juan Singapore
Sydney Tokyo Toronto

McGraw-Hill

A Division of The **McGraw-Hill** *Companies*

1 2 3 4 5 6 7 8 9 0 VNH/VNH 9 0 2 1 0 9 8 7

ISBN 0-07-066892-2

The sponsoring editor for this book was Kevin Commins, the editing supervisor was Donna Namorato, and the production supervisor was Suzanne W. B. Rapcavage. It was set in Caslon 224 Book by Electronic Publishing Services, Inc.

Printed and bound by Von Hoffmann Press, Inc.

The previous edition of this book was published under the title *Investing During Retirement.*

This publication is designed to provide accurate and authoritative information in regard to the subject matter covered. It is sold with the understanding that neither the author nor the publisher is engaged in rendering legal, accounting, or other professional service. If legal advice or other expert assistance is required, the services of a competent professional person should be sought.

—From a Declaration of Principles jointly adopted by a Committee of the American Bar Association and a Committee of Publishers.

McGraw-Hill books are available at special quantity discounts to use as premiums and sales promotions, or for use in corporate training programs. For more information, please write to the Director of Special Sales, McGraw-Hill, 11 West 19th Street, New York, NY 10011. Or contact your local bookstore.

This book is printed on recycled, acid-free paper containing a minimum of 50% recycled de-inked fiber.

Preface

Investing well is important for everyone, but for some 30 million Americans who are retired or nearing retirement, the decisions they make about their investment dollars—how they are allocated, how they are spent, and how they are managed—will have important ramifications for the living standards they can maintain in the later years of their lives. For most retirees, generating current income from their investments is crucial to enjoying a comfortable and secure retirement. It makes the difference between "living well" and merely "getting by." Yet inflation and an increasing life span mean that retirees' investments also must continue to grow in value during at least part of their retirement if their resources are to stretch far enough. These critical issues must be faced against a backdrop of confusing and often conflicting information and media sound bites about the economy, the financial markets, and the Social Security system.

The task of preparing for retirement has received considerable attention over the past few years, sparking the creation of dozens of books, computer programs, and other sources of information. Unfortunately, as hard as it is to properly plan and invest *before* you retire, it may be even harder—and more stressful—*after* you retire. After all, during your working years, you can recover from an investment mistake by either saving more or working harder to earn more; however, once you have retired, both your ability to earn and your ability to save are sharply curtailed.

This guide recognizes the special needs and fears of the retired or nearly retired person and is designed to prepare retirees to make good decisions about their pensions, Social Security benefits, and the handling of their personal retirement savings and investments. The opening chapter begins with a broad overview of the challenges facing the retired person, including the effects of inflation, the increasing span of retirement, the need to supplement Social Security and pension income, and the importance of estate planning. Chapter 2 follows up with the most important question a prospective retiree must resolve: Can you afford to retire? This chapter should also be helpful to current retirees who are uncertain whether they have sufficient financial resources to last for the remainder of their retirement years. The chapter provides simple worksheets to help you decide how much of your savings or investments you can prudently spend each month.

Chapter 3 provides an overview of employer pensions, one leg of the traditional "three-legged stool" model for retirement income. For those not yet retired, the chapter provides guidance on whether to take your pension in the form of a lump-sum payout, regular monthly payments guaranteed for life, or some combination of the two. It also addresses the taxation of pension benefits and ends with a section on evaluating early-retirement offers, which have become prevalent in a downsizing corporate America.

Chapter 4 explores the basics of investing, discussing the three primary classes of financial assets—common stocks, bonds, and short-term reserves—and the historical returns and risks associated with each. Chapter 5 discusses the advantages and disadvantages of investing through mutual funds and provides basic explanations of the many types of mutual funds. In Chapter 6, you'll receive guidance on how to research and select mutual funds that fit your investment needs. This chapter also covers important tax issues for mutual fund investors.

Chapter 7 explores the myriad issues of asset allocation, the heart of successful investing. The chapter recommends portfolios that provide a balance between current income and growth in capital for various stages of retirement. It will help you to fine-tune a portfolio of stocks, bonds, and short-term reserves that meets your financial situation and temperament.

It provides guidance on adjusting your portfolio over time and on low-risk ways to increase the returns from your savings and investments.

Chapter 8 discusses how to draw down your accumulated savings and investments to provide income during retirement. This is the second leg of retirement's three-legged stool. You'll learn how to estimate a "safe" withdrawal rate that will provide the most income while minimizing your chances of running out of money. The chapter also covers the tax rules that apply to withdrawals received from your retirement savings plans.

Social Security, the foundation of the American retirement system and the third leg of the retirement-income model, is the primary topic of Chapter 9. The chapter discusses the financial viability of the Social Security system today, the rules governing Social Security benefits, and how these benefits are taxed. It will also help you decide whether to begin taking Social Security benefits immediately upon retirement or to delay receiving them. Because health care expenses are such a critical factor in the financial security of retirees, Chapter 9 also addresses Medicare, the national health-insurance program for those 65 and older. The chapter ends with an overview of insurance policies that supplement Medicare and insurance for nursing or home health care.

Many retirees fully expect to have assets left over after their death, assets that they will leave to their children or to religious or charitable institutions. Chapter 10 covers the estate planning process and offers guidance on how to bequeath your assets. It also suggests ways to minimize the taxation of your estate.

Finally, Chapter 11 touches on some of the special circumstances that confront many retirees. Among these are the selling of your home, what to do if your money is running short, the problems of divorce during retirement, investment considerations after the death of a spouse, and preparing for the possibility of mental or physical incapacity. The chapter concludes with a summary of the important action steps that investors should consider during their retirement.

At the end of the book, you'll find a glossary of important terms and appendixes with worksheets for preparing a budget, estimating the amount you can withdraw from your savings, and recording important financial information.

In keeping with Vanguard's overall approach to investment education, this guide strives to provide plain and candid information about investment matters. However, given the complexity and detail of many topics broached in this guide, it should not be considered the final word on the subject of personal finance for retirees. Indeed, some subjects addressed here in just a few pages are the grist for entire books. So, for some of your concerns or questions, you may need to consult a more detailed, definitive source or seek the guidance of an investment professional or specialist in taxes or estate planning.

Nonetheless, the fundamentals of investing during retirement may be grasped firmly by the investor who is willing to take the time to learn about the subject and apply those lessons in a disciplined and conservative manner. By investing your time today, you can reap the rewards of a more secure, enjoyable retirement tomorrow.

Contents

The Vanguard Guide To

INVESTING DURING RETIREMENT

TAKE CONTROL OF YOUR RETIREMENT FINANCES

So, You Want to Retire

Chapter 1

The long and fulfilling retirement that we expect today is actually a fairly recent phenomenon. Most of our ancestors did not live long enough to enjoy a lengthy retirement, and most of those who did had too little income to permit them the luxury of not working as they got older. But most Americans today take for granted that their retirement will offer a chance for leisure and freedom from the rigors of their regular jobs. Greater longevity, economic growth, the advent of Social Security, and the widespread growth in private pension plans have all contributed to this dramatic change in the way that most people view retirement.

"The question isn't at what age I want to retire, it's at what income."

George Foreman

Until the second half of this century, personal savings were the primary financial resource for retired Americans. The creation of a federal Social Security program and an expansion of corporate pension plans during and after World War II provided, for the first time, a dependable source of retirement income for a majority of workers. But, even today, Social Security and employer-sponsored pension plans by themselves will not provide most retirees with sufficient income to maintain the lifestyle they enjoyed during their working years. Personal retirement savings and investments are essential to ensure a comfortable retirement. A familiar refrain among retirees is that Social Security and pension benefits cover their base-level expenses, but travel, club memberships, dining out, and other leisure activities must generally be paid for out of personal savings.

The Challenges of Retirement

The difficulty for retired investors is that their personal savings must now perform double duty. Retirees' investments must provide a stream of income to supplement Social

Security and pension benefits, and also provide growth in capital to combat the erosion in purchasing power that occurs over time because of inflation. This challenge is complicated by the fact that the retired investor has considerably less room for error than an investor who is still earning a steady wage. If you make mistakes during your working years, you can often surmount them over time, either by saving more or by working harder or longer. Once you are retired, however, your investment horizon shrinks, and there are fewer practical options available to recover from investing errors.

Embarking on your retirement, then, can be a scary step, because it's difficult to ever know for certain whether you're really financially prepared. If you are like most people, the uncertainty that you feel as you enter your retirement revolves around four major issues:

1. How long will your retirement last?
2. How much will your living expenses increase over time?
3. How much income are you likely to need from your personal investments?
4. How much can you leave behind for your heirs?

The Longevity Challenge

The life span of the typical American has increased dramatically over the past few decades, largely as a result of advances in health care and nutrition. In 1900, a 65-year-old American had an average life expectancy of 1.2 more years; today, a 65-year-old man has a life expectancy of 15.4 years while a 65-year-old woman has an average life expectancy of 19.2 years. What's more, the average 65-year-old has a 56% chance of living to age 80 and a 36% chance of living to age 85. A longer life span may be good news for retirees, but the financial implications are sobering. Longer life spans require exponentially greater financial resources, as the financial burdens of medical care, nursing homes, and hospice care begin to mount.

Table 1–1
Average Life Expectancy (in years)

Your Age	Male	Female	Your Age	Male	Female	Your Age	Male	Female
55	22.7	27.2	65	15.4	19.2	75	9.6	12.2
56	21.9	26.4	66	14.8	18.4	76	9.1	11.6
57	21.1	25.5	67	14.2	17.7	77	8.6	10.9
58	20.4	24.7	68	13.5	16.9	78	8.1	10.3
59	19.6	23.9	69	12.9	16.2	79	7.7	9.7
60	18.9	23.1	70	12.4	15.5	80	7.2	9.2
61	18.2	22.3	71	11.8	14.8	81	6.8	8.6
62	17.5	21.5	72	11.2	14.1	82	6.4	8.1
63	16.8	20.7	73	10.7	13.5	83	6.0	7.6
64	16.1	19.9	74	10.1	12.8	84	5.6	7.1
						85	5.3	6.6

Source: U.S. Department of Health and Human Services, 1992.

It is surprising that many Americans *underestimate* their likely life spans and therefore the length of their retirements. While the average American plans on a retirement period of about 15 years, most will be retired for longer periods. At age 62 (currently the most common retirement age), the average life expectancy is 17.5 years for men and 21.5 years for women. Importantly, these figures are *average* expectancies. In other words, many retirees will beat the averages and live far longer. In any event, Table 1–1 shows the average life expectancy for men and women at various ages.

If you plan your finances based on an average life span, you are taking roughly a 50–50 chance that you will outlive your retirement assets. So you should take into account your family history and your current health when you project your expected life span. In planning for your financial needs during retirement, it's best to add five or 10 years to whatever projection you make. This conservative methodology will reduce the amount of money that you'll be able to spend each year, but it also will sharply reduce the chance that you'll run out of money during retirement.

Understandably, "running out of money" is one of the biggest worries that retirees face. Unfortunately, this situation occurs with some frequency. Many older Americans will outlive their savings, and will be forced to exist on subsistence incomes. Indeed, people age 85 or older are twice as likely to be living below the poverty line as those between the ages of 65 and 74.

According to Dallas Salisbury, president of the Employee Benefit Research Institute, a nonprofit think tank in Washington, "It appears that some Americans are not counting on the extended retirement they will experience." By underestimating the typical length of retirement, Salisbury notes, many Americans also underestimate the amount of savings they will need and overestimate the amount they can safely spend from their retirement savings.

The Inflation Challenge

During a lengthy retirement, you'll need to prepare for the debilitating effects of inflation. The uncertainty of future living costs is one of the great complications in the retirement planning process. Since 1960, consumer prices have risen an average of 4.7% a year; in recent years, inflation has been relatively tame, averaging about 3.5% annually, or just about the long-run average going back to the turn of the century. Unfortunately, no one knows whether inflation will decline even further—or return to the double-digit rates seen in the 1970s and early 1980s.

Whatever happens, there is no doubt that inflation is a powerful force even at relatively low levels, steadily and surely eroding the purchasing power of your income. For example, if you simply want to maintain your purchasing power in the face of a 4% annual inflation rate, you must increase your income by roughly 50% every 10 years. To say the least, that is no mean feat. Figure 1–1 dramatically illustrates the growth in income required over time simply to maintain a stable standard of living.

Although your Social Security payments are indexed to rise with inflation, payments from most corporate pension plans are not. So your investment portfolio must be allocated

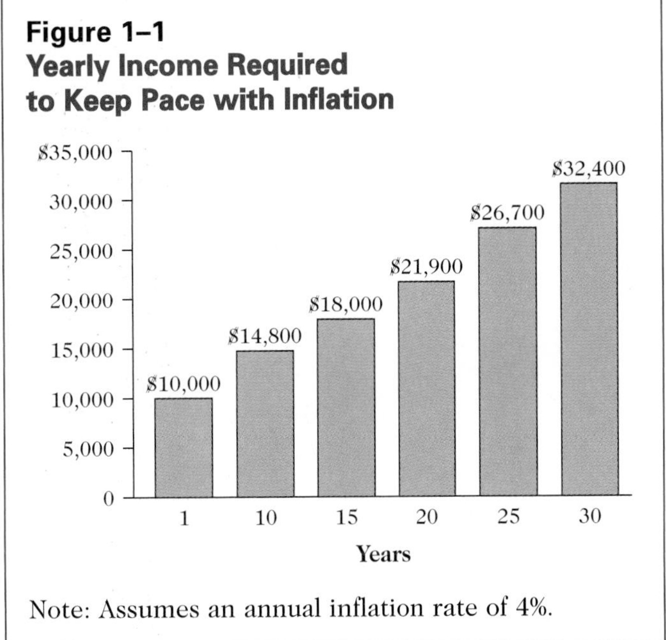

Figure 1–1
Yearly Income Required to Keep Pace with Inflation

Note: Assumes an annual inflation rate of 4%.

to provide the growth in capital that you'll need to keep up with rising prices. A level of investment income that seems adequate when you first retire will seem much less so after several years have passed and the costs of the services and products you consume have risen substantially.

The combination of inflation and a longer retirement makes prudent investing even more important once you've retired. While the potential loss of investment principal is understandably a frightening prospect to someone who is barely making ends meet, "playing it safe" is dangerous, too, since it leaves you vulnerable to diminished purchasing power. As you will see in Chapter 7, finding a proper balance among risk, return, income, and growth will be a critical aspect of your retirement strategy.

The Income Challenge

The presence of inflation is a difficult obstacle for the retiree, but the good news is that you are likely to need less income during retirement than during your working years. The standard rule of thumb is that a retiree needs about 80% of the before-tax income earned in the final working years. But be wary of "standards." Just as one coat does not fit everyone, the 80% rule will not be appropriate for every retiree. The actual level of income you will need during retirement will depend on many variables, including your income before retirement, your health, your age, and, most importantly, your expected lifestyle. Don't underestimate the dramatic impact that your lifestyle choices will have on your income needs. For example, travel and golf are obviously much more

"How are you supposed to know if you have enough saved? Everything is so uncertain."

Michigan

expensive than reading or walking. When in doubt, plan for a higher spending level than you actually expect. Of course, you'll also want to avoid being so fearful of running out of money that you are overly cautious about spending and deny yourself the fruits of your long years of labor.

The Estate Planning Challenge

The level of income that you will have available during your retirement will also depend in part on whether you intend to leave assets behind for your children or other heirs. Because most retirees will need to draw on their accumulated savings and investments, their desire to leave behind an estate for their children or to provide gifts to a church or charity often conflicts with their desire to live as fulfilling a retirement as they possibly can.

Figure 1–2
Annual Retirement Withdrawal Patterns

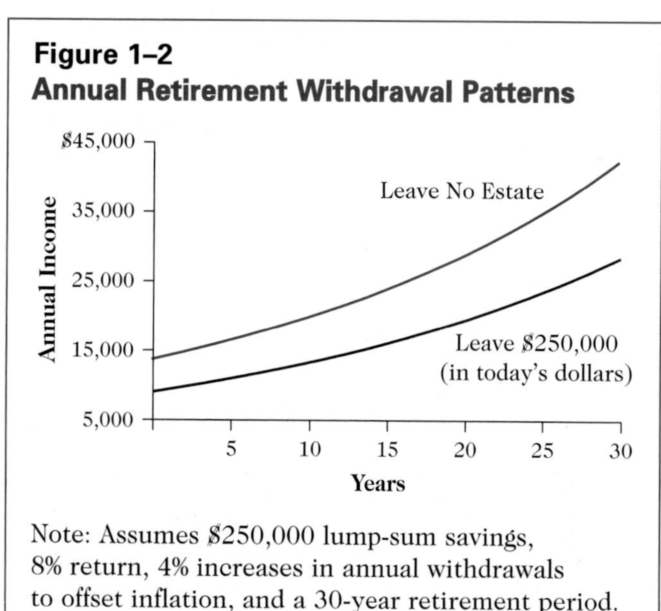

Note: Assumes $250,000 lump-sum savings, 8% return, 4% increases in annual withdrawals to offset inflation, and a 30-year retirement period.

If you definitely plan to leave behind an estate of a particular amount, you may have to accept a lower income level and standard of living. Figure 1–2 shows the diminished level of annual income a retiree can expect by planning to leave behind a $250,000 estate versus the income available for a retiree who is willing to spend down retirement assets over a 30-year retirement. Only you can decide how to balance your income needs with your estate plans, but Chapter 10 will offer some guidelines on developing a long-range estate plan.

This is probably a good time to point out that your estate planning should include a thorough review of where your assets reside. For couples in retirement, ignorance about finances is definitely not bliss. Too often, a partner who is not familiar with financial matters is suddenly confronted with this new responsibility but lacks the crucial background and information, including such basics as the location of documents and bank or investment accounts. Both spouses must be familiar with a couple's finances. If one spouse has always handled financial matters, the other partner should be brought up to speed as soon as possible. One useful way to make sure that both of you know how and where your money is invested is to prepare an inventory of important documents, including savings accounts, mutual funds, brokerage accounts, life insurance statements, and any other financial records. In Appendix B on pages 285-292, you'll find a worksheet for recording these essential documents. You should also provide a copy of this record to either the executor of your will or your children.

Final Thoughts

That was a considerable amount of ground to cover in so few pages, but as you make your way through this guide, the pieces will begin to fall neatly into place. While the challenges you'll face during retirement may seem daunting, you can take heart in that millions of others are facing the same challenges. What's more, opinion surveys have found that retirees are generally happy with their retirement, despite their anxieties about financial security. This guide should help to alleviate these anxieties by identifying the problems you are likely to face and establishing a plan of action.

Overall, you can best overcome the challenges of retirement by clearly assessing your situation, employing some sensible strategies, and avoiding some common errors. This process starts with an assessment of where things stand with your finances today, an exercise that is undertaken in Chapter 2. Plenty of retirees have shown that you don't have to be wealthy to feel financially secure in retirement as long as you establish—and then adhere to—a financial plan. If you've already been following a financial blueprint, you may want to give yourself a financial checkup to ensure that your retirement plans are still on course. After all, it's much easier to get where you want to go if you know where your journey is starting.

Can You Afford Retirement?

Chapter 2

It's hard to really be sure that you're financially prepared for retirement (even if you've already retired), because there are three unknowns that will greatly affect your finances. The first is how long you'll be retired. After all, you cannot accurately predict your own life span. The second is the amount of your future income, which isn't known because the future returns on your financial assets are unpredictable. The third is your future living expenses, which depend on the unpredictable variables of future inflation and taxes.

Although these uncertainties make retirement planning difficult, they are not an excuse for failing to plan. Indeed, uncertainty is precisely why you *need* to plan. You stand a better chance of coping with surprises during retirement if you make an effort to reasonably estimate your retirement income and expenses and then adhere to an appropriate budget. Your estimates will provide a blueprint you can use to monitor your basic assumptions and make mid-course corrections if you find that your actual income and expenses differ from your expectations. Remember, the fact that you're making ends meet in retirement now is no guarantee that your income will continue to be sufficient in the future.

As you make your way through this chapter, a series of worksheets will help you to estimate your annual expenses and income. These steps are essential to knowing whether your retirement foundation is on solid ground. Without a realistic idea of how much money will be going out and how much will be coming in, it's almost impossible to know whether you can count on a secure retirement.

You may want to complete the worksheets in this chapter several times using different estimates and assumptions for your living expenses, inflation, and the returns from your investments. These different scenarios will help you to visualize a variety of possible outcomes for your finances during retirement and will give you an idea of how sensitive your retirement security is to events beyond your control.

Your Net Worth: A Financial Snapshot

"I don't know how much I have in the bank. I haven't shaken it lately."

Milton Berle

The logical place to begin mapping your finances is to add up all of your assets (the things you own) and subtract all of your liabilities (what you owe) to calculate your net worth. You should prepare this snapshot of your financial status once each year as a way to measure your ongoing financial well-being. The worksheet in Table 2–1 will help you determine your net worth. A rising net worth means that your income and any gains on your investments exceed your annual spending. A falling net worth means that you are spending more than your combined income and investment growth. Obviously, a substantial decline in the financial markets will diminish the current value of your investments and cause your net worth to fall, even if you spend less than you earn.

For most retirees, net worth declines over time as they dip into their investments to supplement income from Social Security, pensions, and other sources. While this may seem imprudent, it is the normal pattern for the majority of Americans. As Figure 2–1 illustrates, savings and net worth typically rise sharply in the years leading up to retirement, after many people have finished rearing and educating their children and have paid for their homes. After retirement, most people will see a gradual decline in their net worth as they begin to spend their accumulated savings. This decline in net worth needn't be too worrisome, provided it is a gradual process. Later in this guide, you will learn ways to judge how long your savings and investments will last and how much you can safely spend without exhausting your financial resources.

Figure 2–1
The Retirement Life Cycle

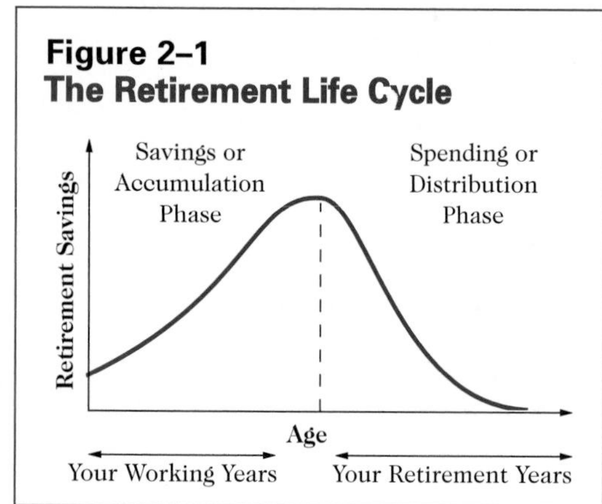

Table 2–1
Net Worth Worksheet

Assets	Current Value
Short-Term Reserves	
Checking account	$ ________
Savings account	________
Money market mutual funds	________
Certificates of deposit	________
U.S. Treasury bills	________
Cash value of life insurance	________
Taxable Accounts	
Stocks	________
Bonds	________
Stock mutual funds	________
Bond mutual funds	________
Tax-Exempt Accounts	
Municipal bonds	________
Municipal bond mutual funds	________
Tax-Deferred Investments	
IRA/Keogh accounts	________
Employer savings plan (e.g., 401(k), 403(b), profit-sharing)	________
Pension (lump-sum value)	________
Accumulated value of annuity (fixed or variable)	________
Personal Property	
Principal home	________
Vacation home	________
Rental property	________
Partnership or business ownership	________
Cars, trucks, boats	________
Home furnishings	________
Art, antiques, coins, collectibles	________
Jewelry, furs	________
Other assets	________
TOTAL ASSETS	$ ________

Liabilities	Current Value
Current	
Credit card balances	$ ________
Margin loans on securities	________
Estimated income tax owed	________
Other outstanding bills	________
Long-Term	
Home mortgage balance	________
Home equity loan	________
Mortgage on rental property	________
Car loans	________
Tuition loans	________
Life insurance policy loan	________
Other long-term debt	________
TOTAL LIABILITIES	$ ________
NET WORTH (Assets − Liabilities)	$ ________

When determining the value of your assets for this worksheet, use their current market value, not the price you paid for them. Thus, if your house originally cost $60,000 but is now worth $200,000, list its value as $200,000. Some of your assets—such as mutual funds, stocks, or bonds—you can value precisely because their prices are established daily. For others, however, you'll have to estimate the value. It's best to use conservative estimates, especially for household goods that may not have as high a resale value as you'd expect. (Consider excluding from your net worth calculation any assets that you do not intend to use as a source of income during retirement.) For real estate, reduce your estimate of its value by the expected sales commission and other closing costs that will arise from the sale of the property. If you don't know current housing prices, ask a real estate agent about the prices paid for houses that have recently sold in your neighborhood.

Don't worry too much about the "answer" provided by the bottom line of this worksheet. There is no right or wrong result. The idea of the exercise is to find out where things stand today so that you can plan for the rest of your retirement. And remember, you are estimating your *financial* net worth, not your worth as a person. Ideally, your assets will outweigh your liabilities and you'll have a positive net worth. If you owe more than you own, that could be a problem. But in Chapter 11, we will discuss options available to you if your resources come up short of what's needed to fulfill your retirement goals.

Estimating Your Expenses

Arriving at a spending budget can be anything but enjoyable. Like counting calories, tracking your spending is an exercise in denial. Yet it is crucial to have a firm grip on your living expenses. Those retirees who find their finances in good order invariably are those who have a firm sense of how much they're spending and what they're spending it on. If you're like most folks, however, an astonishing amount of your money just sort of disappears, spent on incidental items and impulse buys. That's why it is so easy to underestimate your living expenses.

The worksheet in Table 2–2 is designed to help you record and track your expenses. If you're already tracking your expenses, it should be a snap to fill out. If not, try keeping a careful record of all your expenditures during the next few months. Often the mere act of recording them is revealing, as you see for the first time how you really spend your money. If you use an automated teller machine to get cash, make sure to jot down cash purchases so that you can reconstruct where your money went. Gather your canceled checks and credit card receipts for the past six to 12 months so you can look back on the big-ticket items. You may not want to break down your purchases into such small categories, but the detail can be helpful in illuminating where your money goes and making sure you don't forget any significant expense items. It's important to be as complete as possible and not to underestimate your spending, because that would give you a false picture of your financial needs.

"We kept meticulous records of our expenses on a personal computer, using a good personal finance program."

New Jersey

Some items on your expense worksheet, such as a mortgage or rent payment, are recurring. Other expenses crop up only occasionally, which is why you may need to go back through your canceled checks for up to a year to jog your memory. You should also factor in any expected big-ticket purchases, such as a new car or occasional repairs or maintenance on your home. If it has been 10 years since you last replaced your roof or your washing machine, budget for a replacement during your retirement. You may wish to estimate a monthly amount needed to cover such items and put it in a savings account or money market fund earmarked for the occasional big-ticket expense. Or perhaps you'll want to designate a particular bond or bank certificate of deposit (CD) as your repair fund or car fund. Similarly, you may want to include a category in your budget for emergency expenses and set aside a particular amount in savings to cover these contingencies.

If you own a personal computer, consider using any of a number of good, relatively inexpensive programs that can

Table 2–2
Budget Worksheet

Your Projected Expenses	Monthly Amount	× 12	Annual Amount
Housing			
Mortgage/rent payment	$ ________		$ ________
Utilities			
Heat	________		________
Electricity	________		________
Sewer	________		________
Trash removal	________		________
Water	________		________
Telephone	________		________
Cable television	________		________
Property taxes	________		________
Homeowners'/renters' insurance	________		________
Maintenance/repairs	________		________
Association/management fees	________		________
Furniture/appliances	________		________
Household incidental items	________		________
Transportation			
Auto expenditures			
Auto loan	________		________
Auto insurance	________		________
License/registration fees	________		________
Maintenance	________		________
Gasoline	________		________
Public transportation	________		________
Food			
Groceries and beverages	________		________
Dining out	________		________
Health Care and Personal			
Health care			
Insurance			
Health	________		________
Life	________		________
Disability	________		________
Medicare Part B	________		________
Medigap	________		________
Long-term care	________		________
Out-of-pocket medical	________		________
Out-of-pocket dental	________		________

Table 2–2 *(continued)*

Your Projected Expenses	Monthly Amount	× 12	Annual Amount
Health care *(continued)*			
Out-of-pocket vision	$ ______		$ ______
Prescriptions	______		______
Other	______		______
Personal care			
Clothing	______		______
Cosmetics/toiletries	______		______
Barber/beauty care	______		______
Dry cleaning	______		______
Other Expenditures			
Entertainment			
Club dues	______		______
Movies	______		______
Activities/admission fees	______		______
Hobbies	______		______
Subscriptions	______		______
Travel/vacation			
Airfare	______		______
Train	______		______
Hotel/motel	______		______
Other	______		______
Taxes			
Personal property taxes	______		______
Other taxes	______		______
Other debt			
Credit card debt	______		______
Home equity loan	______		______
Other	______		______
Gifts			
Family/friends	______		______
Charitable contributions	______		______
Alimony	______		______
Dependent care	______		______
Education	______		______
Professional dues	______		______
Pet care	______		______
Other ______	______		______
Other ______	______		______
Other ______	______		______
TOTAL PROJECTED EXPENSES	$ ______		$ ______

record your expenses, maintain a household budget, and keep track of your investments. Among the more popular money-management programs are Quicken™, Microsoft® Money™, and Wealthbuilder by *Money* magazine. If you don't have a computer, don't fret—budgeting has been done on paper for centuries.

If you have just entered retirement or are not yet retired, you'll want to adjust the expenses that you incur while working for the changes that you expect during retirement. To do this, you'll have to answer several questions about your retirement goals. For example, will you work part-time or not at all? This decision obviously affects your income, but it also has an impact on your expenses, such as taxes, commuting costs, and clothing costs. Will you move or stay in your current home? What kind of insurance will you need? What sort of lifestyle do you expect to maintain during retirement? Do you intend to travel? Depending on how you respond to these questions, your required income level might actually be higher than it was during your working years. Whatever you decide, a number of expenses will likely diminish or disappear when you enter retirement and stop working:

Table 2–3
1997 Schedule of Social Security and Medicare Taxes

Income	Taxes Paid by Employee and Employer	Taxes Paid by Self-Employed Person
$ 10,000	$ 765	$ 1,530
25,000	1,913	3,825
50,000	3,825	7,650
75,000	5,143	10,285
100,000	5,505	11,010
125,000	5,868	11,735
150,000	6,230	12,460

Source: Internal Revenue Service.

- The amount you were saving for retirement won't have to be deducted from your income. If you were earning $60,000 a year and putting 10% of your salary into retirement savings, you were effectively living on $54,000. You can deduct that 10% from the income you'll need in retirement. By saving during your working years, you not only accumulated a retirement fund but also got acclimated to a lower spending level than your income may have permitted.

- Payroll taxes disappear. If you're no longer drawing a paycheck, you can subtract from your required income the amount you were paying in Social Security taxes (6.2% of gross pay up to $65,400 in 1997), Medicare taxes (1.45% of all pay), and any local taxes. Table 2–3 shows Social Security and Medicare taxes for various income levels in 1997.
- If you haven't already paid off your home mortgage loan, you may be close to it. Once you've finished off the debt, you'll see a nice drop in your expenses.
- Income taxes probably will decline. If you are 65 or older and are among the 70% of individual taxpayers who take the standard deduction instead of itemizing, your standard deduction is increased. If you are a single taxpayer age 65 or older, your deduction is higher by $1,000, which cuts your tax bill by at least $150. If you file a joint return and your spouse is also 65 or older, the standard deduction is boosted by a total of $1,600, or $800 each. Also, if your income declines during retirement, your tax bill will decline as well.
- You'll trim or eliminate work-related expenses, such as clothing for work, commuting, lunches at work, donations for parties or other work celebrations, and dues paid as a member of a union, professional group, or social club. These combined savings can be substantial. For example, some retirees can get by with one car instead of two when they no longer have to commute to work daily; this reduces insurance, maintenance, and other expenses.
- Senior-citizen discounts will cut some costs. Reduced prices are available to senior citizens on a wide variety of products and services, from restaurant meals to prescription drugs to transportation. These discounts can trim 5% to 15% from the costs of many goods and services you buy.

Unfortunately, not all your costs will decline when you retire. Here are some areas where your spending could rise after you stop working:

- You'll almost certainly pay more for medical and dental care, prescriptions, health insurance, and long-term care insurance than you did before retirement. Indeed, the average retiree spends more than $500 a year on prescription drugs alone. (Although Medicare will cover much of your medical costs, it does not cover prescription drugs.) What's more, Medicare comes with its own premiums and deductibles, which rise almost every year. Since your health may decline as you get older, medication or therapies you don't need now may be prescribed for you a decade from now. Even if you are fortunate and your health doesn't deteriorate as you age, the costs of health care can be expected to rise over time. In the past, medical care costs have risen at a rate nearly twice that of overall inflation.
- You'll have more leisure time in retirement, and you may be looking forward to the chance to do more traveling. The typical retiree spends a larger proportion of income on travel, vacations, recreation, and dining out than the typical working person. This is especially true early in retirement, as you visit many of the places on your travel wish list.
- Although you'll have more time on your hands during retirement, you may not be able or willing to do all of the home maintenance and repair work that you have been doing yourself. So expect to spend more on lawn care, painting, and other chores.
- You'll probably spend more time at home than you did when you were working, which will drive your heating and air conditioning costs higher. Also, you may spend more on local and long-distance phone calls to keep in touch with friends, children, and grandchildren.
- Because of the extraordinary rise in longevity in the United States, an increasing number of retirees have aged parents to care for during retirement. Parents who have been getting by in retirement may need your help as their own financial resources dwindle. Alternatively,

divorce, job loss, or some other problem could result in your own child returning to your previously empty nest.

Inflation and Your Expenses

Inflation can be thought of as the silent killer of household budgets. It may be tempting to trivialize the effects of inflation, especially in periods like the 1990s, during which prices have risen at the relatively low rate of around 3% a year. However, even at low rates, inflation can greatly erode the purchasing power of a retiree's income.

"It costs me more every year just to get by. My property taxes keep going up. And medicine—I'm spending a fortune on my prescriptions."

Pennsylvania

From 1985 through 1997, the Consumer Price Index increased at an average annual rate of 3.5%. To get a feel for how even this moderate rate of inflation affects consumers, note the price changes from 1985 to 1997 for an assortment of goods and services listed in Table 2–4.

Although this list does not reflect a comprehensive "market basket," it should serve as a reminder of how small price changes, nearly imperceptible from year to year, can mount up. At an annual inflation rate of 3.5%, your income would need to double over a period of 20 years simply to maintain the identical purchasing power.

Table 2–5 provides inflation factors that you can use to project the effect inflation will have on your retirement income. Suppose, for example, that your property taxes are now $2,500 annually and you expect them to rise by an average of

Table 2–4
Selected Consumer Prices, 1985–97

Item	1985 Price	1997 Price	Change
Gallon of unleaded gasoline (average U.S. price)	$ 1.216	$ 1.235	1.6%
Hardback book on best-seller list (average cost)	19.83	23.36	17.8
Amtrak Metroliner fare, Washington–Philadelphia	35.00	79.00	125.7
One pound of margarine	0.89	1.39	56.2
One pound of filet mignon	4.59	5.49	19.6
Electricity (average residential rate, 500 kilowatt hours)	41.00	49.51	20.7
Arrow dress shirt (on sale)	12.99	18.99	46.2
Auto service (lubrication, oil, and oil filter change)	15.95	19.95	25.1
Medicare Part B (monthly premium)	15.50	42.50	174.2
Ford Taurus GL (1986, 1997 model years)	11,322	26,460	133.7

5% per year over the next decade. At the intersection of the row for 10 years and the column for 5%, you'll find an inflation factor of 1.63. Multiply your property tax bill by the inflation factor ($2,500 × 1.63 = $4,075) to estimate your annual property taxes 10 years from now.

Table 2–5
Inflation Factors

Retirement Period (Years)	Inflation						
	2%	3%	4%	5%	6%	7%	8%
5	1.10	1.16	1.22	1.28	1.34	1.40	1.47
10	1.22	1.34	1.48	1.63	1.79	1.97	2.16
15	1.35	1.56	1.80	2.08	2.40	2.76	3.17
20	1.49	1.81	2.19	2.65	3.21	3.87	4.66
25	1.64	2.09	2.67	3.39	4.29	5.43	6.85
30	1.81	2.43	3.24	4.32	5.74	7.61	10.06

The inflation assumption you use when preparing your worksheet will have a powerful impact on your future income needs. So what number should you use? Since no one can predict future price increases with certainty, the lessons of the past, imperfect as they may be, will have to be your guide. A reasonable notion would be to use some rate between 3.1% (the long-term average inflation rate) and 4.8% (the inflation rate over the past 35 years), keeping in mind that inflation may move beyond these parameters at any time. To provide some perspective, Figure 2–2 shows price trends over various periods going back to 1926, including both deflationary and inflationary periods.

"Inflation is not all bad. After all, it has allowed every American to live in a more expensive neighborhood without moving."

Sen. Alan Cranston

You can see how vital it is to consider inflation in your financial planning, even though the actual inflation rate is virtually certain to differ from your assumptions. The insidious impact of inflation requires retired investors to plan for a rising level of income, which brings you to the next step in the budgeting process.

Estimating Your Income

Retirees, it is often said, are "living on fixed incomes." If that's true, then retirees are in for trouble. To live on a truly fixed income means to live with a steadily *declining* standard of living, as inflation relentlessly increases the costs of the products and services you will use during your retirement. But the reality is that while some sources of income for the typical retiree are fixed, others are not. The difference depends on how you deploy your assets and how much of your investment income and principal you spend.

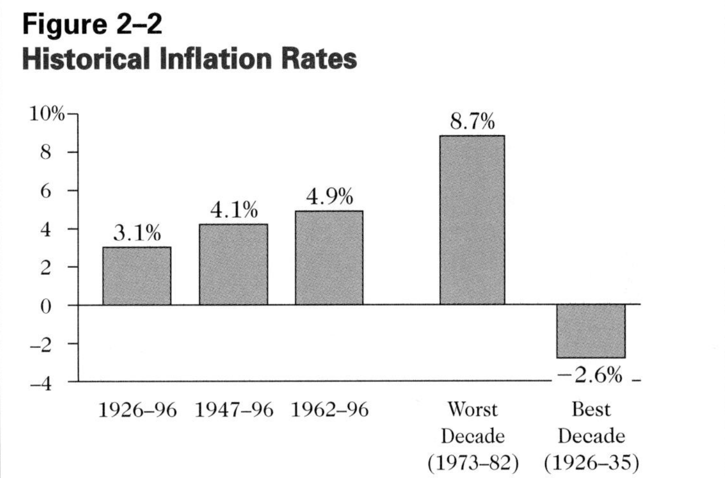

Figure 2–2
Historical Inflation Rates

Source: © *Stocks, Bonds, Bills, and Inflation 1997 Yearbook*™, Ibbotson Associates, Chicago. (Annually updates work by Roger G. Ibbotson and Rex A. Sinquefield.) Used with permission. All rights reserved.

The traditional image for financing your retirement is a three-legged stool: one leg is income from an employer's pension plan, one leg is the personal savings that you have amassed over the years, and one leg is Social Security benefits. Unfortunately, this image is not a reality for many retirees, as some lack one or even two of the legs. For example, almost half of all Americans age 65 or older receive no pension income from their former employers. Those who do receive pension benefits often get relatively small sums, and few such plans are indexed to inflation. Even more surprising, roughly 5% of current retirees receive no Social Security retirement benefits, usually because they did not work enough years or earn enough money to qualify. And a good many Americans reach retirement age without having accumulated much in the way of personal savings or investments. All told, according to the Social Security Administration, less than half of individuals or couples 65 or older get more than $200 a month from their combined savings, investments, and other assets.

It's clear, then, that there is no single blueprint for financing your retirement. Table 2–6 provides a worksheet to identify the sources of your retirement income and to help you project changes you can expect in your income stream.

Table 2–6
Income Worksheet

Your Projected Income	Monthly Amount	× 12	Annual Amount
Social Security			
You	$ ________		$ ________
Your spouse	________		________
Wages			
You	________		________
Your spouse	________		________
Pension			
You	________		________
Your spouse	________		________
Other Income			
Income from your home	________		________
Rental income	________		________
Trust income	________		________
Dividend income	________		________
Interest	________		________
Annuities	________		________
Royalties	________		________
Veterans' benefits	________		________
Other income	________		________
TOTAL INCOME	$ ________		$ ________

In filling out this income worksheet, use the after-tax amounts you receive. If you customarily receive a refund on your income taxes, add your best estimate of the refund to your income before arriving at a figure for your total income. If you expect to owe additional income taxes, be sure to account for this expense either on your expense worksheet or by subtracting this estimate from your income before arriving at total income.

Social Security

This bedrock source of income for most retirees accounts for approximately 40% of the total income for singles and couples age 65 or older. Enter your current monthly benefit on the income worksheet in Table 2–6 and multiply it by 12 to arrive at an annual figure.

Social Security is one source of income that is not fixed, thanks to a 1972 law that requires benefits to increase along with changes in the Consumer Price Index. This annual cost-of-living adjustment (COLA) means that Social Security benefits should generally keep pace with inflation. (However, you should be aware that the COLA could change. Some economists, statisticians, and influential members of Congress argue that the Consumer Price Index actually overstates inflation. They advocate changes in the Index or in the Social Security COLA formula to reduce the inflation adjustments. Reducing the COLA has obvious attractions for politicians seeking to reduce spending by the federal government.)

If you're not yet receiving Social Security benefits, you can get an estimate of your future benefits by calling 1-800-772-1213 and asking for a form called "Request for Earnings and Benefit Estimate Statement." Within a few weeks of completing the form, you'll get a document showing your past wage earnings under Social Security and an estimate of the benefits you've accrued.

Wages

Salary or wage income is an important source of income for many "retirees" who continue to work part-time. Nearly 20% of the income reported by Americans 65 and older comes from wages. Some retirees keep working or return to work because they need the extra income; others choose to keep working simply because they enjoy the activity. After all, the idea that retirement is supposed to start by the time you're 65 is an artificial—and, some would argue, outdated—concept.

"I do secretarial work two days a week for a temp agency. I need the money, and since I live alone, I also like the chance to be around other people."

Iowa

In any case, if you will continue to earn a salary during retirement, you should enter your estimated annual wages on the worksheet. (For information on how wage income affects Social Security benefits, see Chapter 9.) For longer-range financial planning, it's important to think about how long you will continue to work. At some point you will probably be unwilling or unable to continue your job. Your financial plans should take into account this eventual loss of wage income.

Pension Benefit

If you receive a monthly pension check from one or more employers, enter this amount on the worksheet. If you haven't yet retired, your employer should provide the figure as part of your annual benefits statement. Or you can ask your employer's benefit representative to provide a benefits statement or pension estimate. If your employer has a defined benefit pension plan—the type of plan that pays benefits based on how long you've worked and how much you've earned—the employer is required to provide a statement showing the benefit you've earned. Check the benefits statement to verify its information: your name, Social Security number, birth date, years of service, and address.

Just 4% of defined benefit pension plans provide automatic cost-of-living adjustments to compensate for inflation. Thus, with most pension plans, the benefit you receive when you first retire will never increase. If you haven't yet retired and want to learn more about your pension options, be sure to read Chapter 3.

Home Equity

You may be living in one of the most important sources of your retirement income—your home. For millions of Americans, the equity in their home is their largest asset. If you plan to use your home equity to help finance your retirement, you have three main options:

- First, you can sell your home and trade down to a less expensive residence. The difference in price can then be invested and drawn down over the years to provide supplemental income. A favorable provision of the tax code makes it possible to "capture" some of your home equity without paying taxes on it.

- Second, you can use a reverse mortgage loan to get a steady stream of income from your home while still living in it.
- Third, you may be able to arrange a sale–leaseback arrangement with your children so that you can continue to live in your home while getting income from it.

Each method of tapping into your home equity has advantages and potential drawbacks, all of which are discussed in Chapter 11. For example, trading down means that you'll have to move out of your home. It may also mean that you'll have to leave the community where you have put down roots. Reverse mortgage loans and sale–leaseback arrangements raise tax and estate planning issues that require careful consideration. For these reasons, some retirees consider home equity a financial backstop to be used only if other resources prove inadequate.

If you are certain you want to use your home equity as part of your retirement nest egg, it is best to be conservative in estimating the amount that you'll be able to realize from the sale of the home. Once you've actually sold your home, taken out a reverse mortgage loan, or arranged a sale–leaseback of your home, you can adjust your income estimates to reflect the actual amount you'll have to work with.

Savings and Investments

As noted earlier, many retirees receive little or no income from personal savings or investments. In some cases they never accumulated a pool of savings in the first place; in other cases, they've simply used up their personal nest eggs prematurely. Whether you've accumulated a lot or a little, it's important to take into account the income available from your savings or investments when formulating your financial plans.

Once you've entered all your investments on the worksheet and calculated the current income that each is likely to produce, total the figures. Combine your investment income with your current income from other sources to arrive at your total retirement income. Keep in mind that this figure represents the income generated by your *current* mix of investments. You may be able to increase your income by altering your investment mix or by using up some of the principal that you've accumulated. More on these topics comes later in this guide.

How to Calculate Yield

To calculate the yield on an investment, start with the current dollar income from the investment. If it's a monthly amount, multiply it by 12 to annualize the income. If the income is paid quarterly, as with stock dividends, multiply by 4. If you receive the income semiannually, as with interest on Treasury bonds, multiply by 2. Then divide the annualized income by the amount in the account or the current value of the investment. That is the approximate annual yield of the investment. (Do not count any distributions of capital gains as "income." Capital gains represent the profit from the sale of securities and are not regular income.)

Examples:

You have $5,000 in a money market fund. Last month it earned $24.
Income: $24 × 12 = $288, the annualized income.
$288 ÷ $5,000 = 5.76%, the annualized yield from your money fund.

You own 100 shares of a common stock that is currently trading at $40 a share. It pays a quarterly dividend of 30 cents a share.
Income: $0.30 × 4 = $1.20, annualized income per share.
$1.20 ÷ $40 = 3.00%, the annualized dividend yield from the stock.

You own a $10,000 Treasury note. Twice a year you receive $345 in interest.
Income: $345 × 2 = $690, the annualized income.
$690 ÷ $10,000 = 6.90%, the annualized yield of the note.

Forecasting Future Income

Determining how much annual income you are likely to have five years from now isn't much easier than estimating the cost of groceries in five years. Some of your income sources are probably fixed, others may produce increased income over the years, and still others, such as money market accounts,

Treasury bills, and CDs, will produce income that can vary sharply from year to year.

As noted earlier, the monthly payments from an employer's pension plan usually are fixed, so the monthly benefit you receive today is the same as that which you'll receive in 5 or 10 years. If your pension is adjusted for inflation, refer to Table 2–5 and use the same inflation factor you used for estimating your future expenses. This inflation factor can also be used to adjust your Social Security benefits. (This assumption may have to change if, as some members of Congress have proposed, the Social Security cost-of-living adjustments or the government's official measures of inflation are changed.)

Whether your investments will produce higher or lower income as the years go by will depend on several factors, including (1) whether you spend all of your investment income or reinvest some portion; (2) the mix of your investments; and (3) the vagaries of the financial markets. Your investment mix, or asset allocation, will be particularly important to your future income level.

Chapter 7 will go into considerable detail on asset allocation and selecting the right mix of investments. In general, if your money is invested mainly in interest-bearing bank accounts or money market mutual funds, your investment income will tend to vary widely from year to year as interest rates fluctuate. Investments in bonds and bond mutual funds will exhibit much less year-to-year variability in income. What's more, fixed-income investments offer no opportunity for long-term growth in capital and income, resulting in a gradual decline in purchasing power in an inflationary environment. On the other hand, the value of investments in common stocks tends to fluctuate considerably from one year to the next, but stocks tend to produce a durable and rising stream of dividend payments.

When you come right down to it, your level of income during retirement will depend largely on the financial markets, which are unpredictable by nature. In Chapter 4, you will learn a straightforward method of making rational judgments about the future long-term returns on your portfolio.

The Bottom Line

Now that you've estimated your expenses and your income, you should have a pretty good picture of your current finances. And by making an attempt to adjust your expenses and income for inflation, you at least have an idea of what the future may hold. If the picture that emerges from this initial analysis of your finances is not a pretty one, don't despair. There are ways to both reduce your expenses and augment your income. Your financial outlook may also improve once you revisit your current asset allocation and consider changes that may be able to boost your investment returns.

Keep in mind that the simplest way to increase your retirement income is to systematically dip into your personal savings and investments. Although this can be a frightening prospect for many retirees, it is often a necessity. Planning to draw down your capital can make a big difference in the amount of money you have available to meet your living expenses. Consider, for example, a 65-year-old couple with savings and investments worth $400,000. They plan on 25 years of retirement and estimate that their investments will provide an average total return of 7% annually. If they want to preserve the entire $400,000 as an inheritance, they'll be able to draw no more than $26,000 a year. If they are unconcerned about leaving an estate for their heirs, they'll be able to spend $32,000 a year, a monthly increase in income of $500, or 23%. For a more thorough discussion of drawing income from your investment principal, refer to Chapter 8.

Final Thoughts

Developing a financial plan for your retirement is crucial. Without the sort of analysis you've completed in this chapter, you would have no road map for your retirement journey and only a vague notion of whether your resources are adequate to complete the trip.

It's a good idea to revisit this chapter from time to time, perhaps once a year, to check your estimates and assumptions against your actual experience. You may find that you're doing better than expected, which could allow you to loosen your purse strings a bit. Or you may see the need for some economizing. Either way, by tracking your finances regularly, you can respond to changing circumstances by making modest adjustments rather than having to confront a precipitate change in your living standard.

Getting the Most from Your Pension

Chapter 3

The first corporate retirement plan in the United States was created in 1875 by the American Express Co. This novel idea of employers providing a retirement income to their workers spread slowly. Thirty-five years later, in 1910, there were still only 60 established corporate retirement plans nationwide. But during and after World War II, employer-sponsored pension plans proliferated, and they have become a major factor in the improved financial status of older Americans. By the end of 1995 (the latest year for which data are available), 24% of Americans age 65 or older were receiving some level of income from private pension plans, almost triple the 9% rate in 1962. Private pensions in 1995 provided 9% of the total income received by people 65 or older, up from 3% in 1962.

If you've worked many years for a single employer, your pension plan may be the largest asset you have, worth even more than your home. While this may seem startling, consider that a worker who has put in 35 years at a company and retires at a final salary of $60,000 a year could retire at age 65 with a monthly pension benefit of about $2,500. Based on the average life expectancy of a 65-year-old man, such a monthly benefit is roughly equivalent to a lump-sum pension payment of around $300,000.

Given the magnitude of this kind of payout, it's clear that deciding how to manage these assets warrants careful consideration. This chapter is aimed primarily at those who are about to retire and have yet to decide how to receive the pension benefits they've earned over the years. You may have to choose between taking your entire pension benefit as a lump-sum payment or taking it as a series of payments throughout your lifetime.

If you decide (or are required) to take the monthly payments, you'll almost certainly have to choose among several options that have important financial implications for you and your spouse. To make the right decisions, you'll need to consider such factors as your financial needs, your health, your tax situation, and your ability and willingness to take on more investing responsibilities. This chapter is designed to help you understand your choices and get the most out of your pension benefits. The chapter also discusses early retirement offers and the factors you should consider if such an opportunity presents itself. Because this chapter is aimed at people about to retire, you may want to skip it if you're already in retirement and have made your pension decisions.

A Pension Plan Overview

About half of all American workers today are covered by a pension plan sponsored by their employers. Most workers are covered by one of two main types of retirement plans: the defined benefit plan and the defined contribution plan.

The Defined Benefit Plan

The traditional type of pension arrangement is the *defined benefit plan*, under which the employer promises a retirement benefit or pension based on two factors: (1) your salary before retirement and (2) your length of service with the employer. Typically, a defined benefit plan pays a retirement benefit based on a formula that multiplies a percentage factor, say, 1.5%, by the total number of years you worked for the company. The resulting percentage is multiplied by the average salary you earned during your final (or highest-paid) several years with the company. Under this formula, an employee who worked 35 years with a company and had a final average salary of $60,000 would be entitled to a pension benefit of $31,500 a year, or 53% of the final salary.

In a defined benefit plan, the money to fund the pension benefit payouts comes from the employer, who makes periodic contributions to a pension fund. This system puts the employer at risk if the plan doesn't accumulate enough assets to pay the promised benefits. If the assets contributed to the plan do not earn enough to meet future benefit obligations, the employer must invest more cash or securities into the pension fund.

Defined benefit plans are regulated by federal law and guaranteed (up to $2,761.36 per month or $33,136.32 per year in 1997) by a federal agency, the Pension Benefit Guaranty Corporation (PBGC). Federal law limits the annual amount that you may receive from a defined benefit plan. The limit in 1997 is the lower of $125,000 or 100% of your average annual pay during your three years of employment with the highest consecutive salary.

The Defined Contribution Plan

The second category of pensions is called a *defined contribution plan*. This pension plan is generally simpler, more flexible, and less expensive for an employer to administer than a defined benefit plan. For these reasons, defined contribution plans have become increasingly popular with employers. Many large, established companies have adopted defined contribution plans to supplement their existing defined benefit plans, while newer, smaller companies have tended to adopt one or more defined contribution plans to provide retirement benefits. Many hospitals, universities, nonprofit agencies, and governments also offer defined contribution plans for their employees.

In a defined contribution plan, unlike a defined benefit plan, a separate account is established in your name. Contributions to the plan—by you, your employer, or both—are credited to your account, as are any investment gains or losses. No particular benefit level is promised to you when you retire. The benefits you will ultimately receive will depend on the contributions made to the plan by you and your employer and on the investment returns you achieve on these contributions.

Many defined contribution plans allow you to allocate your investments among a variety of options. Such an arrangement is called a participant-directed plan. It effectively shifts the responsibility for investing wisely from the employer to the employee, so that the risks of investing poorly or of contributing too little are borne by you rather than your employer. Contributions to defined contribution plans are made with pretax dollars, and the earnings on your contributions are exempt from federal income taxes until you withdraw the money.

Federal law limits the amount that an employer can contribute to your account each year to $30,000 or 25% of your pay, whichever is less. There is no federal guarantee for your pension money in a defined contribution plan.

The Pension Payout

When you retire, there are two basic ways to receive the pension that you've amassed in a defined benefit plan. The most common choice is to receive a monthly check, or annuity payment, from the pension plan. The other method—offered as an option by about one-third of defined benefit pension plans—is to receive your benefits all at once in a single lump-sum payment. In either case, the total amount of your benefit will depend on how long you worked for your employer, your age and life expectancy, the type of payment option you select, and the interest-rate assumption used in the benefits calculation.

Even if you're among the majority of retirees who do not have the lump-sum alternative, you must choose the type of monthly annuity payment you wish to receive. Most pension plans offer participants at least two annuity payment options. The first is called the single-life option. This option allows you to collect a monthly benefit for as long as you live. The payments start when you retire and continue until you die, at which point they stop. A permutation of this type of annuity is single-life with a guaranty. You could get a lower amount than with a normal single-life annuity, but it would be ensured for a specific amount of time. The second type of pension payout is called the joint-and-survivor option. This option provides a reduced benefit while you're alive but continues to pay a benefit to your spouse or other beneficiary after you die.

As shown in Table 3–1, the initial payments under the joint-and-survivor option typically are lower than payments under the single-life payout. That's because the pension plan may have to keep making payments to your surviving spouse after you die. In general, the younger your spouse, the lower the monthly payment you receive. The reduced monthly payment is, in a sense, the price you pay for ensuring that payments will continue after you die.

The two most common joint-and-survivor options are the 50% joint-and-survivor annuity, which pays half the amount of your pension to your surviving spouse, and the 100% joint-and-survivor annuity, which pays your surviving spouse the same monthly pension that you received while you were alive. If you choose the 100% option for your survivor, the monthly payments naturally will be lower than if you choose the 50% option.

Table 3–1
Typical Annuity Payment Schedules

$200,000 purchase price; age 65; spouse age 62

Single-Life Annuity
- $1,820 per month for life of pensioner

Single-Life with Guaranty
- 10-year guaranty: $1,710 per month for life or at least 10 years
- 20-year guaranty: $1,560 per month for life or at least 20 years

Joint-and-Survivor Annuity
- 50% survivor benefit: $1,700 per month for life ($850 per month for life if pensioner dies first)
- 100% survivor benefit: $1,500 per month for life ($1,500 per month for life if pensioner dies first)

If you're married, federal law requires you to select the joint-and-survivor option unless your spouse explicitly approves the choice of the single-life annuity or the lump-sum payout. This rule is meant to make sure that your spouse isn't unknowingly deprived of a pension income and that both marriage partners understand the primary risk of the single-life annuity: namely, that the pension income ceases when the pensioner dies.

Ordinarily, taking the survivor option is a good idea because it ensures pension income for your spouse if you die first. But there are circumstances when taking the single-life annuity might be sensible—for example, if your spouse has a good pension of his or her own, or if there is a strong likelihood that you will outlive your spouse, perhaps because you are considerably younger or because your spouse's health is poor.

On the other hand, a joint-and-survivor annuity probably makes the most sense in the following situations:

- Your spouse has no pension and may not have enough life insurance proceeds or other assets after your death to meet his or her daily living expenses. In this case, especially if your spouse is likely to outlive you and your pension does not come with cost-of-living adjustments, you should consider the 100% joint-and-survivor benefit.
- Your employer provides medical benefits to both pensioners and their spouses. If you choose a joint-and-survivor annuity, your spouse may be eligible to maintain these medical benefits after you die. If you choose a single-life annuity, medical coverage for your spouse typically ends at your death, when your pension benefits stop.
- You can designate someone other than a spouse as your joint annuitant. Some pension plans allow this option, and it may be attractive to you, for example, if you are single and have an aging parent who depends on you for financial support. If your joint annuitant is much older than you, the benefit reduction for choosing the joint-and-survivor option will be relatively small.

In deciding which annuity option to select, you might want to use the income and expense information from Chapter 2 to test different scenarios. Find out from your employer's benefits representative how much your pension would be under the various options open to you. Then enter on the pension line of your income worksheet the appropriate monthly income from each option under three scenarios: (1) both you and your spouse are living; (2) your spouse dies first; and (3) you die first. This exercise should help to clarify your thinking about which option is most appropriate to your situation.

Pension Maximization

Married retirees who are trying to decide whether to take their pension payment in the form of a single-life annuity or take the smaller joint-and-survivor annuity may be approached by insurance agents offering a pension maximization or "pension max" plan. The idea behind this plan is for you to take the higher, single-life annuity payment and then use the difference between that and the joint-and-survivor payment to buy life insurance on yourself, with your spouse as the beneficiary. If you die first, the insurance proceeds will be used to purchase an annuity that will provide your spouse with at least as much income as he or she would have gotten from the pension under the joint-and-survivor annuity. If your spouse dies first, you can stop paying for the life insurance, leaving you with more spending money, or you can keep paying and let the life insurance proceeds pass to your beneficiaries after you die.

To see how this scheme would work, assume that your pension plan pays $1,500 per month under the single-life annuity option and $1,250 under the joint-and-survivor option. In essence, you are "paying" $250 a month in "premiums" (in the form of benefits not received) to ensure the continuance of pension payments after your death. If you can buy enough insurance for $250 (or less) a month to provide adequately for your spouse after your death, the pension maximization deal may well make sense. But when you consider the challenge facing the insurer—providing an amount equal to what your spouse would have received from your pension, while also covering its expenses, its profit, and an agent's sales commission—you can appreciate how difficult it will be to get a better deal from an insurer.

Most financial planners agree that pension maximization plans usually don't work unless you bought the insurance coverage some years before you retired, when premiums were lower. If you are buying the insurance at retirement, the premiums usually are higher than the extra income you'll get from taking the single-life annuity. In any event, when evaluating a pension max proposal, consider these factors:

- Are you sure the insurance you'll be buying will be sufficient to buy a lifetime annuity that will provide the monthly income your spouse will need if you die first? The insurance benefit should be sufficient right from the start; it should not depend on a buildup in value according to projections the agent shows you. Also, you should be certain that your spouse can get the annuity income necessary. What happens if rates paid by annuities fall in the future?
- A pension max plan works only if your premium for the insurance policy is less than the difference, after taxes, between the single-life annuity payment and the joint-and-survivor annuity from your pension plan. If you're buying universal life insurance or interest-sensitive whole life insurance, changing market conditions might cause the premium to rise in future years to provide the level of insurance coverage that you need.
- Your spouse is taking a risk with the pension max option. If you got divorced, if you couldn't pay the insurance premiums, or if the insurance company failed, your spouse would have signed away the rights to part of your pension benefit and received nothing in return. At a minimum, your spouse should be the owner and named beneficiary of the life insurance policy.
- Your pension payments are insured by the PBGC, while the annuity payments from an insurance company are not backed by federal insurance.

In short, pension maximization can be a mistake if you haven't carefully reviewed the proposal. Before giving up the proverbial bird in the hand—the joint-and-survivor pension benefit—make certain you'll really get the two in the bush.

The Lump-Sum Alternative

If your employer provides a defined benefit pension plan, you may also have the option at retirement of taking the pension benefit in a lump sum. If you've participated in a defined contribution pension arrangement, such as a 401(k) plan, you can always withdraw your account balance in a lump sum upon retirement.

"Most of my retirement money came from my lump sum, and my strategy was to put it away for 10 years. Little did I know that I would need it to live on during those 10 years."

Connecticut

Retirees often find the choice between taking a lump sum or the monthly payments difficult, and for good reason: from a financial viewpoint, the lump sum and the annuity are designed to be equivalent on a present-value basis. The lump sum is calculated to be equal to the amount of money it would take to provide the equivalent monthly pension payments for the rest of your life based on your benefit level, the average life expectancy for someone your age, and an estimate of the income you could earn on the lump sum. In short, the lump sum simply allows you to create your own annuity.

Deciding how to invest a lump-sum distribution can be intimidating, particularly since the amount of the distribution can be stunning. Indeed, it is likely to be more money than you've ever had available all at one time in your entire life. However, although it may seem like a great deal of money, it has a very big job to do. The money and the income it generates must provide a stream of income for you, and perhaps for your spouse, until you die.

Choosing a lump-sum payout is certainly the more flexible option; it allows you to decide when and how you use the money, when and how you pay taxes on it (some favorable tax treatments may apply), and when and how you invest it. Also, depending on your spending habits and how you invest the lump-sum proceeds, this option gives you the possibility of a growing stream of income that will allow you to keep pace with inflation. The annuity payout in most cases will never rise once you start receiving payments.

Annuity versus Lump Sum

This section delineates the pros and cons associated with taking your pension benefits as a stream of monthly payments or in one single distribution.

Advantages of Monthly Annuity Payments

Simplicity. Once you decide to take the monthly annuity payment, there's nothing else to consider. Financial planning and tax planning are simple because you know the amount you'll be receiving each month. Nor does the pension complicate your estate planning, since there is no sum of money left to pass on to your heirs.

Certainty. Your payment doesn't depend on your investment results. A fall in interest rates or in the stock market won't result in a decline in your pension income. You also don't need to hire an investment adviser or make investment decisions.

Durability. You can't outlive your money. If you're fortunate enough to live a very long time after you retire, the annuity option will prove quite beneficial.

Disadvantages of Monthly Annuity Payments

No growth. Few pension plans boost monthly pension payments to account for inflation. At even a "modest" inflation rate of 3.5% a year, your fixed pension payment will lose half of its buying power in 20 years.

Rigidity. Once you've made your decision, you can't elect to postpone or accelerate the payments if your health or financial situation changes.

Nothing to pass on to your heirs. Once you (and your spouse, if you choose the survivor option) die, there is nothing left to bequeath to your heirs. If you die before reaching the actuarial average life expectancy, your family is shortchanged because you didn't receive the full benefits you earned while working.

Insurance limitations. If your pension plan becomes insolvent and the government has to take over the plan's obligations, you could lose some of your pension benefit. Specifically, if your monthly benefit is above the limit covered by the federal PBGC ($2,761.36 a month in 1997), your check will be reduced.

Advantages of the Lump-Sum Payment

Control and flexibility. When you take the lump-sum payment, you control how fast you spend it and how it's invested. If you need it for an emergency or for an investment or business opportunity, you have easy access to it.

Potentially higher income. You may be able to invest your lump-sum proceeds so that you get more income than you'd have received from the annuity payout of your pension plan. This is particularly true if you're an experienced investor willing to hold a diversified portfolio. Your pension income also has the potential to increase over time, keeping pace with inflation.

Income isn't cut when you die. Most pension annuity payments stop or decline when you die, so the income available to your spouse falls. Income from your lump sum won't fall because of your death.

Leaving an estate. If you die earlier than expected, the unspent portion of your lump sum can be left to your heirs as part of your estate.

Disadvantages of the Lump-Sum Payment

Temptation. A big chunk of cash can be extremely tempting, especially if you've never had such a large amount of money all at once. Some retirees go through a lot of the money quickly, perhaps to help family members or to enjoy a big trip, a fishing boat, or some other reward for a lifetime of toil. Then they must sacrifice when the money isn't available to produce needed income in their later years. A U.S. Department of Labor study of workers who had received lump-sum distributions found that 20% of workers between ages 55 and 64 spent the entire distribution when they received it. About 20% of workers spent part of their lump sums. Only 60% put all the money directly into savings.

Investment risks. In financial markets, risk is accepted as part of the landscape. Your portfolio may not provide as much income as you expected, and you could end up with less money than if you'd taken the monthly benefit. The responsibility for investing rests on your shoulders. If you are not comfortable with taking risks, you probably will feel more at ease taking the annuity payments.

Complexity. Not only will you face tax issues in deciding how to take the lump sum, you'll also have to make investment decisions and include the pension lump sum in devising an estate plan.

Running out of money. Even if you make good investment decisions, you may outlive the money if you are blessed with a long life.

Buying an Annuity with Your Lump-Sum Payout

"My wife and I have gone into annuities. We feel that this is not necessarily going to give us as substantial a return as we'd like to see, but we think it's a reasonably safe way to go."

Ohio

Before choosing whether to take the annuity or the lump-sum payout from your employer-sponsored pension plan, you should also consider the possibility of buying your own annuity with your lump-sum payout. Compare the payments under your employer's annuity options with the payments you could get from a direct annuity bought from a commercial insurance company. It is possible that you'll find a better deal from an insurer.

To give you annuity price quotations, an insurance agent will need to know the amount of the lump-sum distribution, your birth date, and your spouse's birth date (if you're married). When you shop for an annuity, look only at insurers that have received top ratings for financial strength from at least two rating agencies. This is crucial because the only guarantee that you'll receive the annuity payments you've paid for is the financial ability of the insurer to make the payments. Table 3–2 lists rating agencies and the top ratings they bestow.

Quotations on insurance annuities are usually expressed as the amount of monthly income you will receive for each $1,000 you invest in the annuity. Once you receive several quotations, compare the monthly annuity benefits offered by the various insurers. Obviously, you want to be sure that all the annuities are of the same type. If you're comparing a 100% joint-and-survivor option from your employer, the insurance companies' annuities also should be 100% joint-and-survivor contracts.

It can pay substantially to shop around. In mid-1995, monthly payments from direct annuities offered by companies with top financial ratings differed by as much as 14%, or by $1.09 per month per $1,000 invested, for a 65-year-old man. If you find an insurance company offering a higher payment than your employer's plan, consider having all or part of your distribution transferred directly to the insurance company to buy the annuity. If the assets are transferred directly, no taxes are due—except, of course, on the monthly payments from the annuity. If you find several highly rated

Table 3–2
Insurance Company Ratings

Five independent rating agencies analyze insurance companies for their financial strength and ability to pay claims. The agencies and their top ratings are shown below:

Rating Agency	Top Ratings	Percentage of Insurers Receiving Top Ratings
A. M. Best Co.	A++	6%
Standard & Poor's Corp.	AAA	25
Moody's Investors Service	Aaa	9
Duff & Phelps	AAA	30
Weiss Research	A+	1

Source: *Annuity & Life Insurance Shopper.*

insurers offering better deals than your pension's annuity, you might consider splitting your lump sum between the two highest-paying annuities to reduce your risk of financial difficulties with any single insurer.

For more information on annuities, The American Council on Life Insurance, Consumer Dept., 1001 Pennsylvania Ave. N.W., Washington, D.C. 20004-2599 offers a free booklet, *A Consumer's Guide to Annuities.* A good source for comparing annuities is the *Annuity & Life Insurance Shopper*, a quarterly publication that reviews the annuities offered by about 50 insurers and shows the ratings financial analysts have given to each insurer. A single issue of the *Shopper* sells for $20; you can order it by calling 1-800-872-6684 or writing to U.S. Annuities, 8 Talmadge Drive, Monroe Township, NJ 08831.

Taxes and Your Retirement Plan

As a rule, you must pay federal income tax on any money you receive from a retirement plan—including lump-sum distributions, monthly pension checks, and withdrawals from individual retirement accounts (IRAs)—unless you roll the assets over into an IRA or another eligible retirement plan. Any *after-tax* contributions to an IRA, a defined contribution pension plan, or any other retirement plan are not taxable when they are withdrawn, so they are not eligible to be rolled over into an IRA.

If you are under age 59½, not only will you pay ordinary income taxes on the taxable portion of your retirement plan income but you'll also pay a 10% penalty tax. The tax penalty is waived if you are disabled or if you die and the money is distributed to your beneficiary or your estate, if you use the funds to meet medical expenses that exceed 7.5% of your adjusted gross income, or if you use them to pay health-insurance premiums when you are unemployed. With the exception of IRAs, you do not pay a penalty tax on retirement distributions that result from a job termination, provided the withdrawal occurs during or after the year in which you turn age 55.

A few states exempt private pension income from income taxes, and about 15 states provide a partial income tax exemption. Consult your tax adviser for details about the tax treatment of pensions in your state.

Taxation of Lump-Sum Distributions

As noted earlier, distributions from a pension plan are taxable for federal income tax purposes, with the exception of after-tax contributions you have made to the plan. Ordinarily, the taxable portion of a lump-sum distribution is taxed as regular income in the year it is received. However, you can postpone or reduce the taxes due on a lump-sum payout through an IRA rollover or by using a technique called forward averaging.

The IRA Rollover You can defer taxes on your lump sum through a direct rollover to an IRA. If you directly roll over your proceeds into an IRA, the money can continue to grow, free of taxes, until you're ready to start withdrawing it. By rolling the money into an IRA, you can also control how the assets are invested and how much you withdraw. If you don't have an immediate need for a big portion of the lump-sum proceeds, the rollover is usually your best option.

That said, you must be sure that your pension rollover is done *directly* from your pension plan to the IRA. If you don't choose the direct rollover option *before receiving the distribution*, your employer is required by law to withhold 20% of the sum for taxes. Even if you then put the money into an IRA, you'll have to file a tax return to get the 20% back. If you're not certain how to proceed with a rollover, ask your employer to leave the lump sum in your company plan until you're ready to move ahead. The institution where you want to invest the money should be able to help you accomplish the rollover.

You may start taking money from an IRA with no tax penalty beginning at age 59½. And you *must* begin to take withdrawals from your IRA by April 1 of the year after you turn age 70½ or the year you retire, if you continue working past age 70½. See Chapter 8 for more information on these required minimum distributions.

"Should I use 10-year averaging and take all my money out of a qualified plan, or should I take it out over 16 years? If I do take it now, is there a safe investment that will stay ahead of inflation and have flexibility for occasional withdrawals for major expenses?"

Pennsylvania

Forward Averaging Forward averaging is a technique that can cut the taxes on your lump-sum distribution by allowing you to pay the tax as if you had received the lump sum over a period of years, rather than all at once. It also allows you to exclude all income from other sources when you're calculating the forward-averaging tax. This way, the one-time distribution of a lump-sum payout from your pension should not bump you up to a higher income-tax bracket.

Five-year forward averaging allows you to pay taxes (using current tax rates) as if your lump sum were distributed over a 5-year period and as if you had no other income. However, beginning in the year 2000, 5-year forward averaging will be repealed as a part of the Small Business Protection Act of 1996. Ten-year forward averaging (available only to those who were born before 1936) treats the lump sum as if it had occurred over 10 years, and requires you to use the income tax rates that were in effect in 1986. If you were born before 1936, you may be eligible to treat part of your pension distribution as a long-term capital gain, taxable at a 20% rate. You may use this long-term capital gains treatment on the portion of your lump sum that stems from your participation in the pension plan before 1974. The remaining part of your pension distribution—the part earned from 1974 forward—is taxed under either the 10-year or 5-year forward averaging method.

As Table 3–3 indicates, you are generally better off using 10-year averaging, if you are eligible, on lump sums below $350,000 or so. Five-year averaging is the better method on larger lump-sum payouts. For you to use either method, your lump-sum distribution must meet six requirements:

1. It must be made from a "qualified" retirement plan.
2. It must be prompted by retirement (or by a layoff or other separation from service), death, or attainment of age 59½. (If you're self-employed, the distribution must be prompted by disability, death, or reaching age 59½.)

3. You must have been a participant in the qualified plan for at least five years, unless the payment is being made to your heirs because of your death.
4. The distribution must represent your entire balance in the plan.
5. It must be distributed within a single tax year.
6. It must be distributed on or after the date when you reach age 59½.

Table 3–3
Tax Rates for Forward Averaging

Lump Sum	10-Year Averaging	5-Year Averaging
$ 20,000	5.5%	7.5%
30,000	8.4	11.0
40,000	10.5	12.8
50,000	11.7	13.8
100,000	14.5	15.0
150,000	16.4	17.3
200,000	18.5	20.0
300,000	22.1	22.7
350,000*	23.8	23.8
400,000	25.7	24.8
600,000	31.2	26.8

*Approximate level where 5-year averaging becomes more advantageous.

You may use lump-sum averaging only once in your lifetime. Also, if you choose to use forward averaging with respect to *any* lump-sum distribution you receive during a particular year, you must apply the method to *all* the distributions you receive that year from a qualified plan.

Any lump-sum payouts will be reported to you (and the Internal Revenue Service) on Tax Form 1099-R. To calculate the tax due on the distribution using forward averaging, you'll need to use Form 4972, "Tax on Lump-Sum Distributions."

Rollover versus Forward Averaging Which method is better, IRA rollover or forward averaging? Not surprisingly, the answer is an equivocal "It depends." In general, forward averaging is the better choice if you expect to need all or most of your assets soon—within five years or so, say, to build a house or use as an entrance payment for a continuing care community. Although forward averaging means that you pay taxes up front and miss out on the tax-deferred compounding within the IRA, those disadvantages are outweighed by the fact that withdrawals from an IRA are treated as ordinary income and will typically be taxed at higher rates. Table 3–4 shows an example

Table 3–4
Forward Averaging versus IRA Rollover

	10-Year Averaging	IRA Rollover
Distribution	$200,000	$200,000
Tax at distribution	– 37,000	– 0
Net sum to invest	$163,000	$200,000
Two-year earnings	+ 16,844[1]	+ 28,980[2]
	$179,844	$228,980
Taxes at distribution	– 0	– 64,114
Net sum available	$179,844	$164,866

[1]Assumes 5.04% after-tax return.
[2]Assumes 7.0% pretax return.

for a couple in the 28% marginal tax bracket who have received a $200,000 lump-sum distribution. They expect to earn a 7.0% per year pretax return in the IRA. If forward averaging is used, the money will be invested in a taxable account earning 5.04% (7.0% × 0.72) after taxes. They want to use the money to purchase a vacation home in two years.

Forward averaging results in a 9.1% larger distribution over two years. State and local taxes may be due.

On the other hand, if you want to use your retirement plan money to provide a steady stream of income during your retirement, you'll probably be better off rolling the lump sum into an IRA. Not only do you avoid the initial tax, but you also allow your capital to grow unfettered by income taxes. These two factors allow you to overcome the higher effective tax on your withdrawals from the IRA. You also don't have to worry about a big IRA withdrawal suddenly pushing you into a higher tax bracket.

Table 3–5 provides another illustration for a couple in the 28% marginal tax bracket, again with a $200,000 distribution that is expected to earn a 7.0% pretax return in an IRA or 5.04% after taxes outside the IRA. The couple wants the assets to last for 15 years. You can see in the table that the tax-deferred compounding of assets in the IRA provides an edge over the forward averaging method, producing a monthly payment, *net of taxes*, that is larger by a tidy (if unspectacular) 6.4%.

Table 3–5
Forward Averaging versus IRA Rollover

	10-Year Averaging	IRA Rollover
Distribution	$200,000	$200,000
Tax on distribution	– 37,000	– 0
Sum left to invest	$163,000	$200,000
Monthly payment for 15 yrs at 5.04% ÷ 7.00%	$ 1,292	$ 1,798
Less tax at 28%	– 0	– 503
Net monthly payment	$ 1,292	$ 1,295
After-tax total over 15 years	$232,560	$233,100

Investing a Lump-Sum Distribution

If you decide to take your pension as a lump-sum distribution, investing the proceeds is an enormous responsibility. The next several chapters provide considerable background and guidance on key issues about investing during retirement, particularly how to determine the most appropriate mix of investments to meet your goals. But this is a good place to address a critical investing issue: Should a lump sum be invested all at once, or should you gradually invest the cash into mutual funds through a technique called dollar-cost averaging?

Dollar-cost averaging is a disciplined, steady program of systematic investments in the stock and bond markets. You decide on the amount you ultimately want to put into stocks and bonds and then invest equal portions of that amount at regular intervals over some predetermined period of time. This method helps to make market fluctuations work for you rather than against you. When prices of financial assets decline, your regular investment will buy more shares in a mutual fund. When prices rise, your investment will automatically buy fewer high-priced shares.

As an example, assume that you had a lump sum of $100,000 that you wanted to invest in stocks. One alternative would be to invest $5,000 into a stock fund (or group of stock funds) each month for 20 months. Table 3–6 provides a simple illustration of how dollar-cost averaging might work over six months in a fluctuating market. Because you buy fewer shares when prices are higher and more shares when prices are lower, the average cost for your shares is always lower than the average market price for the period in which you are investing.

If you are investing a lump sum from a self-directed retirement plan for which you have made the investment decisions, there is little problem in immediately moving the money into a similar mix of stocks and long-term bonds. For instance, if you've split your retirement plan assets evenly between stocks and bonds, you won't be taking any additional risk by moving your money to, say, an IRA with a mix of half stocks and half bonds.

The question of whether to use dollar-cost averaging really arises when you receive a big lump sum from an inheritance or as a distribution from a defined benefit plan, where the investment risk was borne by your employer. Some investment advisers say that, after determining how to allocate your assets among short-term "cash" reserves, bonds, and stocks, you should simply plunge ahead and invest your assets all at once. If your plan is to invest 50% of your lump sum in stocks, 35% in bonds, and 15% in cash reserves, these advisers recommend that you "just do it." Their advice is based on two empirical points. First, the stock and bond markets are unpredictable, so you can't predict the best time to invest. Second, bonds and stocks historically have provided higher returns than cash reserves, so why waste any of that return potential through a gradual investment approach? Other advisers concede these two points, but they still argue that you should put your lump sum to work in stages by dollar-cost averaging.

Table 3–6
Dollar-Cost Averaging

Month	Investment	Price per Share	Shares Purchased
1	$5,000	$25.00	200.000
2	5,000	27.50	181.818
3	5,000	21.00	238.095
4	5,000	24.00	208.333
5	5,000	22.50	222.222
6	5,000	24.50	204.082
Total shares purchased			1,254.550
Total investment			$30,000
Average price per share			$24.08
Average cost per share			$23.91

In studies that have compared an "all-at-once" strategy of investing in stocks with a dollar-cost averaging strategy, the all-at-once approach has tended to produce better results on average. For example, a recent study in the *American Association of Individual Investors Journal* compared the all-at-once strategy to dollar-cost averaging over rolling 12-month periods from 1926 through 1991 (January 1, 1926, through December 31, 1926; February 1926 through January 1927; and so on). Out of 780 12-month periods, the all-at-once strategy would have provided better returns in 503 periods, or 65% of the cases.

Despite the impressive margin for the all-at-once strategy, there are still reasons to strongly consider dollar-cost averaging.

First and foremost, the historical averages are of little use to the individual investor, since you have only one lump sum to invest. If you happen to invest it all at once just before a severe downturn in the markets, you will not receive the *average* returns of the past—you will earn a big loss. As a retiree, you may not have the luxury of riding out such a severe downturn and waiting years for your assets to recover. While the odds of such a severe downturn may not be very high, they are certainly greater than zero.

Dollar-cost averaging also mitigates the all-too-human tendency for emotions to overrule judgment. Few of us could accept with equanimity a sudden drop of −10% to −20% in the value of a large investment we had just made, especially if that investment represented a major portion of our net worth. Yet a typical bear market results in a −20% decline in stock prices. (You may recall that on October 19, 1987, the stock market declined an astounding −20.5% in a single day.) Some investors react to such downturns by yanking money out of stocks, not only missing the chance for any rebound, but turning a "paper" loss into a "real" loss.

If you're unwilling—or unable—to suffer a significant interim decline in the value of your lump-sum distribution, but you still want to invest some of your lump sum in stocks and long-term bonds to earn potentially superior returns, dollar-cost averaging is an eminently sensible approach. It may modestly reduce the returns you could have gotten by investing all at once, but it will strongly reduce the chance of a large, sudden loss.

Over what period should you use dollar-cost averaging? There is no magic formula. However, since stock market cycles tend to take place over periods of three to five years, that may be an appropriate time frame. Of course, aggressive investors may wish to complete their investment programs in as little as one year. Ultimately, only you can decide whether investing all at once or dollar-cost averaging is right for you, weighing the potential for higher returns against the risks of committing your lump sum all at once.

Early Retirement Offers

Corporate downsizings and restructurings in recent years have affected millions of workers. One method hundreds of employers have used to reduce their workforces is to offer early retirement incentives. Although some companies have discovered after the fact that they have lost many valuable employees through these retirement offers, there is every indication that the early retirement offer will remain in the corporate manager's toolkit. This section will describe common features of early retirement packages and raise some important issues you should consider if confronted with such an offer.

Types of Early Retirement Offers

Although the details of early retirement offers are as varied as the companies that make them, there are two main types. The first is often called a "voluntary separation" or "voluntary retirement" offer. Such an offer might be extended to all employees, not just to older employees, and would typically provide slightly improved severance benefits—say, two or three weeks' pay for each year of service with the company, up to a maximum of one year's pay. A particularly attractive offer might include paid health insurance for one year after your departure. And, of course, if you are vested in your employer's pension plan, you'll get your pension benefits when you reach retirement age. In thinking about the cash portion of the package, be sure to consider taxes. Income taxes will be withheld from the final check, and they can take a surprisingly large bite out of the payment.

The second, more extensive type of early retirement package is typically offered only to employees who are over age 50 or 55. These offers usually provide cash severance payments and adjustments to your defined benefit pension plan to make the pension benefit larger than it otherwise would have been. For example, the employer might add three years to your age and to the length of your employment for purposes of calculating your pension benefit. These changes will boost your monthly benefit check or the lump-sum payout your pension will provide. Some packages also contain employer-paid medical insurance for some period after your departure. The employer might also offer monthly "bridge" payments to boost your pension until you reach age 62 and are eligible for Social Security benefits. Bridge payments are, in effect, the equivalent of getting your Social Security payments early.

"As early retirees, my wife and I spent a lot of time determining whether we could afford to quit the fast track and go sailing. Our income is much less than it was three years ago, but we aren't aware of a decline in our quality of life. We used a computer-software program to help with setting our objectives, assessing our current assets, making inflation adjustments, and our asset allocation."

Maryland

Evaluating the Offer

The first consideration in evaluating an early retirement offer is whether it really is a voluntary offer. Under federal law, you can't be required to take an early retirement offer. However, the law doesn't protect you if the company later fires you, saying your job has been eliminated. You could also be demoted later, or the duties of your job could be changed in ways that make it unbearable to you. Indeed, companies often announce that there may be layoffs if they don't get enough volunteers for early retirement offers. So, before rejecting an offer, try to make sure that your superior is happy with your work and that your position is secure. And keep in mind that even if your boss likes your work, entire departments sometimes get wiped out in corporate staff reductions.

If you have the opportunity and desire to take another job or to start your own business, you may be in a position to accept a less-than-ideal early retirement offer. If working part-time is attractive to you, ask about the possibility of doing work for your old employer on a freelance or consulting basis. For those who truly intend to retire, the income provided in the retirement package—whether from severance or from pension payments—must be sufficient to meet their living needs. Do projections of your expenses and income several years out to get a feel for how inflation will affect your finances. A deal that looks good today may not look so good several years from now as prices rise and your pension payments remain the same.

If you retire early and begin accessing your IRA or other investments early, you'll be hurting yourself in two ways.

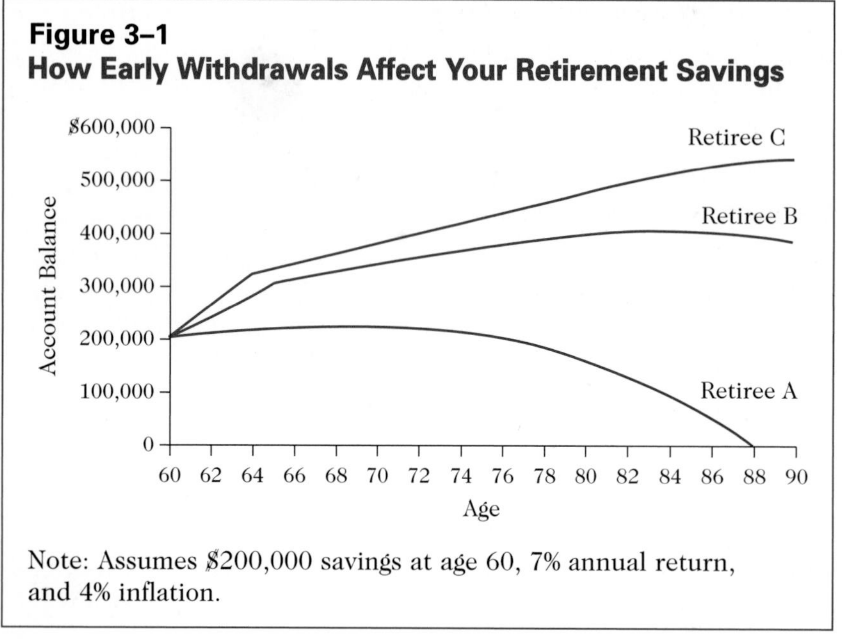

Figure 3–1
How Early Withdrawals Affect Your Retirement Savings

Note: Assumes $200,000 savings at age 60, 7% annual return, and 4% inflation.

First, your contributions to the retirement accounts will cease. Second, you'll be interrupting the compounding of investment earnings and thus reducing the ultimate growth in your investment assets. This will mean getting less income from your investments than would be available if you had waited until your normal retirement age to begin using your retirement savings. These two factors are quite powerful, as illustrated in Figure 3–1, which is based on three coworkers (conveniently named A, B, and C), each with $200,000 in tax-deferred accounts at age 60. We'll assume that each earned 7% on the accounts and that inflation will average 4% annually. If Retiree A retires at age 60 and takes an initial withdrawal of $10,000 from his tax-deferred account, with withdrawals rising 4% annually to account for inflation, the account will run out of money when he is 88 years old.

Retiree B stops adding to the tax-deferred savings at age 60 but waits until age 65 to retire, by which time the $200,000 in retirement savings has grown to $280,500. In the first year of retirement, he withdraws $12,170 ($10,000 adjusted for five years of inflation at 4% per year). When he is 90 years old, the annual withdrawal has grown to $32,440, but the retirement account still contains more than $382,000.

Retiree C continues to contribute to her tax-deferred retirement account from age 60 until retirement at age 65, starting with a $6,000 contribution at age 60 and boosting the amount by 4% a year. The extra contributions, plus earnings on the account, push its value to $320,300 when she retires at age 65. She takes the same withdrawal from the retirement account as her friend Retiree B, starting at $12,170 at age 65 and rising to $32,440 at age 90, when Retiree C's account contains $543,000 and is still growing.

Retiring early will also reduce the amount of your Social Security benefits, since the earnings used to calculate your benefits will include more of your low or nonearning years and exclude the higher later earnings that you will forgo by retiring. (You'll find more on early retirement and Social Security in Chapter 9.) Even if early retirement incentives include pension "sweeteners," you will probably get a lower pension benefit from your employer than if you'd continued to work until normal retirement age. That's because your final average salary—the base usually used for determining pension payments—will probably be lower than it would have been if you'd kept working. It's very important that you make careful estimates of your future living costs and income; don't just rely on a "feeling" that you'll be financially secure.

The costs of health care and health care insurance will be critical factors in deciding whether to accept an early retirement offer. If the offer includes continued insurance coverage from your employer, that is a very big savings for you. If you're not yet age 65 and eligible for Medicare, you could spend $5,000 a year or more for private insurance coverage. If you have health problems, you may not be able to get insurance at any price. You always have the right under COBRA, a federal law, to buy health insurance coverage under your employer's plan for at least 18 months after your departure. You may buy coverage for the same cost your employer pays for the coverage, plus an administrative fee of up to 2%. Make certain that you understand the health care coverage under the early retirement offer. Most early retirement offers give the employer the right to change the terms of insurance coverage in the future—and many companies have done just that, trimming or even eliminating coverage they had promised to retirees.

You should also take into account other benefits that your employer provided or subsidized, such as group disability insurance or life insurance. Find out whether coverage continues for some period after you depart, and find out what it will cost you to replace any coverage that you still need after leaving your job.

A final word about early retirement offers: don't procrastinate in researching and thinking it over. Employers typically put a time limit of a month or two on considering an offer. If you wait too long to study it, you may have to make crucial decisions while feeling rushed and pressured as the deadline looms.

Final Thoughts

Benefits from employer-sponsored pension plans are a critical source of retirement income, so it's important to understand the payment options available to you as a pensioner and the tax treatment of distributions from pensions. Once made, pension decisions are usually irreversible, so it is vitally important to take the time to learn the details of your employer's plan and consider your options in light of your own income needs and tax situation.

Of course, income from employer-sponsored pension plans is only one of the three legs in the traditional model of retirement income. The second leg is income from your personal investments, which may have been amassed through regular savings and investment accounts, or perhaps through investments in retirement savings plans. This guide now turns to the issues of how you go about investing and managing those assets.

MAKE THE MOST FROM YOUR RETIREMENT INVESTMENTS

Part **2**

Basic Principles of Investing

Chapter **4**

While investing can be made to sound incredibly complicated, the process can really be reduced to analyzing three basic types of assets: short-term cash reserves, long-term bonds, and common stocks. If you have a basic understanding of these three asset classes, you're well on the way to becoming a capable investor.

"In investing, the return you want should depend on whether you want to eat well or sleep well."

J. Kenfield Morley

Unfortunately, an enduring myth of investing is that good long-term results depend on brilliant timing of moves into or out of the financial markets or on shrewd selections of individual stocks, bonds, or mutual funds. In reality, as numerous studies have shown, an investor's long-term investment results will be largely determined by how the investor's portfolio is split, or allocated, among the three primary classes of assets.

This chapter will try to demystify the investing process and show how even neophyte investors can develop a diversified portfolio that meets their long-term financial needs. The chapter starts by discussing the three types of assets, the risks and rewards of each type, and how different combinations provide different risks and rewards. Next, to assist you in your retirement planning, the chapter explores an easy method for projecting likely returns on stocks and bonds. The chapter closes with a discussion of other investment options that may be appropriate in a diversified retirement investment portfolio.

The Three Primary Asset Classes

The three primary financial asset classes are short-term cash reserves, long-term bonds, and common stocks.

Short-Term Cash Reserves

Even if you're a novice investor, you are probably familiar with short-term reserves, the asset class held by the greatest number of investors. Reserves are short-term IOUs issued by high-quality borrowers. These IOUs can take many forms: bank money market deposit accounts, certificates of deposit (CDs) issued by banks, Treasury bills guaranteed by the U.S. government, short-term bonds, or commercial paper issued by corporations. Money market mutual funds may hold any or all of these securities.

The way that all of these instruments work is that, in return for your investment, the borrower agrees to pay you a stated interest rate for a predetermined length of time. For "money market" instruments, the lending period is usually less than one year, although CDs typically are offered with maturities up to 10 years. Because the loan period is so short, there is very little risk that your investment will not be repaid in full when the money market instrument matures. This low level of *principal risk* makes short-term reserves especially attractive to retirement investors who are extremely concerned about the risks of losing principal.

As you might expect, there are critical trade-offs associated with this lower risk. First, short-term reserves typically pay lower yields than longer-term bonds or other fixed-income securities. Historically, the returns on short-term reserves have barely exceeded the rate of inflation. Second, short-term reserves carry a very high *income risk,* meaning that the income generated by your investment in cash reserves may vary sharply from year to year.

Certificates of Deposit Certificates of deposit, or CDs, are basically IOUs issued by banks. They are available with many different maturity levels, from 30 days to 10 years, and are insured up to a maximum of $100,000 by a government agency, the Federal Deposit Insurance Corporation (FDIC).

This insurance feature of CDs is a key attraction to retirement investors, as is the assurance that the principal value of the certificate will not fall. However, CDs do have some drawbacks. First, the interest paid usually is lower than that available on Treasury securities or corporate bonds of similar maturities. Second, banks usually charge substantial interest penalties if you withdraw your money from a CD before it matures. The penalty—and the difficulty of selling a CD to a second party if you need access to your money before the certificate matures—means that CDs are not as liquid, or convertible to cash, as many bonds or bond mutual funds. One way to improve liquidity is to buy CDs "brokered" for banks by brokerage firms, which will make a secondary market in the certificates. Before investing in CDs, shop around. Rates paid vary substantially from bank to bank and from one city to the next.

Long-Term Bonds

Bonds are another form of IOU, but with a longer period until maturity (repayment by the borrower). Bonds are issued by the U.S. government and its agencies, by corporations, and by states and municipalities for periods of up to 30 years (even longer in a few cases). Bonds typically pay interest at a set "coupon" rate twice a year and repay the original investment, or principal, at the end of the bond's term.

"I am very confused right now. Do I invest in bonds and take income, without future growth? Do I invest in stocks, pull out what I need each year for income, and let the rest grow? Do I just keep my money in money market funds, where it just sits there earning a small amount of interest?

Pennsylvania

Because you are lending your money for such a long period, bonds have greater risks than short-term reserves. First, there is uncertainty as to whether the borrower will be able to continue making interest payments and to repay your principal at maturity. For bonds issued by corporations, there is no guarantee that a company will stay in business long enough to repay the full amount of your loan. A second risk is that you are locked into the interest payments agreed upon when you bought the bond. To see why this presents a risk to you, suppose that you hold a 20-year bond paying 7% annual interest. If interest rates move to, say, 8% right after you buy the bond, you are still locked into a 7%-per-year interest payment. You could, of course, sell your current bond and buy a new 8% coupon bond, but when you sell your lower-coupon bond, you will receive a lower price than you paid for it when interest rates were at 7%.

This inverse relationship between interest rates and bond prices is called *interest-rate risk.* Using the previous example, it follows that if interest rates fall to 6%, you will be able to sell your 7% bond for a higher price than you paid for it, since the bond is locked into a higher interest payment. To compensate them for this interest-rate risk, investors in long-term bonds typically command higher yields than investors in short-term reserves. These higher, locked-in yields are why long-term bonds probably should make up a substantial part of the typical retiree's investment portfolio. Of course, in exchange for the higher, relatively predictable stream of income, the retired investor must be willing to accept some interim price volatility.

Common Stocks

Common stocks, the third primary class of financial assets, represent partial ownership in corporations, rather than a corporate loan. As an owner of stock in a company, you earn a proportional interest in all corporate profits paid out in dividends, as well as any rise or fall in the market value of the company's stock. Of the three main asset classes, stocks are the only security that provides both an income component and a long-term growth component.

Dividend payments on common stock are not fixed, as are interest payments on most bonds. Nevertheless, unlike interest on bonds, dividends on stocks tend to rise over time as corporate profits increase. Indeed, some companies have increased their dividend payouts each year for several decades. But since dividends are not a contractual obligation, like interest payments on bonds, companies sometimes reduce or eliminate dividend payments in tough times. Stocks, unlike short-term reserves and bonds, have no fixed maturity date, so a stockholder may receive a rising stream of cash dividends for as long as a company prospers. But dividend payments from stocks can also stagnate or even drop. After all, dividends are paid after a company meets all its other financial obligations, including wages, taxes, raw materials and supplies, rent, and interest payments to bondholders. When a company has financial problems, dividends on common stock are first in line to be eliminated.

Another risk of owning common stocks is that the market value of your shares will fluctuate, often widely, with changes in investors' perceptions about the prospects for the economy and for corporate profits. As compensation for this high price volatility, stocks historically have provided much higher returns than either short-term reserves or long-term bonds. Because these higher returns have in the past helped investors to stay ahead of inflation, a diversified portfolio of stocks (as opposed to just a few individual stocks) should be a major component of most retired investors' investment portfolios.

An Overview of Risks and Returns on Financial Assets

Investors are inundated with investment information through advertisements, stockbrokers, journalists, and authors. Much of this information, particularly advertising and promotional material, focuses heavily (if not exclusively) on returns, but pays little attention to risk. This section will build on the background you've learned about the three major asset classes and discuss how to evaluate the trade-off between risk and return.

This guide focuses primarily on "total return," which includes the income an investment produces (from interest or dividends) plus any rise or fall in the value of the asset. Because retirees are especially sensitive to the income portion of total return, the guide will generally separate total return into both its income and capital components.

In the abstract, absolute total returns are relatively simple to evaluate: a 10% return is better than an 8% return, but worse than a 12% return. But evaluating the risk of an investment is more complex. It involves three primary elements: principal, inflation, and income. Some investors focus solely on principal risk—the chance that they could lose money. This is hardly surprising, since the emotional impact of seeing your investment decline in value is powerful, even for investors who realize that such declines occur frequently and may only be temporary.

"I'm spreading the risk. You don't want to put it all into one thing, so you spread it around. Some of my investments are aggressive, some are conservative."

Virginia

Table 4–1
Risks and Returns of Financial Assets

	Short-Term Reserves	Long-Term Bonds	Common Stocks
Long-term total return potential	Low	Moderate	High
Inflation risk	High	Moderate	Low
Principal risk	Low	Moderate	High
Income risk	High	Low	Low

For retirees, there is another investment hazard that may be less obvious but can be just as damaging as principal risk. This second danger is the risk that inflation will erode the value and purchasing power of your assets. As noted in Chapter 2, this inflation risk is why an investment should be evaluated on the basis of both its *nominal return* (before inflation) and its *real return* (after inflation).

Unfortunately, investments that offer the highest potential returns, and therefore the best chance of overcoming inflation risk, tend to have correspondingly higher levels of principal risk. When it comes to principal risk, short-term reserves, long-term bonds, and common stocks fall along a continuum. At the far left lie short-term reserves, with their low-risk/low-return profile. On the far right lie common stocks, with their high-risk/high-return characteristics. Long-term bonds lie somewhere in between.

Another type of risk that must be considered, especially by retirees, is income risk—the chance that the income stream from your investments will decline. Short-term cash reserves, which have the lowest principal risk, carry the highest income risk, as shown in the risk/return overview in Table 4–1. Stocks, which have high principal risk, have low income risk because dividends paid on a diversified portfolio of stocks rarely decline substantially from one year to the next, and in fact tend to grow over time. As a retiree who relies on income from your investments to make ends meet, you must strike a balance between achieving a long-lasting stream of income that keeps up with inflation and avoiding undue risks to the value of your investment principal.

The Risks and Returns of Short-Term Reserves

Short-term reserves provide a safe haven for money that will be needed within a relatively short period. Historically, short-term reserves have provided average returns only a bit higher than the rate of inflation. As shown in Figure 4–1, a $1 investment in U.S. Treasury bills on December 31, 1925, would have grown to $13.54 on December 31, 1996, equivalent to a 3.7% average annual return. However, after adjusting for an annual inflation rate of 3.1% over the same period, the final value of the $1 investment in today's dollars would be just $1.53. Short-term reserves have fared slightly better in recent times, as investors have insisted on higher yields to compensate them for a greater perceived (and at times, actual) risk of inflation. From 1962 through 1996, short-term reserves provided an average annual return of 6.3%, compared with average inflation of 4.9% a year, for a real return (nominal return minus the inflation rate) of 1.4% annually.

Over both the 1926–96 and 1962–96 periods, the impact of inflation has been hard to overcome for short-term investments; inflation has eaten up roughly 80% of the return on U.S. Treasury bills. In the 62 "rolling" 10-year periods since 1926 (1926–35, 1927–36, etc.), Treasury bills provided a negative real return in 27 periods, or nearly half the time. In only nine periods did Treasury bills provide a real return of more than 3% per year. Thus, while short-term reserves may be a necessary component of a retiree's portfolio, their returns have not been nearly generous enough to justify making them the sole investment vehicle for your retirement assets.

Figure 4–1
Growth of $1 Invested in U.S. Treasury Bills, 1926–96

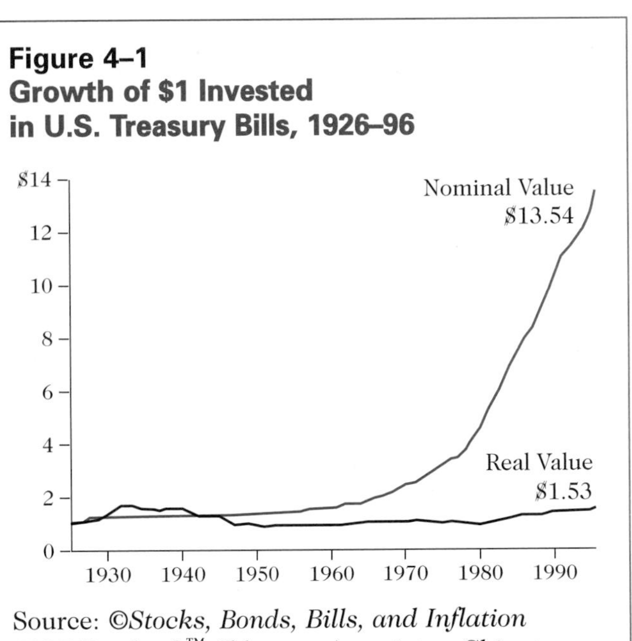

Source: ©*Stocks, Bonds, Bills, and Inflation 1997 Yearbook*™, Ibbotson Associates, Chicago. (Annually updates work by Roger G. Ibbotson and Rex A. Sinquefield.) Used with permission.

Because the risk to both principal and interest is essentially zero in U.S. Treasury bills and in CDs from FDIC-insured banks, most investors view these investments as unequivocally safe. But the penalty for this level of security is a sharp reduction in investment returns, which exposes your assets to erosion by inflation. Additionally, investors in short-term reserves incur the greatest risk of income fluctuations. Recall the "income shock" suffered by many retirees in the early 1990s, as short-term interest rates fell from 8% in 1990 to less than 3% in 1993. This rate decline cut the income earned on a $200,000 investment by more than 60%, from $16,000 annually to $6,000 annually.

In sum, short-term reserves provide welcome peace of mind when it comes to safety of principal; however, this attribute must be weighed against the lower returns they have provided historically. Retirees also must keep in mind that the wide variability of income returns from short-term reserves makes them a surprisingly risky investment option. This variability makes retirees vulnerable to the temptation to move out of short-term reserves when interest rates are at their lowest and to reach for higher yields on long-term bonds. Switching from short-term reserves to long-term bonds at the bottom of an interest-rate cycle can be a costly move, as many investors discovered when interest rates moved sharply higher during 1994, causing bond prices to plummet some −25%. The best protection against such missteps is a diversified portfolio of short-term reserves, common stocks, and bonds.

The Risks and Returns of Bonds

Over time, the returns on long-term bonds are largely determined by their coupon payments and the compounding of reinvested interest income. As shown in Figure 4–2, a $1 investment in long-term U.S. government bonds on December 31, 1925, would have grown to $33.73 on December 31, 1996, representing an annual rate of return of 5%. Taking into account an inflation rate of 3.1% over the same period, the

5% nominal return translates to a 1.9% real return, and the final real value of the $1 investment drops to $3.82.

Although the returns from long-term bonds have, on average, beaten inflation, the averages obscure a good deal of variability. In 34 of the 62 ten-year periods beginning in 1926 (1926–35, 1927–36, etc.), bonds produced average annual returns that were less than inflation. In the 10-year periods from 1933–42 through 1976–85, long-term government bonds never beat inflation by more than 2% annually. Results were particularly poor during the decades beginning in 1960 through 1975, when high inflation rates pushed up interest rates, which caused bond prices to decline sharply.

Figure 4–2
Growth of $1 Investment in Long-Term U.S. Government Bonds, 1926–96

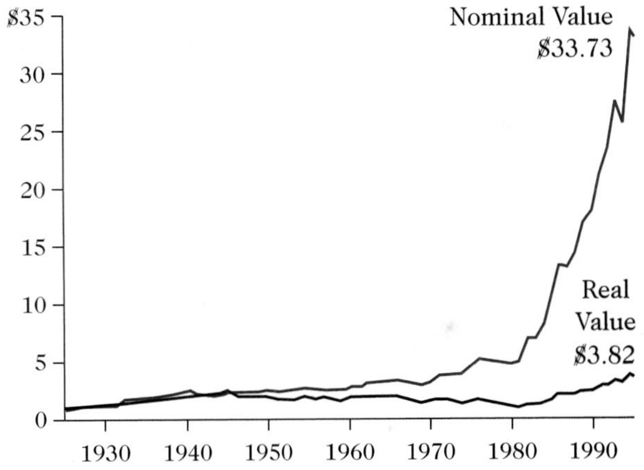

Nominal Value $33.73
Real Value $3.82
$35, 30, 25, 20, 15, 10, 5, 0
1930 1940 1950 1960 1970 1980 1990

Source: ©*Stocks, Bonds, Bills, and Inflation 1997 Yearbook*™, Ibbotson Associates, Chicago. (Annually updates work by Roger G. Ibbotson and Rex A. Sinquefield.) Used with permission.

In assessing the future performance of bonds over longer periods—say, 10 years—your best indicator of likely returns is the yield at the beginning of the investment period. For example, with long-term U.S. Treasury bonds yielding about 6% at year-end 1996, the return from long-term bonds from 1995 to 2005 may reasonably be expected to average about 6% a year. This rate of return is about halfway between the 7% average annual return from bonds over the 1960–96 period and the longer-term average annual return of 5% from 1926 through 1996.

As with U.S. Treasury bills and insured bank CDs, investors who hold long-term U.S. Treasury bonds can be sure of being paid both their interest income payments and, at maturity, their original principal. In this sense, U.S. Treasury bonds offer an unparalleled degree of safety. However, if you own Treasury bonds and need to sell them before their stated maturity, the price you receive may be higher or lower than the price you paid for them. The reason, as noted earlier, is that bond prices move in the opposite direction from interest rates. Rising interest rates make existing bonds, which pay a lower rate of interest, less attractive compared to new bonds, which pay a higher rate of interest. Therefore, the prices of the lower-yielding bonds fall when interest rates rise. Conversely, falling interest rates make existing bonds, with their higher yields, relatively more attractive than newly issued bonds. Thus, the prices of existing bonds rise when interest rates decline.

Table 4–2 illustrates the effect of rising interest rates on the price of a $1,000 bond with a 7% coupon, assuming a range of maturities. As the table shows, the longer the maturity of a particular bond, the more its price falls in response to a rise in rates. For example, the price of a 20-year bond would decline by roughly −10% (from $1,000 to $901) if interest rates rose by one percentage point, and by −18% (from $1,000 to $816) if they rose two percentage points. This principal volatility explains why rising interest rates—which typically accompany accelerating inflation—are so worrisome to bond investors. However, if you're reinvesting the interest income from your bonds and you have a long-term investment horizon, the price risk of bonds is not such a big concern. That's because after a rise in rates you are able to invest the interest income from the existing bonds at higher rates, which can be expected to offset at least part of the decline in the bonds' price. (Of course, if you hold a bond until it matures, you will receive your full original investment.)

Table 4–2
Price Change of Bonds When Interest Rates Rise

Bond Maturity (Years)	Value if Interest Rates Increase by					
	0.5%	1%	1.5%	2%	2.5%	3%
2	$991	$982	$973	$964	$955	$947
5	979	959	940	921	902	884
10	965	932	900	870	841	813
20	949	901	857	816	778	743

Note: Assumes $1,000 face value and 7% coupon.

Table 4–3 shows how a *decline* in interest rates *boosts* the prices of bonds. The table suggests why the bond market was so favorable during the period from year-end 1983 through 1993. During this decade, the yield on long-term Treasury bonds fell from 11% to 6.4%. This rate decline boosted the price of long-term bonds by more than 60%, for an average annual gain of 4%. So holders of long-term bonds not only were paid a relatively high level of annual interest income, but also benefited from a substantial rise in the value of their holdings.

Table 4–3
Price Change of Bonds When Interest Rates Decline

Bond Maturity (Years)	Value if Interest Rates Decline by					
	0.5%	1%	1.5%	2%	2.5%	3%
2	$1,009	$1,019	$1,028	$1,038	$1,047	$1,057
5	1,021	1,043	1,065	1,088	1,111	1,135
10	1,036	1,074	1,114	1,156	1,200	1,245
20	1,056	1,116	1,181	1,251	1,327	1,410

Note: Assumes $1,000 face value and 7% coupon.

There is one negative aspect of falling interest rates for the holder of long-term bonds: income from your existing bonds or the proceeds from maturing bonds can't be invested at the old, higher rates. So, as old bonds mature, you'll be forced to replace them with bonds paying lower rates of income. For a retiree who is using the interest from bonds for current expenses, this can be a serious problem. Consider, for example, Figure 4–3, which shows the fluctuations in income derived from a $100,000 investment in one-year Treasury bills. Each year, as the bills come due and are rolled over into new one-year securities, the interest earned fluctuates considerably.

Figure 4–3
Income from $100,000 Invested in One-Year U.S. Treasury Bills

Source: Salomon Brothers, Inc.

Of course, there are ways to mitigate the risks that go hand in hand with bonds. First, you can choose a maturity level that suits your needs and the amount of risk you're willing to take. In Tables 4–2 and 4–3, you can see the level of risk at each step-up in maturity. If you plan to use some of the principal in a few years, you might want to steer clear of longer-term bonds. A second way to mitigate interest-rate risk is to stagger, or "ladder," the maturities of the bonds or bond funds that you own.

You can build a laddered portfolio with mutual funds by splitting your investment among bond funds with differing average maturities: short-term, intermediate-term, and long-term. Or you can build a bond ladder with individual bonds by purchasing securities with differing maturity dates. For example, you can split your money equally among 10 individual Treasury securities, ranging from a one-year bill to a 10-year note. Each year, as one matures, you can keep the ladder going by buying a 10-year note. If you want to shorten the average maturity of the ladder, reinvest the maturing security in a shorter-term security. To lengthen the maturity and lock in a high rate, buy a longer-term bond with the proceeds from a maturing bond.

Another type of risk to consider when buying bonds is "credit risk"—the risk that a bond issuer will not pay the interest or principal as it has promised. Standard & Poor's Corp., one of several bond-rating agencies, evaluates the creditworthiness of bonds using grades ranging from the top-quality AAA to C, for "junk," or high-yield, bonds. Table 4–4

Table 4–4
Bond Credit Ratings

Standard & Poor's	Moody's	Description
AAA	Aaa	Highest quality, an indication that the issuer's finances are extremely strong.
AA	Aa	Very high quality, indicating that the issuer is highly secure.
A	A	Upper medium grade.
BBB	Baa	The lowest investment grade, indicating that the issue is creditworthy but that there is a moderate risk to payment of principal and income on the bond.
CCC	Caa	Speculative grade, indicating substantial risk of default.

defines bond credit ratings for Standard & Poor's and Moody's Investors Service, Inc.

In general, the lower the quality of a bond, the higher the yield it will offer. U.S. government bonds, with the very highest credit quality, typically offer the lowest available yields. Yields on AAA corporate bonds are slightly higher, and yields generally rise further as credit quality declines and there is less certainty about the ability of the bond issuer to honor its obligation. Retired investors, especially those who own bonds primarily for the interest income they generate, should generally stick with investment-grade (BBB or better) bonds to reduce the chance that their income will decline because of a bankruptcy or default.

A final risk applies to most corporate or municipal bonds, whose issuers have the right to "call," or redeem, the bonds earlier than the stated maturity date. (Almost all U.S. Treasury bonds are non-callable.) Typically, call provisions allow the issuer to redeem the bonds after five or 10 years from the date they were issued. Obviously, a company isn't going to redeem its bonds early unless it gains an advantage. That's why bonds are called when interest rates drop, and the issuer can sell new bonds at a lower rate than it's paying on the older bonds. The call means you get your money back early. Instead of receiving the interest you had expected from the bond, you're faced with reinvesting the proceeds, almost surely at lower interest rates than those that prevailed when you bought the bond. If you buy a corporate or municipal bond, make sure you understand whether and when it can be called. Also, find out the bond's yield to its call date, not just the yield to its maturity date.

Municipal Bonds Taxable U.S. government and corporate bonds are the right choice for most retirees, the large majority of whom are in low income tax brackets. But if you're in a higher tax bracket, the tax-exempt interest available from municipal bonds may provide you with a higher after-tax return than higher-yielding taxable bonds. Municipal bonds are issued by cities, counties, states, and various local government authorities. The interest paid on these bonds is exempt from federal income tax and may be exempt from state and local income taxes too.

Because of this tax-exempt advantage, yields on municipal bonds are usually below the yields available on taxable bonds of similar maturities. There is a straightforward calculation you can use to compare the yields on tax-exempt bonds with the yields available on taxable bonds of comparable quality and maturity. Simply multiply the taxable bond's yield by 1 minus your income tax rate. If your income is taxed at the 31% marginal tax rate, a taxable bond yielding 7% would pay an after-tax yield of 4.83% (0.07 × [1−0.31]). Thus, any municipal bond that yields more than 4.83%—provided it is of comparable quality and maturity—should be favored over the taxable alternative.

The Risks and Returns of Common Stocks

Common stocks have in the past provided the highest rate of return of the three major classes of financial assets. Figure 4–4, using the Standard & Poor's 500 Composite Stock Price Index to represent stocks, shows how dramatically the value of an investment in stocks has grown over time. A $1 investment in a diversified basket of stocks at year-end 1925 would have grown to $1,370.95 by year-end 1996, an average annual growth rate of 10.7%. After adjustment for inflation, the $1 investment would have grown to $156.39, which means that, even after accounting for a 3.1% inflation rate, stocks provided an average return of 7.6% a year.

"Don't gamble; take all your savings and buy some good stock, and hold it 'til it goes up, then sell it. If it don't go up, don't buy it."

Will Rogers

To achieve such remarkable long-term results, investors in common stocks have had to endure dramatic year-to-year fluctuations in their returns. In 1931, the worst year for stocks, investors saw the value of a diversified basket of common stocks plummet −43%, even after reinvestment of dividends. In 1933, the best year ever, the return from stocks was 54%. The spread between the worst and best years was a staggering 97 percentage points. Volatility is not a relic of the Great Depression. In 1974, stock prices fell nearly −30% and the total return for the year—including dividends—was −26%. During the "Great

Crash" of October 19, 1987, stock prices fell more than −20% *in a single day.* Investors who sold their stock holdings during these market declines suffered significant losses.

This volatility risk is precisely what most concerns retired investors about the stock market. Fear of sharp declines in stock prices keeps many retirees away from stocks entirely. As a result, these play-it-safe investors miss out on the benefits of stock ownership—higher long-term returns and relatively stable, but rising, income from stock dividends.

Figure 4–4
Growth of $1 Invested in Common Stocks, 1926–96

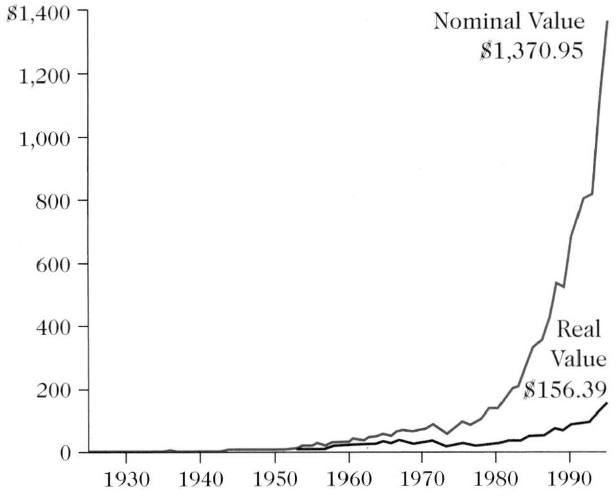

Source: ©*Stocks, Bonds, Bills, and Inflation 1997 Yearbook*™, Ibbotson Associates, Chicago. (Annually updates work by Roger G. Ibbotson and Rex A. Sinquefield.) Used with permission.

There are ways to tame the volatility risk that accompanies common stocks. The first way to reduce risk is to adopt a long-term time horizon. In general, the longer the holding period for a basket of stocks, the lower your price volatility, as shown in Figure 4–5. As noted earlier, the worst one-year loss for stocks was −43.3% in 1931. Compare that figure with the worst five-year period (1928–32), when stocks fell an average of −12.5% a year, even after reinvestment of dividends. The worst 10-year period was 1929–38, when stocks lost an average of −0.9% a year, taking the value of a $1,000 investment at the start of 1929 to $915 by the end of 1938. In all but one other rolling 10-year period, stocks provided a positive total return. Put another way, stocks lost money in only two of 62 10-year periods starting with 1926–35. And in *every* rolling 15-year, 20-year, or 25-year period from 1926 through 1995, stocks provided a positive average total return.

Why are price fluctuations in the stock market so wide over shorter periods and so muted over longer periods? The

Figure 4–5
Range of Returns on Common Stocks, 1926–96

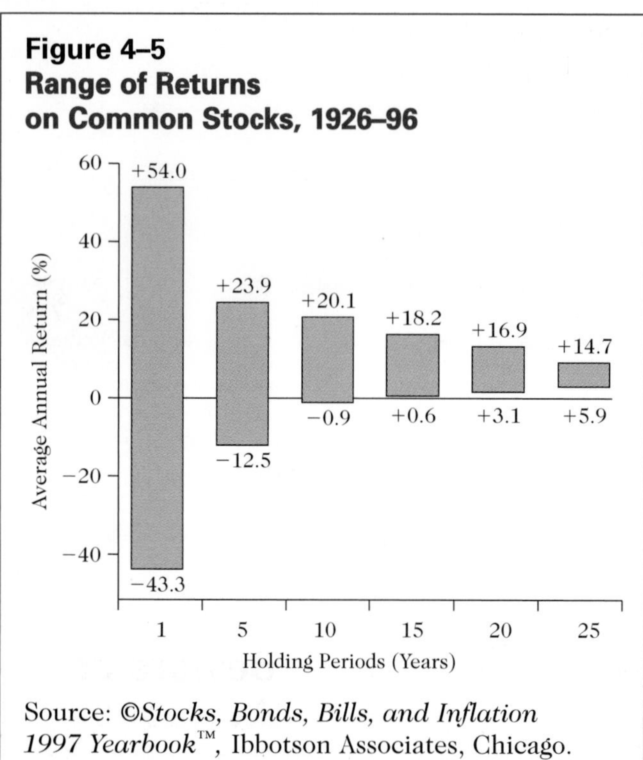

Source: ©*Stocks, Bonds, Bills, and Inflation 1997 Yearbook*™, Ibbotson Associates, Chicago. (Annually updates work by Roger G. Ibbotson and Rex A. Sinquefield.) Used with permission. All rights reserved.

main reason is that stock prices in the short term, even over periods of a few years, are influenced very heavily by investors' hopes and fears about the economy, inflation, political upheaval, and the like. Over the long run, however, stock prices are determined mainly by growth in corporate profits and the dividends paid on common stock. The longer your investment time horizon, then, the more likely you are to be able to ride out the gyrations of the emotional stock market. Since most Americans now retire between the ages of 60 and 65 and can reasonably expect to live past age 80, most investors early in retirement have a time horizon long enough to make common stocks a sensible part of an overall investment portfolio. (As discussed in Chapter 3, retired investors who receive a large lump-sum distribution from a pension can use dollar-cost averaging—the regular, systematic investing of money regardless of market conditions—to reduce the risks from a sudden decline in stock prices.)

Unlike the prices of common stocks, the dividends paid on common stocks are remarkably durable. In the 71 years from 1926 through 1996, the dividends paid on a diversified basket of stocks declined in nine years, increased in 61 years, and remained unchanged in one year. Dividends increased at an average annual rate of 4.5%, handily beating the annual inflation rate of 3.1% and producing real income growth of 1.4% a year.

You can also mitigate the risks of owning common stocks by holding a diversified portfolio that contains a healthy proportion of bonds and cash reserves. The returns from stocks and bonds do not always move in lockstep, and bond prices generally fluctuate less than stock prices. So owning both stocks and bonds can smooth out some of the fluctuations from either asset class. The third component of a balanced portfolio—cash reserves—provides stability of principal and a certain (if usually modest) stream of income.

In combination, these three asset classes can provide what most retired investors need: a reasonable level of current income as well as long-term growth in income. Instead of focusing on the risks or rewards inherent in any *one* part of a balanced portfolio, an investor should consider the risk and return characteristics of the *overall* mix of investments.

Beware of Averages

Why should you forecast the returns you expect from your investments, rather than simply project forward the historical average returns from the past? After all, many investors—indeed, many financial planners—do precisely that. But this crude methodology can be as dangerous as assuming that you can safely wade across a river with an average depth of four feet.

The returns from financial assets during the recent past have been extraordinarily high, as you can see from Table 4–5. However, an investor today would be ill-advised to count on a continuation of the high returns of the 1980s and early 1990s. Results in any particular decade have a very good chance of being far different from the long-term historical averages. For each of the three principal classes of assets—short-term reserves, bonds, and stocks—there have been extended periods of unusually high and unusually low returns.

Table 4–5
Average Annual Returns

	1926–96	1982–96	1987–96
Common stocks	10.7%	16.8%	15.3%
Long-term bonds	5.1	13.3	9.4
Cash reserves	3.7	6.5	5.5
Inflation	3.1	3.6	3.7

Source: ©*Stocks, Bonds, Bills, and Inflation 1997 Yearbook*™, Ibbotson Associates, Chicago. (Annually updates work by Roger G. Ibbotson and Rex A. Sinquefield.) Used with permission. All rights reserved.

"I just want to keep making about 10% a year. I'll be happy with that."

Texas

The prudent investor should consider the possibility of having to endure periods when returns are well below the much-quoted long-term averages.

It's probably safe to assume that retired investors are not worried about the "risk" that their investment returns will be *better* than the long-term averages suggest. Rather they are concerned that their investments will badly *underperform* compared with recent experience. In 62 rolling 10-year periods from 1926 through 1996 (1926–35, 1927–36, and so on), common stocks provided average annual returns of 8.7% or lower in 24 of those decade-long slices. Thus, in 39% of the decades, stocks underperformed the long-term historical average by more than two percentage points annually. In 14 of the 62 periods—about one in four of the decades—the average annual return from common stocks lagged behind the long-term average by *four percentage points or more.* Although history does not always repeat itself, the record suggests that there is more than a remote possibility of suffering through such periods of subpar performance.

Periods of significant underperformance and significant outperformance tend to run in cycles. As Figure 4–6 shows, 11 of the 24 decades in which stocks provided returns that badly lagged behind (by more than two percentage points) the long-term average included at least part of the Great Depression of the 1930s. The 13 other periods of significant underperformance coincided with the run-up in inflation during the late 1960s and 1970s. On the positive side, common stocks provided above-average returns in every 10-year period from 1941–50 through 1956–65 and again from 1974–83 through 1987–96.

For long-term bonds, average returns have been two percentage points or more below the long-term annual average of 5.2% in 28 of the 62 10-year periods from 1926 through 1996. Remarkably, 26 of the subpar decades were consecutive, from the decade beginning January 1, 1941, through the decade beginning January 1, 1966. In every decade from 1973–82 through 1986–95, bonds provided annual returns above the

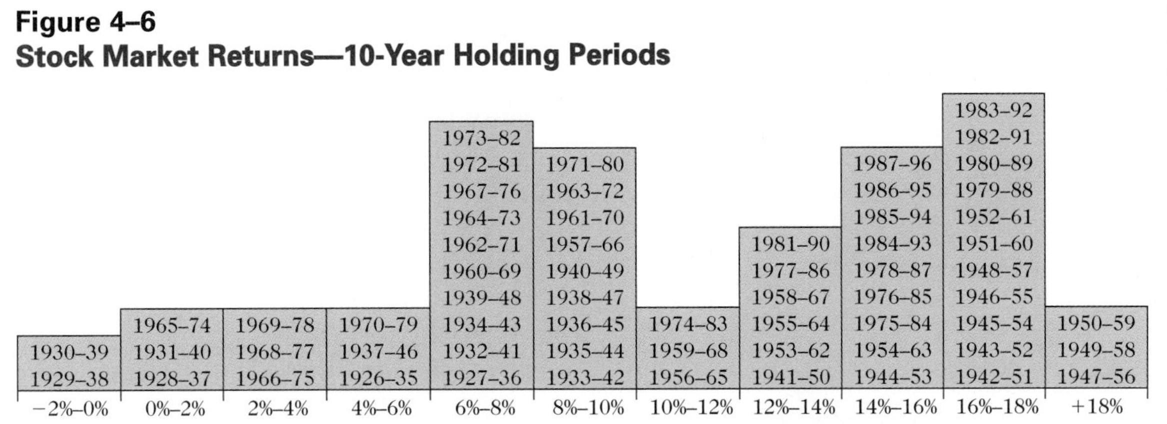

Figure 4–6
Stock Market Returns—10-Year Holding Periods

Source: ©*Stocks, Bonds, Bills, and Inflation 1997 Yearbook*™, Ibbotson Associates, Chicago. (Annually updates work by Roger G. Ibbotson and Rex A. Sinquefield.) Used with permission.

long-term average of 5.2%. Bonds provided double-digit annual returns during every decade from 1979–88 through 1986–95. Keep in mind that the past returns on bonds have absolutely no relevance to the prospective returns on bonds in the future. The return you will earn from long-term bonds, as noted earlier, will depend almost entirely on the current level of long-term interest rates.

Returns on short-term reserves averaged 3.7% a year for the entire period from 1926 through 1996. But that average is a bit misleading, because there have been essentially two "eras" when it comes to returns from cash reserves. Not once in the decades from 1926–35 through 1959–68 did short-term reserves provide average returns as high as the long-term annual average of 3.7%. However, in every 10-year period since, from 1960–69 through 1987–96, short-term reserves have provided an average annual return exceeding the long-term average of 3.7%. In every decade from 1968–77 through 1985–94, short-term reserves provided average annual returns of 5.6% or above.

The purpose of this brief digression is to remind you that averages can be misleading when it comes to forecasting the returns you may get from your portfolio. Although you can look to the long-term averages as your guide, extrapolating the past into the future is a hazardous exercise. The underlying economic and investment forces at work during the coming decade—not those of the past—will determine the financial returns you earn during your retirement, and these returns will affect your ability to meet your financial goals.

The Annuity

Cash reserves, bonds, and stocks are the building blocks that should dominate a retired investor's portfolio, but there are thousands of other potential investments, most of them variations within the three asset classes. This section discusses one option that may be of particular interest to retired investors: the annuity.

As noted in Chapter 3, an annuity is an investment contract between you and an insurance company. You can invest in either fixed or variable annuities. With a fixed annuity, you invest a sum of money, and the insurance company promises to make a series of payments to you for a set number of years or for your lifetime. You can choose annuities that begin making payments immediately, or you can choose a "deferred" annuity that delays the regular payments until some future date.

A big advantage of annuities is that the investment earnings you get are not subject to income tax until you withdraw the money. (Like several other tax-deferred investments, annuities are subject to a tax penalty if funds are withdrawn before you reach age 59½.) Unlike IRAs or employer-sponsored retirement plans, annuities are without limits on how much you may invest or how much you may withdraw in a single year. However, most insurers charge redemption fees, or "loads," if you take money out of an annuity within five to seven years of your initial investment. These redemption fees can be a big drawback for retired investors if they need to withdraw money for some emergency.

Fixed Annuities

Fixed annuities are somewhat like bank CDs, in that interest is credited to your account. The interest rate is reset from time to time, usually annually. To entice investors, fixed annuities sometimes offer a high "teaser" rate for the first year or so, after which the interest rate paid on the annuity typically declines. It is crucial to know not just the guaranteed interest rate for the first year or first few years of the annuity, but also the guaranteed *minimum* rate, or floor, since this may be the long-term rate you will earn.

In general, you should avoid annuities that offer extraordinarily high teaser rates, since the high rates almost surely will drop in later years, perhaps to below-normal levels as the insurer tries to compensate for overpaying in the early years. Concentrate on the offerings of insurance companies that have consistently paid competitive rates on their fixed annuities each year, not just in the first year or two of the contract. Make sure the agent selling the annuity gives you its interest-rate history. If you can't get information going back at least five years, don't buy that annuity.

Variable Annuities

With variable annuities, you choose how to invest the money; the amount you receive later depends on how well you select your investments. Variable annuities provide several investment options, analogous to stock, bond, or money market mutual funds. You may switch among the options within the annuity—say, from a stock fund to a bond fund—without triggering any capital gains tax. Your variable annuity accounts are subject to the same risks as the asset classes in which you decide to invest. For example, a variable annuity invested in a stock or bond fund will fluctuate in value, although the annuity contract guarantees that your heirs will never receive less than you invested in the annuity, even if your account value declines after you invest. And, as with common stocks generally, a variable annuity in stocks has the potential to earn higher returns than a fixed annuity or a variable annuity invested in bonds.

As a rule, in order for the tax-deferral advantage to outweigh the higher costs associated with variable annuities—taking into account mortality expenses, annual fees, and the like—an investment usually must remain in the annuity for at least 10 years. This lengthy time horizon makes variable annuities impractical for many retirees, particularly those planning to draw income from the investment. The Roth IRA, which allows those eligible to make after-tax contributions that can be withdrawn tax-free at maturity, can be an attractive alternative to variable annuities.

What to Ask Before Buying an Annuity

Fixed Annuity

- Is the insurance company financially strong?
- What is the initial interest rate? How long is the rate effective?
- What sort of interest rates has the insurer credited to annuities in the past?
- What is the minimum guaranteed rate?
- What are the surrender charges?
- Can I end the arrangement, penalty-free, if I don't like the renewal rate on the annuity?
- Under what conditions can I withdraw my money without paying a surrender charge?

Variable Annuity

- Is there a wide variety of investment options?
- Am I able to move my money around easily?
- Have the investment options provided competitive returns in the past?
- Is there a sales charge or load?
- What are the annual charges and expenses?
- Is there a redemption fee or surrender charge?
- Would a Roth IRA make even more sense?

Final Thoughts

By now you should have a solid understanding of the potential risks and rewards inherent in the three primary classes of financial assets. If you take nothing else away from this chapter, remember that there is no way to eliminate all risks from investing. In order to totally protect yourself from price fluctuations, you will incur the risk of inflation and the risk of wide fluctuations in the year-to-year income you receive from your investments. In order to earn a higher, relatively stable income stream in a bond fund, you will incur the risk of share price declines when interest rates rise. In order to combat inflation, you will need to commit a large portion of your assets to common stocks, which have provided superior long-term returns but have also subjected investors to wide price fluctuations.

Although you can never totally eliminate these risks, you can mitigate them by owning a diversified investment portfolio, including holdings in each of the three classes of financial assets. Before deciding the right mix of assets for you given your financial situation, your retirement goals, and your risk tolerance, you should consider how mutual funds might fit into your investment plans. To assist in this analysis, Chapter 5 provides a broad overview of mutual funds, and Chapter 6 provides specific guidance on how to choose the right funds for you out of the burgeoning universe of more than 6,000 mutual funds.

A Mutual Funds Primer

Chapter 5

Individual investors have increasingly turned to mutual funds as their preferred vehicle for investing in stocks, bonds, and even cash reserves. Evidence of this trend can be seen in the rapid growth over the past two decades in mutual fund assets and in the number of mutual funds. Indeed, mutual fund assets have grown at a rate of more than 20% a year since 1975 and now exceed $3.5 trillion. That is more than the deposits of all the commercial banks in the United States. The number of mutual funds has mushroomed, too, from 400 funds in 1975 to more than 6,000 today. Figure 5–1 illustrates this tremendous growth.

This chapter is intended as a primer on mutual funds, explaining the characteristics of funds and highlighting their advantages and disadvantages. If you're an experienced mutual

Figure 5–1
Growth of the Mutual Fund Industry

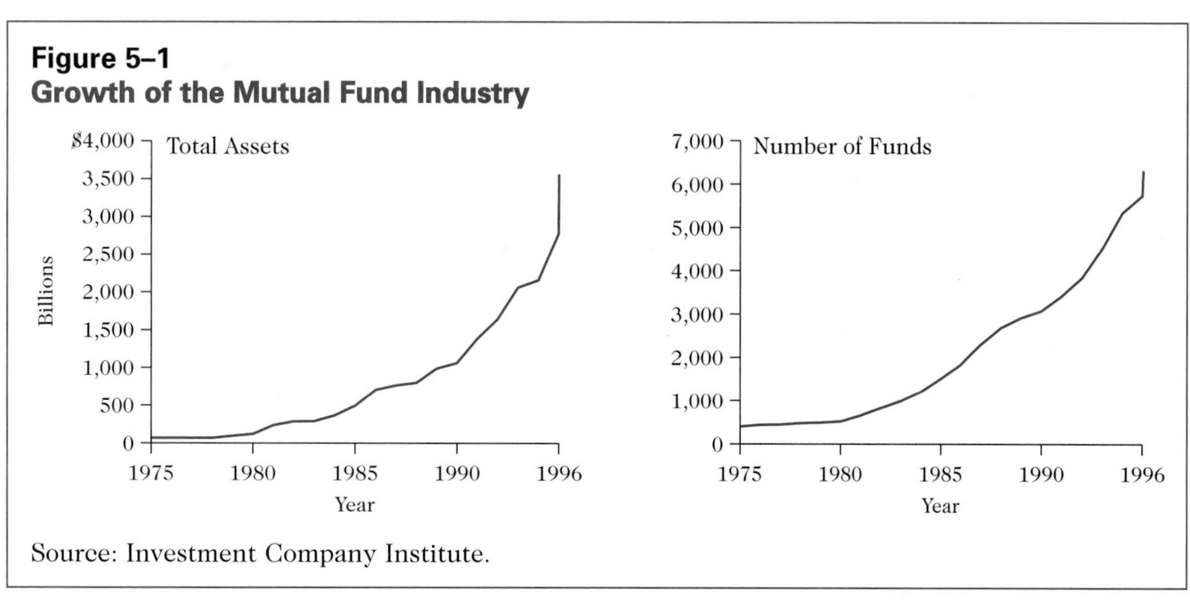

Source: Investment Company Institute.

"Mutual funds offer a simple, low-cost way to build a tailor-made portfolio."

Albert J. Fredman and Russ Wiles
Building Your Mutual Fund Portfolio

fund investor, you may want to skim over this chapter and Chapter 6, which discusses how to gather information on mutual funds and how to select specific mutual funds to meet your personal objectives.

Although the popularity of mutual funds has exploded during the past two decades, they have been around for more than 70 years. The idea is pretty simple: a group of investors pools resources to invest in various types of securities, primarily common stocks, bonds, and money market instruments or some combination of the three. Each investor owns part of the pool, proportionate to his or her share of the assets in the fund, and each investor shares proportionately in the income or investment gains and losses that the fund as a whole produces.

Each mutual fund (formally known as an "open-end investment company") has a manager, or investment adviser, who invests the pooled money according to the objectives and limitations set forth in the fund's prospectus. A fund's investment objective might be to produce current income, to produce long-term growth in capital, or to produce a mixture of current income and long-term growth. The fund might try to meet its objective by investing in stocks of companies based in the United States, in U.S. government bonds, or in securities of foreign companies. Mutual funds are called "open-end" because investors may sell their shares or purchase new shares every business day. Because of this ability to convert shares into cash on a daily basis, mutual funds are generally regarded as highly liquid investments.

Mutual fund shares can be bought through two main channels: (1) directly from the fund's sponsor or (2) through an intermediary such as a stockbroker, insurance agent, bank, or financial planner. Funds that are sold through an intermediary usually charge some form of sales commission, or "sales load," which reduces—dollar for dollar—the ultimate return the fund provides to the investor. Most funds that sell shares directly to the investor do not assess a sales load and thus are called "no-load" funds. However, some mutual funds disguise their sales charges through ongoing distribution fees. You'll learn more about such fees later.

The share price of a mutual fund fluctuates daily depending on the total change in value of the securities it holds. (Money market mutual funds are an exception. They aim to keep a constant net asset value of $1 per share, although there is no guarantee that they will meet this objective.) At the close of trading each business day, a fund determines the current market value of all the securities and cash in its portfolio. It then deducts any accrued expenses and divides this net value by the total number of shares outstanding on that day. The result of this calculation is the net asset value (NAV) of each share in the fund. Most major newspapers carry a daily listing of net asset values of mutual funds.

Mutual funds are regulated by federal and state agencies, the most powerful being the U.S. Securities and Exchange Commission (SEC). Funds are required to provide full disclosure about their investment objectives, policies, and risks, as well as thorough information about any fees, commissions, and operating expenses. These disclosures are made in the fund's prospectus, which must be provided to prospective investors either before or at the time they buy shares in a fund. The main federal law regulating mutual funds is the Investment Company Act of 1940, which contains numerous provisions designed to make sure that mutual funds are operated in the interests of shareholders rather than the interests of fund sponsors.

The Advantages of Mutual Funds

One of the primary reasons for the rapid growth in mutual fund assets over the past 20 years is the extraordinarily favorable investment climate that has existed for much of that period. Otherwise, no single factor explains the astounding success of mutual funds and the large increase in households that invest in funds. On balance, four time-honored attributes seem to lie at the heart of the mutual fund explosion: diversification, professional management, liquidity, and convenience.

Diversification

Investing in a mutual fund provides immediate portfolio diversification, even for an investor of relatively modest means. To acquire a diversified portfolio of individual common stocks on your own would mean buying 30 to 60 different stocks and could easily require $100,000 or more in financial resources. But an investor with only a few thousand dollars can acquire a widely diversified portfolio comprising hundreds of stocks by purchasing shares in just one mutual fund. Because your money is pooled with money from thousands of other investors, your fund can invest in a wide array of companies. Such diversification is of crucial importance in a long-term investment program because it can reduce (though not eliminate) the volatility of investing in individual securities.

Professional Management

"I've gotten bored and tired trying to read the financial pages and pick individual stocks, which is why I'm in mutual funds."

New Jersey

The decisions on buying and selling securities for a mutual fund are overseen by a professional investment manager, who charges the fund a fee for this service. The job of the investment manager is to establish a portfolio that is consistent with the fund's investment objectives, as set forth in the fund's prospectus. This professional management can be a valuable service, since few investors have the time or expertise to manage their personal investments on a day-to-day basis and to investigate all the securities available for investment. (In Chapter 7, you will learn of an alternative to "active" management of mutual funds that has proved extremely effective in providing competitive long-term returns.)

Liquidity

Shares in a mutual fund may be sold whenever the investor chooses. A fund is required to redeem shares on each business day at their net asset value. While the same level of liquidity is often available for individual stocks or other securities, as a mutual fund investor, you may redeem your shares at no cost to you, provided that you are invested in a no-load fund.

Convenience

Mutual funds offer a variety of services that can make things easier for investors. For example, you may buy fund shares by mail, by phone, or from any number of outside sources, including stockbrokers, banks, and insurance agents. You can arrange to make regular purchases of mutual fund shares through automatic deductions from your paycheck or your bank account. Or you may automatically sell some shares in your fund account and have the proceeds regularly deposited to your bank account. You may choose to have all distributions of fund income from interest, dividends, or capital gains paid directly to you or automatically reinvested in more shares of the fund.

"I like being able to write checks against my account. It's convenient."

Oregon

Just as you can conveniently buy or sell fund shares, you may easily exchange them for shares of another mutual fund within the same fund complex, or family, often at no cost to you. Mutual funds also provide extensive recordkeeping services to help you keep track of transactions and any distributions of income. Each day you can monitor and evaluate your fund's performance through newspapers, investment magazines, independent fund-rating services, or computer online services. You'll also get regular shareholder reports on the fund's performance, including a discussion of its investment activities. At the end of each calendar year, mutual funds provide important tax-reporting information to help you complete your income tax returns. Many fund groups provide information on the cost basis of your shares to make it easier for you to report any capital gains or losses on your sales of fund shares.

The Disadvantages of Mutual Funds

In fairness, there are some disadvantages associated with investing in mutual funds, which you should consider before investing your money.

No "Guarantees"

Unlike bank accounts, mutual funds are not insured or guaranteed by the FDIC or any other agency of the U.S.

government. Mutual funds are regulated by the SEC and by state securities regulators, whose oversight is aimed at assuring full disclosure of all the pertinent information an investor needs to make an informed investment decision. Securities regulators can help to protect you from fraudulent activity, but they cannot protect you from the risk of an investment falling in value.

Manager Risk

Gaining access to professional investment managers is an important advantage of investing in mutual funds. However, evidence suggests that few professional managers consistently exceed the results you could achieve simply by owning an index fund, which mirrors the performance of a broad segment of the market. There are, to be sure, some notable exceptions. But identifying these star performers in advance is extremely difficult, if not impossible. (Even the managers who produce returns that exceed those of the broad market averages often fall short after their expenses and transaction costs are taken into account.) There is also no guarantee that a particular fund manager will stay with a given fund after you have made your investment. Alternatively, the excellent performance that attracted you to a particular fund may actually have been achieved by a former manager. It is up to you as the prospective investor to find out whether a fund's record can be attributed to its current manager.

The Diversification "Penalty"

The diversification of mutual funds means that the returns of even the best-performing mutual funds will rarely approach the returns of the best-performing individual common stocks. By spreading your bets in a diversified mutual fund, you eliminate the chance of a big score from a single stock doubling or tripling in value in a brief period. On the other hand, the diversification of mutual funds also helps you to avoid the substantial losses—up to 100%—that the worst-performing stocks incur. Nonetheless, while diversification reduces the risk of price swings in comparison with an investment in a single security, it will not eliminate the market risk associated with an overall decline in the financial markets.

Potentially High Costs

Mutual funds can offer investors lower costs than buying individual securities through a broker. However, in many cases, a combination of sales commissions and high, ongoing operating expenses offsets these efficiencies. Funds that are sold through brokers and other financial intermediaries usually charge sales commissions of one kind or another. Sometimes these charges take the form of front-end loads (typically in the range of 4% to 6%) taken off the top of your investment.

Sometimes the front-end load is eliminated and replaced with a contingent deferred sales load. In this case, an annual charge is assessed equal to 1% of the value of your investment. At the same time, a redemption fee is imposed that begins at 5% in the first year and declines by one percentage point each year that you hold your shares. By the sixth year, the redemption fee may be eliminated. But by then, you've paid a total of 6% in annual sales expenses. If your fund shares have increased in value over the years, you will actually pay more through the annual charges than you would have paid with a front-end load. In recent years, many mutual funds have added annual "12b-1" fees ranging from 0.25% to 1% of average net assets, or from $2.50 to $10 per $1,000 of assets. The 12b-1 fee is typically paid directly to the fund's sponsor to help offset the costs of advertising or otherwise marketing shares in the fund.

In addition to these sales-related charges, all mutual funds incur annual expenses for operating the fund—fees paid to the investment adviser and accountants, mailing and bookkeeping costs, and so on. These operating expenses are expressed as a percentage of a fund's average net assets. The ratio of annual fund expenses to average net assets may range from as low as 0.2% ($2 per $1,000 of assets) to more than 3% ($30 per $1,000 of assets).

Taken together, the sales commissions, 12b-1 fees, and fund operating expenses reduce the net returns that mutual fund shareholders receive from the gross returns achieved by the fund. Obviously, funds with extremely high expenses will, over time, have difficulty achieving competitive after-expense returns for their shareholders. Before investing in a mutual fund, read its prospectus to find out how much you'll be paying in fees and expenses. All else being equal, funds with high ongoing expenses should be avoided.

Types of Mutual Funds

With more than 6,000 mutual funds available to investors, you can find funds that invest in just about any type of security traded in the financial markets, from the staid and predictable to the exotic and erratic. Some funds maintain well-diversified portfolios and follow carefully disciplined investment strategies in order to provide relatively predictable performance. Such funds should compose the core portion of your retirement portfolio. Other funds invest in highly specialized securities that may be subject to wide, unpredictable swings in price and performance. Such funds may be suitable for a very small part of your investment dollars, but for many retired investors they will not be suitable at all. This section provides an overview of the major types of mutual funds offered within the three primary classes of financial assets: stocks, bonds, and short-term cash reserves. Figure 5–2 illustrates how mutual fund assets are distributed among the major market sectors.

Money Market Funds

Money market funds seek to provide a stable net asset value of $1 per share while providing current dividend income. As a result, the investment return you earn from these funds comes solely from reinvested daily dividends paid from interest earned on the fund's investments. Keep in mind that, while all money market funds expect to keep their net asset values at a steady $1 per share, there is no guarantee that they will be able to do so. Remember, too, that an investment in a money market fund is neither guaranteed nor insured by the U.S. government, unlike bank accounts, which are insured up to $100,000.

Figure 5–2
Allocation of Mutual Fund Assets, December 31, 1996

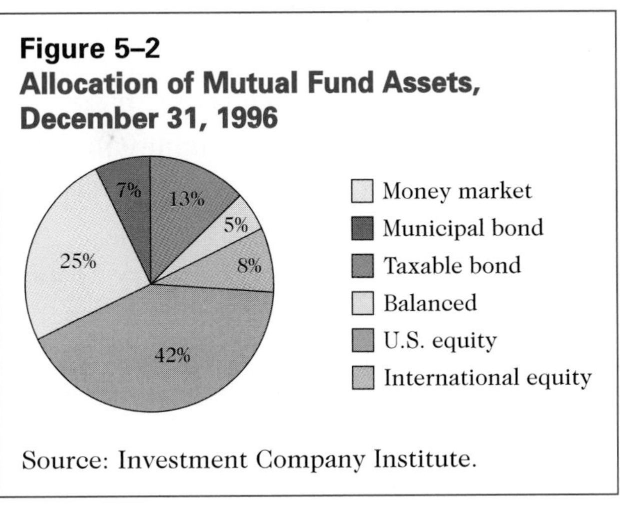

Source: Investment Company Institute.

Money market funds purchase short-term debt, or IOUs, with maturities typically ranging from one day to one year. SEC regulations mandate that the *average* maturity of all the securities held by a money market fund may not exceed 90 days. By keeping this very short average maturity, money market funds have virtually no exposure to the risk of losses from changes in interest rates. However, as noted in Chapter 4, low interest-rate risk goes hand in hand with a high risk of short-term fluctuations in the level of income provided by an investment. So while you have virtually no worry that the price of your shares in a money market fund will fall, it is quite possible for the dividend income from the fund to fall sharply over a short period of time. Figure 5–3 shows the interest rate paid by the average money market mutual fund over the five-year period ended December 31, 1996. As you can see, the level of income earned varied widely over the period.

Figure 5–3
Money Market Mutual Fund Yields, 1991-96

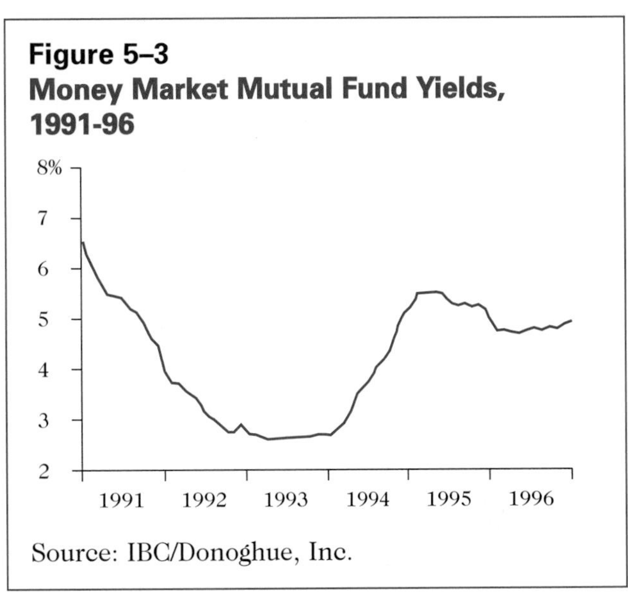

Source: IBC/Donoghue, Inc.

The investment holdings of money market funds are generally of exceptionally high quality, since the SEC requires that all taxable money market funds invest at least 95% of their assets in securities of the highest credit quality, as rated by a major credit-rating agency such as Moody's or Standard & Poor's. Even with these stringent quality regulations, money market mutual funds can be divided into three quality groupings.

U.S. Treasury Money Funds These funds invest mainly in direct obligations, or IOUs, of the U.S. Department of the Treasury. As a result, all or part of the income from them may be exempt from state income taxes.

U.S. Government Money Funds These funds invest in IOUs of the U.S. Treasury and of other agencies of the U.S. government, such as the Federal Home Loan Bank.

"Prime" Money Funds These funds invest mainly in the short-term debt, or IOUs, of large, high-quality corporations and banks.

A separate category of money market funds, the municipal money market fund, invests in short-term IOUs of state and local government agencies. These funds pay income that is exempt from federal, and sometimes state and local, income taxes. (Funds holding only securities issued within a particular state provide income to investors living in that state that is exempt from state income taxes.) These funds may provide very attractive after-tax yields for investors who pay high tax rates; however, tax-exempt money market funds would not be appropriate for any kind of tax-advantaged retirement account, such as an IRA.

Taxable Bond Funds

In general, bond funds seek to provide a higher, more stable level of current income than money market funds. This is why bond funds are particularly well-suited for retired investors seeking regular income to help pay their monthly bills.

Duration: A Measure of Interest-Rate Risk

To understand the interest-rate risk of a bond mutual fund, it helps to know more than the average maturity of the bonds in the portfolio. The average maturity of a bond fund is simply the average number of years until all the bonds in the portfolio will mature, or be repaid by the issuer. But two funds with the same average maturity may have quite different levels of interest-rate risk. To gauge the level of principal volatility engendered by a particular bond fund, you need to know the *duration* of its portfolio.

A fund's duration, which takes into account the timing of the cash flows from interest payments on bonds, tells you approximately how much the fund's share price, or net asset value, will rise or fall for each percentage point change in interest rates. For example, a fund with an average duration of seven years will rise by 7% in value when interest rates fall by one percentage point. Conversely, the fund's net asset value will fall by −7% if interest rates increase by one percentage point. (Duration figures are, of course, estimates and may change when bonds are redeemed, or *called,* early or when mortgage-backed securities are prepaid early.) The duration of a fund may be disclosed in its annual or semiannual report, or you can call the fund to request the information. Independent information services, such as Morningstar and Value Line, also publish duration figures for bond funds.

Over the long term, virtually all of the total return (capital change plus reinvested interest income) from bond funds comes in the form of reinvested interest income, with a much smaller portion resulting from capital gains or losses. The capital component is primarily a function of changes in interest rates. The reason, as noted in Chapter 4, is that bond prices—and therefore the prices of bond funds—fluctuate in response to changes in the general level of interest rates.

The key factor in measuring the sensitivity of a bond fund's price to changes in interest rates is the duration of the fund, which takes into account the maturity and coupon of each individual bond it owns. The longer the duration of the bond fund, the greater its price will fluctuate when interest rates rise or fall. The trade-off for accepting this higher interest-rate risk is that bond fund investors generally earn a higher income yield as the duration of a fund lengthens.

While many fund sponsors do not regularly report the duration of their bond funds, virtually all fund sponsors provide each bond fund's average maturity. Because of the manner in which these two statistics are calculated, a fund's duration will always be less than its average maturity.

Nevertheless, the same relationship exists: the longer a fund's average maturity, the greater its interest-rate risk and the higher its yield. Figure 5–4 shows this relationship between the yield of a bond fund and its average maturity.

Bond funds can be divided into three major segments in terms of average portfolio maturity:

1. Short-term (average maturity of one to five years).
2. Intermediate-term (average maturity of five to 10 years).
3. Long-term (average maturity of 10 to 30 years).

Figure 5–4
Average Taxable Bond Fund Yields and Maturities December 31, 1996

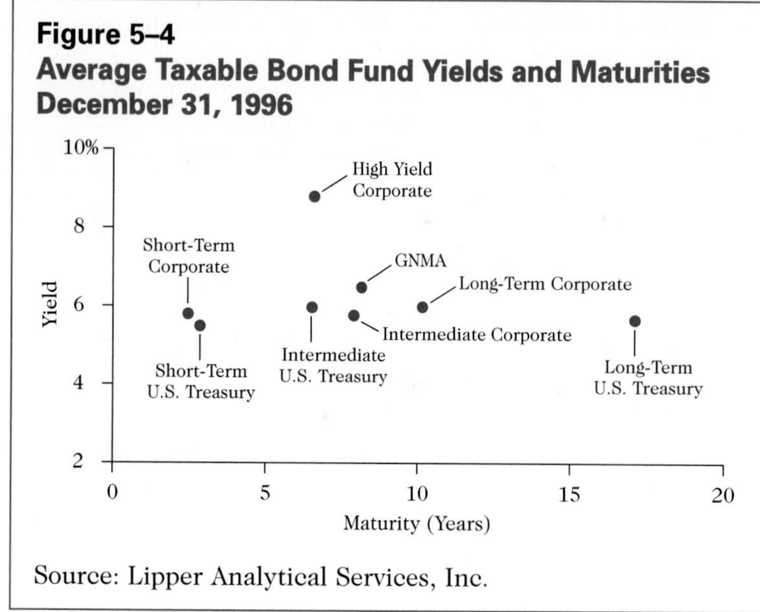

Source: Lipper Analytical Services, Inc.

In addition to these maturity levels, bond funds vary according to their investment objectives. There are four primary bond fund investment categories: U.S. government, mortgage-backed securities, investment-grade corporate, and municipal (tax-exempt) bond funds. (A fifth type—the high-yield, or "junk," bond fund—will be discussed later in this chapter.)

"I want funds that will provide me with a monthly check."

Tennessee

U.S. Government Bond Funds These funds invest in securities issued by the U.S. Treasury or agencies of the U.S. government, such as the Federal National Mortgage Association. (Funds that invest solely in U.S. Treasury securities are known as U.S. Treasury bond funds.) Because these securities are obligations of the U.S. government, they are considered to be of top credit quality. Even government bond funds, however, are subject to the risk of losses due to fluctuations in interest rates. The net asset values of government bond funds fluctuate in relation to their average maturities. Some U.S.

government funds may periodically alter their maturity levels if the investment adviser thinks the fund can profit by doing so; other funds stick closely to a particular maturity level and make no "bets" on the future trend of interest rates.

Mortgage-Backed Securities Funds These funds invest in securities that represent part ownership of pools of home mortgage loans. The most popular mortgage-backed securities fund is the GNMA fund, which holds pools of mortgage loans that are guaranteed by the Government National Mortgage Association, which in turn is backed by the full faith and credit of the U.S. government. (The government guarantee for mortgage securities extends only to the repayment of principal and interest.) Mortgage loan pools are made up of hundreds or thousands of individual home loans that have been purchased and packaged by GNMA or another government-sponsored agency before being resold to investors as a single security. Each month, the investor in the mortgage pool—in this case the mutual fund—receives a payment that represents partly interest income and partly a repayment of principal on each underlying mortgage loan.

Mortgage-backed securities are subject to interest-rate risk, like other bond funds, but they are also subject to *prepayment risk*. That is, when interest rates decline, the total return from mortgage-backed funds may lag behind the return from other bond funds. That is because many homeowners will refinance their mortgage loans at the new, lower interest rates and pay off their old, higher-rate mortgage loans. To compensate investors for this incremental risk, the yields on mortgage-backed funds tend to be higher than the yields on funds that invest solely in U.S. government bonds.

Investment-Grade Corporate Bond Funds These funds invest mainly in the debt obligations of U.S. corporations. Corporate borrowers range from blue chip (large and established) companies with strong, investment-grade credit ratings to financially distressed companies with credit ratings of a speculative grade. Investment-grade corporate bond funds generally buy only bonds that are rated Baa or higher by Moody's or BBB by Standard & Poor's. Despite the relatively low credit risk of investment-grade corporate bond funds, they do not match the quality of U.S. government bond funds. Because their quality is lower, corporate bond funds generally pay higher yields than U.S. government bond funds of similar maturity levels.

Municipal (Tax-Exempt) Bond Funds

These funds invest in the bonds of cities, counties, states, and their related government agencies. The interest income from municipal bonds is generally exempt from federal income taxes, although capital gains earned from the sale of municipal bonds are subject to income tax. If you buy a bond fund that limits its holdings to bonds from the state in which you live, the interest income you earn will usually be exempt from state and local income taxes as well as federal tax. Investors who are taxed at one of the higher marginal income tax rates (above 28%) generally will benefit by investing in a municipal bond fund rather than a taxable bond fund.

Like taxable bond funds, tax-exempt bond funds are available in a range of maturity levels, from short-term to long-term. Most municipal bond funds invest solely in securities with investment-grade credit ratings; some go a step further by investing mainly in bonds that have been insured by private insurance companies. At the other extreme, a few municipal bond funds specialize in high-yield, lower-quality municipal bonds.

Common Stock Funds

Almost all common stock funds seek to provide long-term growth in capital as a primary investment objective. More conservative stock funds may make dividend income a secondary objective. Table 5–1 shows the components of total return for the major categories of common stock funds, breaking out the portion of return provided by dividend income and the portion provided by capital growth. In general, the higher the

Table 5–1
Components of Total Return (10-Years Ended December 31, 1996)

Investment Objective	Income Return	Capital Return	Total Return	Income as a Percentage of Total return
Equity income funds	4.6%	7.0%	11.6%	42%
Growth and income funds	2.8	10.4	13.2	22
Growth funds	1.5	12.0	13.5	12
Small company funds	0.6	13.6	14.2	4

Note: During this period, stocks achieved returns well above their historical average. These results should not be considered indicative of possible future returns.

Source: Lipper Analytical Services, Inc.

proportion of a fund's return that is derived from income, the less its performance is likely to vary from year to year.

Equity Income Funds These funds aim to provide a high level of current income and growth in income by investing in the stocks of well-established companies that pay substantial dividends. In addition to dividend-paying common stocks, equity income funds often invest in other income-producing securities, such as long-term corporate bonds, preferred stocks, and bonds convertible to shares of common stock. Although income is the primary objective of equity income funds, they also seek to provide a reasonable level of long-term capital growth. Because equity income funds tend to have lower price volatility, high dividend yields, and the potential for some moderate capital growth over the long term, they may serve as a core part of your retirement portfolio.

Growth and Income Funds These funds seek to provide a balance between current dividend income and long-term growth of capital and dividend income. The portfolios of growth and income funds vary tremendously from one fund to the next, with some funds heavily stressing growth and others focusing intently on income. Overall, most growth and income funds are well diversified and emphasize the stocks of large and medium-size companies that have demonstrated the ability to pay regular dividends. Growth and income funds are often called "value" funds, because they tend to emphasize companies with below-average price/earnings ratios (the current price of a stock divided by its annual profits, or earnings) and above-average dividend yields. In general, growth and income funds can be considered a middle ground between equity income funds and growth funds. As such, they are also appropriate for a core part of your retirement portfolio.

Growth Funds These funds seek long-term capital growth as their primary objective, with current dividend income a minor, even inconsequential, objective. They typically invest in a mix of established and relatively new companies with good prospects for sustained, rapid growth in profits. Dividend yields on growth funds tend to be quite low in comparison with other types of stock funds. Also, price fluctuations of growth funds tend to be more dramatic than those of value funds or equity income funds. Because of their low level of current income and high level of price volatility, growth funds are rarely appropriate as the cornerstone of a retiree's portfolio. However, if you are in the early stages of retirement or if your primary objective is to build an estate rather than to generate current income, you may want to hold a sizable portion of your portfolio in growth funds.

Small Company Funds These funds typically seek to provide long-term capital growth by investing in the stocks of smaller, emerging companies. (A few small company funds select stocks of companies that, though small, pay relatively high dividends.) Typically, smaller companies do not pay out much of their profits in dividends; they retain their profits to invest in future growth opportunities. The stocks of smaller companies typically trade over the counter rather than on a major stock exchange and tend not to be monitored as closely by Wall Street analysts as the stocks of big corporations. Partly because of this lower level of scrutiny, investment managers of small company funds hope to discover companies whose growth potential has not yet been widely recognized and reflected in the price of their stocks.

The risks of this type of strategy may be substantial, because small companies tend to be less able than large companies to ride out business setbacks. The prices of small company stocks also tend to be more vulnerable to market disappointments than stocks of big companies. As a result, small company funds have had among the highest price fluctuations of all stock funds. Because of the high volatility and low level of dividend income generally associated with small company stock funds, they typically play only a small part in a retired investor's portfolio.

International Stock Funds These funds invest in the stocks of companies that are based outside the United States. Funds that hold only non-U.S. stocks are known as international funds, while those that invest in stocks of both U.S. companies and non-U.S. companies are known as global, or world, funds. Some international funds specialize in stocks of just one country, such as Japan or Germany, or one geographic region, such as the Pacific Basin or Europe. Others specialize in stocks of "emerging markets"—newer, less-established stock markets of nations in Latin America, Asia, Africa, or Eastern Europe.

The risks of these funds vary widely, depending on their individual investment policies. Some funds try to pick countries where they think economic growth and overall stock performance will be strongest, rather than focusing on the selection of individual stocks. Other funds use a traditional, fundamental investment approach, trying to select the most promising companies regardless of the countries in which they operate.

International stock funds provide a way for U.S. investors to participate in stock markets around the world and to diversify their overall investment portfolios. Indeed, diversification is the biggest argument for holding some portion of your portfolio in international stocks. As shown in Figure 5–5, the U.S. stock market now accounts for some 40% of the total

Figure 5–5
Allocation of Global Equity Markets, December 31, 1996

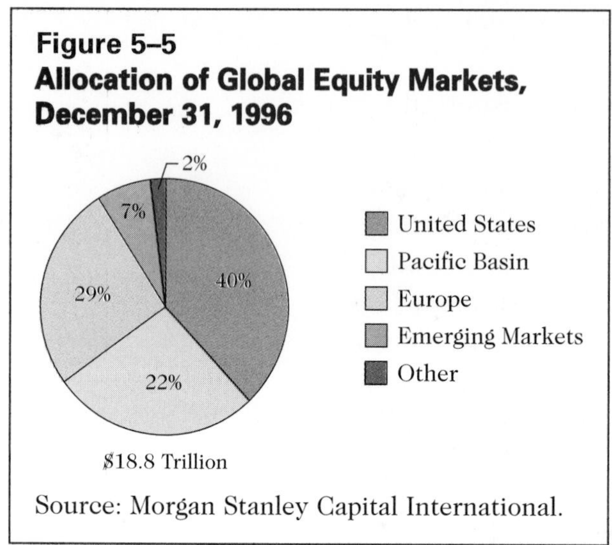

Source: Morgan Stanley Capital International.

market value of all the world's stock markets. Having some portion of your stock holdings outside the United States allows you to participate more broadly in world economies.

It's important to understand that, while international investing provides important opportunities for diversification, it also holds extra risks for the U.S. investor. In addition to the usual risks of stock investing, foreign stocks carry political and currency risk. If the value of the U.S. dollar strengthens versus foreign currencies, your return from foreign stocks is reduced because there is a decline in the dollar value of each German mark, Japanese yen, or British pound you or your mutual fund controls. What's more, many foreign nations, particularly those classified as emerging markets, are more vulnerable to political and social upheaval than the United States. Thus, the investor abroad can see investment values affected by coups, civil unrest, or other conflicts. Given these extra risks, international funds usually should compose a relatively minor portion of a retired investor's portfolio.

Balanced Funds

As the name implies, balanced funds are hybrids—part stock fund, part bond fund. There are two basic types of balanced fund: traditional and asset allocation. These two varieties share some portfolio characteristics and investment objectives but use very different methods to try to meet their objectives.

Traditional Balanced Funds These funds seek to provide a combination of growth, income, and conservation of capital. The typical balanced fund invests 50% to 60% of its assets in common stocks, usually those paying higher than average dividend yields. The rest of the fund is invested in bonds and short-term reserves. Thus, a traditional balanced fund is considered to be a relatively conservative, middle-of-the-road investment option. The net asset value of a balanced fund will fluctuate as bond and stock markets move up and down, but its price fluctuations tend to be less extreme than the price swings of a fund that invests only in common stocks. Because a traditional balanced fund produces relatively high income, a reasonable opportunity for long-term growth, and a moderate level of price volatility, it is a solid choice for a core part of a retiree's portfolio.

A relatively new wrinkle in traditional balanced funds is the "life cycle" or "lifestyle" fund. These funds provide a preset mix of assets targeted to specific stages of a person's life cycle. For example, an income portfolio aimed at retirees might contain 20% stocks, 60% bonds, and 20% cash reserves, while a growth portfolio aimed at investors with two or more decades to invest before retirement might hold 80% stocks and 20% bonds. Another approach to lifestyle funds is to offer funds with varying target dates for maturity. The mix of investments in such funds shifts from a growth stance to an income stance as the maturity date approaches.

Asset Allocation Funds These funds, like traditional balanced funds, invest in a mixture of stocks, bonds, and short-term reserves. But the similarity ends there. Managers of asset allocation funds have wide flexibility to switch their allocations among the three asset classes, according to the manager's outlook for the different financial markets.

Even among asset allocation funds, investment policies vary widely. Some funds, for example, are allowed to hold all of their assets in stocks, while others may have a much lower limit. However, all asset allocation funds engage in market timing to some degree. And market timing has rarely proved to be a successful strategy, due to the unpredictability of financial markets and economic events. This is why holding an asset allocation fund may entail considerably more risk than holding a traditional balanced fund. It's important that you carefully evaluate the investment policies of these funds before investing. One factor to consider, for example, is how to fit an asset allocation fund into your overall investment mix. Suppose you want to maintain an overall mix of 50% stocks, 30% bonds, and 20% short-term reserves. If you invest in an asset allocation fund and the manager switches from, say, stocks to short-term reserves, the switch may move you away from your desired mix of assets.

Specialty Funds

The fund categories just described can be thought of as the main menu of mutual fund offerings. But, like restaurants, many mutual fund complexes offer some specialties, spicier and riskier than the main dishes. Two examples are high-yield corporate bond funds and sector funds. Both of these specialty funds carry extra risk and therefore may not be appropriate for the portfolios of many retired investors. Yet for investors who understand and accept the risks, these funds may have a place in their portfolios.

High-Yield Corporate Bond Funds These funds—commonly known as "junk bond" funds—invest in the debt of corporations that have credit ratings too low to be considered investment grade. These below-investment-grade ratings are Ba or lower by Moody's and BB or lower by Standard & Poor's. Many of these companies are simply too small or have too short an operating history to earn an investment grade rating; others may be "fallen angels"—formerly solid, blue chip companies whose financial condition has weakened. During the 1980s, a wave of high-yield bonds was issued to finance corporate takeovers and restructurings. Many of these bonds were considered quite speculative because these companies assumed very high levels of debt.

Investors in high-yield bond funds are attracted, of course, by the higher income yields they offer in comparison to bond funds that invest in U.S. government or investment-grade corporate bonds. But, as suggested by their speculative credit ratings and the nickname "junk," there is substantial risk that the companies that issue these bonds will be unable to meet their interest payments or to pay back principal when the bonds mature. This high risk of default means that the attractive stated yields may never actually be received by the investor.

If you are considering an investment in a high-yield bond fund, you should know that they vary tremendously in credit quality. Some funds stick almost exclusively to the highest-quality, least speculative end of the high-yield bond spectrum, while others invest mostly in the lowest grades, which entail the greatest risks. So it's particularly important before you invest to compare the average quality of a fund's portfolio.

Like all bond funds, high-yield bond funds are subject to interest-rate risk. However, the price volatility of high-yield bond funds tends to more closely resemble the price swings of stock funds than those of bond funds. Given the higher risks associated with these securities, it would be wise to hold to a small position (if any) for your portfolio.

Sector Funds These funds invest in the stocks of a single industry, or sector, such as energy, health care, financial services, utilities, precious metals, or technology. Sector funds offer investors a convenient way to participate in a particular industry that they expect will prosper while maintaining a reasonable level of diversification *within* that industry. Although these funds are much riskier than owning a portfolio of stocks that is diversified across a wide band of industry sectors, they are much less risky than buying the stock of a single company.

Final Thoughts

Mutual funds offer compelling advantages for retired investors and are playing an increasing role in the portfolios of millions of retirees. Certainly, there are some disadvantages in comparison with holding individual securities. But they seem to be far outweighed by the benefits of broad diversification, professional management, convenience, and liquidity.

The very success of mutual funds, however, has created a problem for the individual retired investor. With more than 6,000 funds to choose from, the process of selecting funds can seem daunting. Even after you narrow your fund selection to a particular investment objective, such as growth and income funds, you will find that there is extreme diversity in the investment *policies* of funds that claim to have identical investment *objectives*. For instance, most funds use an "active" investment approach in which a professional manager selects investments, but some funds dispense with investment advisers and instead employ an index strategy that seeks to match the performance and risk characteristics of a particular segment of the financial markets. Some funds emphasize technical factors, hoping to identify market trends from the past that will recur in the future; others emphasize research of fundamental measures of value, such as price/earnings ratios, dividend yields, and earnings growth.

The next chapter will guide you through the process of selecting mutual funds, from gathering and sorting through information about funds, to comparing their past results, to understanding the costs associated with them. With this guidance, you'll be able to narrow your search to a manageable number of funds. From these you can select the funds that meet your personal investment objectives.

Investing through Mutual Funds

Chapter 6

After reading Chapter 4, you should have a basic understanding of the risks and rewards of the three asset classes that will comprise the vast majority of a retiree's investment portfolio. In Chapter 5, you learned the advantages and disadvantages of using mutual funds as a way to invest in the three asset classes. You can probably see why mutual funds have become the clear choice of so many investors for building a diversified investment program. Unfortunately, when compared with simple investment choices such as bank CDs or U.S. savings bonds, mutual funds can seem bewildering. The success of mutual funds has resulted in the creation of so many funds and the proliferation of so much advertising and news coverage that it's easy to be intimidated by the process of choosing the right funds. This chapter will guide you through the selection process, explaining how to gather information about mutual funds and use it to select funds that will help you meet your investment goals.

"Everyone says, 'Buy mutual funds.' But there are so many. How do you know which ones to choose?"

New York

Gathering Mutual Fund Information

If anything has grown faster than the mutual fund industry itself, it is the volume of information about funds. Newspapers, magazines, on-line computer services, television, and special fund-rating services provide a vast array of articles, reviews, and rankings of mutual funds. Most major business magazines, including *Business Week, Forbes,* and *Money,* produce annual mutual fund reviews, containing information about fund objectives, performance, costs, and account services. Newspapers have dramatically increased coverage of mutual funds as well. Most major newspapers provide a daily listing of fund net asset values and some data on performance.

The Wall Street Journal publishes detailed quarterly reviews of fund performance and regularly carries articles about fund investing for both novice and experienced investors. *Barron's,* the financial newsweekly aimed at an especially sophisticated audience, provides articles, detailed fund listings, and extensive quarterly reviews of fund performance for mutual fund investors of all stripes.

Several independent services rate mutual funds according to their performance and risk characteristics. Morningstar Mutual Funds is the leading contender in this field. Its single-page reports provide an astounding amount of data on a fund, including long-term performance, portfolio holdings, risk measures, investment manager and tenure, expenses, portfolio turnover rates, potential tax liability, a brief, up-to-date commentary on the fund's performance—the list goes on. A similar service is provided by Value Line, Inc. Other good sources of fund information include Lipper Analytical Services and CDA/Wiesenberger Investment Companies Service. Public libraries often subscribe to one or more of these fund-rating services, or you may subscribe directly. Tables 6–1 and 6–2 show addresses and phone numbers of agencies that provide performance results and other information on mutual funds.

Table 6–1
Mutual Fund Information Sources

American Association of Individual Investors
625 N. Michigan Ave., Suite 1900
Chicago, IL 60611
(312) 280-0170

Investment Company Institute
1401 H St. N.W., Suite 1200
Washington, DC 20005-2148
(202) 326-5800

The Mutual Fund Education Alliance
P.O. Box 419263
Kansas City, MO 64195
(816) 454-9422

Although outside, independent sources can be very helpful in selecting funds, much of the information you'll need will come from mutual fund companies directly. The most important information will be in two documents required by the SEC: the prospectus and the annual shareholder report. These documents provide full disclosure of a fund's risks, costs, and investment strategy. They will alert you to important facts about the fund that won't necessarily be disclosed in advertisements, in marketing literature, or by a stockbroker or financial adviser. Be sure to read the prospectus and annual report to determine whether a fund is suitable for your retirement portfolio. You may find the fund company's marketing and educational materials useful, too, but such information should be read with a more skeptical eye than the official disclosure documents.

Table 6–2
Mutual Fund Performance Services

Morningstar Mutual Funds
225 W. Wacker Drive
Chicago, IL 60606
(312) 424-4288

Lipper Analytical Services, Inc.
47 Maple St.
Summit, NJ 07901
(908) 598-2220

CDA/Wiesenberger Investment Companies Service
1355 Piccard Drive, Suite 220
Rockville, MD 20850
1-800-232-2285

Value Line Mutual Fund Survey
220 E. 42nd St.
New York, NY 10017
1-800-284-7607

Reading a Mutual Fund Prospectus

The mutual fund prospectus is a legal document which even experienced investors can find difficult to read. This is partly because much of the important information is written in legalese, which tends to obscure rather than illuminate. Fund sponsors sometimes magnify this problem by failing to give priority to the most important information. For instance, important risk characteristics may be buried deep in the document or explained only briefly, while extensive explanation is provided to relatively unimportant matters such as how a fund invests its excess cash each night.

To help you quickly review a fund's prospectus, the following section will highlight the key parts that an investor should read and understand. If you have any questions when you're reading a prospectus, you should not hesitate to call the fund's investor information department to get further clarification.

Investment Objective Does the fund seek capital growth? Current income? Stability of principal? A combination of income and growth? The prospectus should clearly state the fund's basic investment objective. For money market funds and bond funds, investment objectives usually are clearly stated; for stock funds, objectives tend to be stated more vaguely and may even be outright misleading.

"There are people who have never met a mutual fund they didn't like, so they're buying the same kinds of funds from a lot of different companies. They think they're diversified, but they're really not."

New York

Investment Policies The prospectus should describe the types of securities that the fund expects to hold and in what percentages. For example, a fund's policies may require the manager to invest at least 80% of the fund's assets in U.S. Treasury bonds. Or a fund's policies may limit investments in foreign stocks to 25% of the fund's total assets. Also, the prospectus should describe the extent to which the fund may buy speculative financial instruments, such as derivatives, and whether the fund intends to use these derivatives to hedge against various risks.

Investment Risks This section of the prospectus explains the risks engendered by the fund's investment objectives and policies. While this section usually is written in very general terms, it's important to read it to get an idea of the risks you'll incur if you invest. If you don't understand the risks involved, ask questions of the fund sponsor before you invest. If the risks aren't explained to you clearly, choose another fund!

Disclosure about risk should relate specifically to the types of securities that the fund holds. For example, money market funds should focus on the credit quality of the portfolio. Bond funds should emphasize credit risk, interest-rate risk, and income risk. Stock funds should compare the fund's expected price fluctuations with the fluctuations of the overall stock market. International funds should provide a full explanation of currency risk, political risk, and the risk of price fluctuations. As a rule, terms such as "speculative," "unseasoned," or "above-average risk" should be a warning to conservative investors.

Fund Costs Given the wide dispersion of fund costs, with high-cost funds charging expenses several times higher than low-cost funds, you should understand all the expenses that you will incur. A fee table, required to be placed near the front of the prospectus, will make it easy to compare costs among different funds. Mutual fund costs are so important to the ultimate investment returns you'll receive that they are discussed in considerable detail near the end of this chapter.

Financial Highlights Table This table, located near the front of every prospectus, provides the financial results of a fund share for the past 10 years (or for the life of the fund, whichever is less). The information in this table may confuse a novice investor, because it is presented for the fund's fiscal year, which is used for legal, tax, and accounting purposes. (A fund's fiscal year may not coincide with the calendar year.) It is important to remember this point when comparing the performance results of funds with different fiscal years.

The financial table includes several useful pieces of information, the most important of which is the total return on a year-by-year basis. (Performance information also may appear elsewhere in the prospectus, in the fund's annual report to shareholders, and in marketing literature.) To get a crude sense of the fund's likely share-price volatility in the future, check the annual changes in the fund's total return going back in time. If income is your main concern, check the fund's annual dividend payments. This line will show you how much income the fund has distributed in the past and will give you a sense of whether that income has fluctuated widely from year to year or remained relatively stable.

If your investment will be made through a taxable account, check on the size and frequency of taxable dividends and distributions of capital gains. This will indicate how frequently you will incur taxable distributions. You also should note the amount of accumulated, unrealized capital gains, since these gains may be realized in the future and become taxable income to you. The fund's portfolio turnover rate will indicate whether the fund buys and sells securities frequently or whether it tends to buy and hold securities, taking a longer-term approach to investment management. Turnover rates also provide an indication of how tax-efficient your investment is likely to be, since the lower a fund's turnover rate, the lower its propensity to realize, and then distribute, taxable capital gains. (An investor in a retirement plan account need not be concerned about such tax issues.) The 10-year table also shows the fund's annual expense ratio, which will indicate whether costs have declined as the fund has grown in size (in general, the expense ratio *should* decline if the fund's assets have grown considerably).

Investment Manager It is good to know the name, qualifications, and tenure of the fund's portfolio manager, since there is some evidence that successful funds tend to be marked by continuity of fund management. For instance, a study by *CDA/Wiesenberger Investment Companies Service* found that changes in investment advisers can have a big effect on a fund's performance. The study found that funds with above-average past performance who changed investment advisers were much more likely in the future to have below-average returns than funds with above-average returns whose managers stayed put. On the other hand, funds with below-average performance tended to improve their results after changing portfolio managers. In any case, you should know whether a fund's record was achieved by its current investment adviser.

Shareholder Services The prospectus will explain how to buy and sell shares of the fund and will highlight related services such as checkwriting, whether free exchanges are permitted to other funds within the fund family, the policy on telephone exchange privileges, the availability of automatic investment programs, and the minimum investment requirements.

Reading an Annual or Semiannual Report

Each mutual fund must provide to shareholders an annual and semiannual performance update. These reports, like the prospectus, often suffer from an excess of legal and accounting jargon. So you must read selectively to find relevant and useful information. Fund reports are also issued on a fiscal-year basis, so be careful when comparing performance results with the results of funds that have different fiscal years.

One of the most useful bits of information in the fund report is the listing of the fund's investment holdings. The holdings should help to clarify the fund's investment policies as stated in the prospectus. For instance, the portfolio holdings will tell you whether a "U.S. government fund" holds all U.S. Treasury securities or invests mainly in non-Treasury securities, including mortgage-backed securities. The list of portfolio holdings will indicate whether a stock fund invests mainly in blue chip stocks whose names you recognize or whether it emphasizes smaller and riskier emerging companies. You may also find out about any "surprise" holdings, such as international stocks in a U.S. stock fund or junk bonds in an investment-grade bond fund.

You can also check the list of holdings to determine the degree of portfolio concentration, which is typically measured by the percentage of fund assets invested in the top 10 securities. A heavily concentrated fund may have 50% or more of its assets in its 10 largest holdings. A more conservative fund offering may limit its 10 largest holdings to no more than 30% of assets. Sometimes the fund report will provide this statistic; other times you will have to calculate the percentage on your own.

Although funds are not required to do so, some will provide other important statistics about their portfolios, such as a breakdown of the credit quality of bonds in a bond fund, the industry concentrations in a stock fund, or recent significant purchases or sales of securities. This information will reinforce and clarify the policies in the fund's prospectus.

In its annual report, the fund is required to compare its 10-year performance record with a relevant broad-based market index and to illustrate the comparison with a line graph covering the past 10 years. This chart should appear in the fund's annual report or prospectus and must be accompanied by a message from the investment adviser explaining the fund's results. You should review this commentary from the fund sponsor and/or portfolio manager. While this report should be the ideal forum for the fund sponsor to offer a candid assessment of the fund's performance and investment strategy, it often contains little more than puffery. Ideally, any message from the fund sponsor should address at least the following issues:

- How has the fund performed? Both short-term and long-term performance should be explained.
- How does the fund's performance record compare with those of funds with similar investment policies? When compared to broad market averages? The report should include long-term performance results for the fund, a group of competitors, and an appropriate market index.
- What factors explain the fund's performance? If a fund has performed well, the report should address the extent to which its returns reflect the skill of the adviser and the extent to which they simply reflect strong performance from the markets in which the fund invests. By the same token, if a fund has not performed well, the factors contributing to the shortfall should be explained.

A thorough fund report will address—at a minimum—all of these questions. If the commentary does not candidly discuss these issues, you should turn to independent sources for insight into the fund's performance.

Understanding Investment Performance

No aspect of mutual funds is more heavily relied upon, or more often misunderstood, by investors than past investment performance. Investors want their mutual funds to "do well" in the future and, in pursuit of that goal, they look for funds that have "done well" in the past. Sadly, it is not so easy to identify funds that will provide superior future results.

"The ad says, 'Past performance does not guarantee future results.' So why is the past performance up there in big print?"

Massachusetts

Many investors make two common mistakes in seeking out the top-performing funds. First, they tend to misinterpret historical performance information. If you don't carefully review a fund's past performance, it is easy to draw the wrong conclusions about its record. Second, they rely too heavily on past performance as a guide to future performance. Surprisingly, numerous studies have indicated that excellent past performance by a mutual fund is not a reliable indicator of excellent future performance. Indeed, a list of last year's winning funds rarely predicts next year's winners. Nor does choosing the best-performing funds from the past three, five, or 10 years guarantee you a winner over the next three, five, or 10 years. In all, there is an overwhelming tendency for the performance of mutual funds to "regress to the mean." In other words, the more extreme—good or bad—a fund's performance is compared with other funds in one period, the more likely it is that the fund's performance will move back toward the average during the next period. Before choosing any fund for your portfolio, you should understand the implications of past performance and the linkage, if any, to future performance.

Evaluating Past Performance

The past performance results for funds appear regularly in fund advertisements, marketing literature, newspaper and magazine articles, and the ratings put out by independent analytical services. Since there are many opportunities for misrepresenting fund returns, it takes a certain skill and skepticism to get at the true meaning of past performance. Consider the following examples:

- On any given day, you might come across five advertisements for funds claiming to be "Number 1" in performance. Such claims are of dubious value unless the reader knows how many other funds were in the "race," the period of time covered, the risks the fund took to achieve its record, and so on.
- A stock fund ad states, "Up over 200% in the past 15 years." That 200% figure seems terrific, until you learn that (1) it is equal to only 8% per year and (2) investors in a stock market index fund over the same period earned 700%, or 15% per year.
- "Invest abroad for higher returns," suggests an ad for an international fund. The ad shows a table that emphasizes recent stellar returns. But the ad fails to mention that most of the fund's recent returns came not from strong foreign stock market returns, but from a weakening U.S. dollar which magnifies returns earned overseas.

As these examples indicate, performance claims of mutual funds should be taken with more than a grain of salt. The following points should help you to sift through the claims and get to the reality of fund performance.

Understand the Components of Total Return Mutual funds report their investment performance in terms of total return, which reflects the reinvestment of all income plus any capital growth. To clearly understand a fund's performance record, you should determine how much of its total return came in the form of income and how much came in the form of capital growth. Income returns tend to be fairly stable from year to year, while capital growth is more spasmodic and unpredictable. By analyzing these two components of total return, you'll have a clearer sense of whether a fund's past performance is likely to be repeated in the future. For instance, a bond fund might accurately claim a double-digit total return after a period of falling interest rates has generated large price increases for bonds. But an investor buying the fund *after* the decline in rates isn't likely to benefit from a repeat performance. An investor who understands the two components of total return is unlikely to make the mistake of comparing a bond fund's return with the yields being offered by money market funds or bank CDs.

Don't Be Misled by Cumulative Returns Investors often are distracted by fund returns reported on a cumulative basis rather than on an average annual basis. The stock fund that boasted a "200% return" for 15 years is using a big number to appeal to investors' emotions. The reality, an average annual return of 8%, is unlikely to impress. It is almost always best to use average annual returns when you compare the performances of various funds.

As you compare these annual rates of return, never underestimate the dramatic impact of compounding over long periods. A $10,000 investment that earns 10% a year for a decade will grow to $25,940; another investment earning 9% a year will grow to $23,675 in a decade. Although the difference of one percentage point a year seems modest, it becomes dramatic as you lengthen the investment period. In this case, the disparity in returns amounts to a difference of nearly 10% in the final value of your investment ($25,940 versus $23,675).

Time Periods Matter The period over which performance is measured matters in several ways. First, all performance results are "period-dependent." In order to judge a fund's performance, you need to understand the underlying financial and economic environment of the period being measured. For example, the 1980s were an exceptional decade for stocks and bonds, a fact reflected in the inordinately high returns that financial assets provided during that period.

Time periods are also a critical consideration when you compare the records of two funds. Even a seemingly inconsequential difference in the measurement period of two funds can reverse their relative performance. For example, if you compared the performance of one stock fund for the year ended October 31, 1987, with the performance of another stock fund for the year ended September 30, 1987, the latter fund's record would exclude the sharp decline in the stock market that took place on October 19, 1987. Obviously, that would put the first fund at a distinct disadvantage in the comparison. To encourage consistent comparisons of performance, the SEC requires that all fund marketing literature and advertisements report one-, five-, and 10-year total returns as of the most recent calendar quarter.

Finally, the longer the period covered by fund performance data, the more reliable your interpretation of the fund's record will be. While comparing returns over just one year is of little value in determining the relative merits of two funds, comparing returns over a decade—especially year-by-year returns, which indicate how a fund's performance varied over time—can be a revealing exercise. Remember also that short-term returns typically depend on short-lived market conditions, such as a sudden change in interest rates, a temporary shift in the relative strength of growth stocks versus value stocks, or short-term currency fluctuations in foreign markets. For periods of less than two years, the best-performing fund is likely to be one with a narrow focus on some segment of the market that is enjoying a sudden surge.

Consider Sales Charges and Taxes When you evaluate past performance, don't forget to consider the impact of any sales charges and taxes. Most reports about mutual fund returns ignore the effect that sales charges would have had on the fund's results. If a fund charges a sales load of 5%, a one-year return of, say, 10% would drop to 4.5%. (That is, after one year, the $9,500 invested after sales charges would have grown 10% to $10,450, which is just 4.5% above the original investment.) Over a five-year period, an average annual return of 10% would decline, after the sales load, to 9% a year—still a −10% reduction to the investor.

Performance results also typically ignore the impact of taxes on your return. If you are investing through a taxable account, you should investigate how the investment policies of a fund (e.g., the rate of portfolio turnover) may affect your after-tax return.

Compare Apples with Apples Evaluations of fund performance are relevant only when you compare funds with similar investment objectives and policies. You cannot fairly compare the return on a money market fund with the return on a stock fund. The risk and return characteristics of the underlying investments are too dissimilar.

Even when comparing two funds within the same asset class, you need to be diligent in your analysis. For example, while both value funds and growth funds invest in common stocks, it is typical for them to provide quite different returns over different periods. When value funds prosper, growth funds often languish, and vice versa. You will have better results with your fund selections if you compare value funds with value funds and growth funds with growth funds. This is where a portfolio's holdings may be a useful reference. If one value fund holds only stocks of U.S. companies and another holds a significant portion of its assets in international stocks and junk bonds, you probably should not be comparing the records of the two funds head to head.

Compare a Fund with an Unmanaged Index You can learn a lot by comparing a fund's performance and volatility with a broad market index. By observing the extent to which a fund falls short of (or exceeds) a stock or bond market index, you can judge how effective the fund's investment manager has been in adding value over the rate of return you could earn by merely holding a market index. (Remember that the performance of an unmanaged index does not include the "real world" costs of investing, so it is extremely tough competition for mutual funds, all of which must incur operating costs.)

When comparing your fund's performance with the performance of a market index, you must also be sure to compare apples with apples. A broad-based U.S. stock fund should be compared with a broad-based index for the U.S. stock market, such as the Standard & Poor's 500 Composite Stock Price Index or the Wilshire 5000 Index. A fund investing in stocks of small companies should be matched with an index of small company stocks, such as the Russell 2000 Index. As shown in Table 6–3, indexes exist to cover most sectors of the stock and bond markets.

Some Pointers for Fund Selection

If past performance isn't a particularly useful guide to selecting mutual funds, what factors should an investor consider? Here are some key pointers.

"My advice is to keep it simple. I use a minimal number of funds."

Arizona

Investing Skill Look for demonstrated investing skill. Although past fund performance doesn't automatically enable you to pick tomorrow's winning funds, it still makes sense to choose funds that have displayed a reasonable level of investment competence in the past. As a rule, limit your selections to funds that have ranked over an extended period at least in the upper half of all funds in their category. See whether the

Table 6–3
The Major Market Indexes

Common Stocks

Standard & Poor's 500 Composite Stock Price Index. Tracks 500 large-capitalization stocks representing about 70% of the value of all U.S. stocks.

Wilshire 4500 Index. Tracks the portion of the U.S. stock market not included in the S&P 500.

Wilshire 5000 Index. Tracks the entire U.S. stock market.

Russell 2000 Index. Tracks small-company stocks.

Morgan Stanley Europe, Australasia, and Far East (EAFE) Index. Tracks the world's major non-U.S. stock markets.

Morgan Stanley Europe Index. Sub-index of the EAFE that tracks European stocks.

Morgan Stanley Pacific Index. Sub-index of the EAFE that tracks Pacific Rim stocks.

S&P/BARRA Growth Index. Sub-index of the S&P 500 that tracks stocks with "higher-than-average" ratios of market price to book.

S&P/BARRA Value Index. Sub-index of the S&P 500 that tracks stocks with "lower-than-average" ratios of market price to book.

Bonds

Lehman Brothers Government Bond Index. Tracks U.S. government agency and Treasury bonds.

Lehman Brothers Corporate Bond Index. Tracks fixed-rate, nonconvertible, investment-grade corporate bonds.

Lehman Brothers Mortgage-Backed Securities Index. Tracks fixed-rate securities of the Government National Mortgage Association (GNMA), Federal National Mortgage Association (FNMA), and Federal National Loan Mortgage Corp. (FHLMC).

Lehman Brothers Aggregate Bond Index. Tracks some 5,000 investment-grade fixed-income securities, weighted by the market value of each security.

fund's returns have been relatively predictable. If a fund's returns seem erratic compared with funds that have similar investment objectives, it could be a sign of an undisciplined investment approach.

Past Performance Avoid the very worst-performing funds. Studies show that while excellent past performance is no guarantee of excellent future performance, really bad performers tend to stay near the bottom of performance rankings. One reason is that the worst-performing funds tend to have the highest operating costs, which represent an ongoing drag on performance.

Costs Consider costs carefully. Although the performance of a fund is not easily predictable, costs tend to be quite predictable. That is, funds that have high operating costs tend to continue to have high operating costs, while funds that have low operating costs tend to maintain their low expenses. While future performance is uncertain, it is absolutely certain that costs will reduce the net investment return that you receive as a fund shareholder.

As noted earlier, cost is almost the sole determinant of performance rankings among money market funds. If you want to own a top-performing money market fund, choose the fund with the lowest operating costs. If you're choosing among index funds, cost is also the crucial determinant of relative fund results. Since index funds should be able to match the performance of the targeted indexes before costs are taken into account, the best-performing index funds will invariably be the lowest-cost of such funds.

In the case of actively managed bond funds, a manager begins to have some ability to differentiate—for better or for worse—a fund's performance relative to a market index. More often than not, however, the relative performance of bond funds is determined by their stated investment policies (the credit quality and the average maturity of the bonds in their portfolios) and their costs. So while costs are not the only factor that determines which bond funds do best and which do worst, fund operating expenses are so influential in the long run that you should always avoid higher-cost bond funds.

In the case of actively managed stock funds, the relationship between costs and performance is tenuous. Stock funds have flexible investment policies, so funds with the same investment objective may incur very different levels of risk. While a stock fund with a 2% operating expense ratio and a 5% front-end sales charge is at a distinct disadvantage compared with a no-load, low-cost stock fund, the high-cost fund may be able to close the cost gap by taking on more risk in the search for higher returns.

Nonetheless, all else held equal, it still makes sense to choose a no-load stock fund over a load fund and a low-cost fund over a fund with a high expense ratio. When in doubt, consider these three rules: (1) Never pay a sales charge; (2) avoid the highest-cost funds; and (3) be very skeptical of all funds with above-average costs.

After you've chosen a specific fund or funds, be realistic about the performance you expect. Some mutual fund companies create unrealistic expectations by touting performance from some unusually favorable period from the past. As a result, many investors fail to realize how difficult it is for any investment manager to provide consistently superior results. A stock fund that consistently beats the market averages by 1% a year—after taking into account the fund's costs—is exceptional. Yet novice investors sometimes expect their funds to beat the market averages by 5% or more each year. That kind of performance rarely—if ever—occurs. If you build your financial plans on expectations of beating the market averages by a substantial margin, you stand an excellent chance of seeing those plans go awry.

Mutual Fund Costs

When it comes to most products and services, consumers are acutely aware of costs. Yet when it comes to investing, many investors don't even know the direct costs they are paying, not to mention the hidden costs. For the most part, mutual fund investors incur costs in three ways: (1) through sales commissions; (2) through expenses incurred in operating and managing the fund; and (3) through transaction costs paid by the fund when it buys and sells securities. As an investor, you can avoid the first cost entirely and, through careful analysis, minimize the second and third costs.

Sales Commissions

For years, all sales commissions on mutual funds were incurred when shares in a fund were purchased. As investors became more aware of how sales charges affected their investment returns, other types of commissions emerged. Today, the most common types of sales commissions are front-end loads, back-end loads, and 12b-1 fees.

Front-End Loads These are the traditional sales commissions, levied up front when you buy fund shares and deducted from your initial investment. They typically range from 4% to 6%, although so-called low-load funds assess sales charges ranging from 1% to 3%.

Back-End Loads These charges are incurred when you sell your fund shares. Back-end loads may be assessed either as a percentage of the value of the shares you redeem or as a flat fee. In many cases, the percentage deducted will decrease by, say, one percentage point for each year that you are invested in the fund, up to a total of six years. In the interim, you typically pay a 1% annual fee based on your average account balance. So, while the load may be eliminated in the seventh year, you will still have paid over the six years the equivalent of a 6% load (or higher if the fund increased in value while you owned it). To make matters worse, many funds continue to assess the 1% annual fee for as long as you hold the fund. Back-end loads assessed in this manner are called contingent deferred sales loads.

12b-1 Fees These fees are used to pay for distribution-related expenses, including advertising and broker fees. Like fund operating expenses, they are assessed as a percentage of your average net assets and must be included in the fund's stated expense ratio.

It's important to note that these sales commissions have no bearing whatsoever on the quality of investment management you get from a fund. Despite the fact that these commissions essentially are fees paid to a salesperson, some investors believe that they get what they pay for—that is, high fees and commissions mean better investment management. If you need advice on choosing particular funds, it may be worth it to you to pay a commission for the services of a stockbroker or financial adviser. But the advice given should be worth at least as much as it costs. Since you can't make that judgment if you don't know what costs you are paying, be sure that you know whether you are paying a sales charge and, if so, how much you're paying.

Operating Expenses

These include the advisory fee charged by the fund manager and the expenses of administering the fund's daily operations—everything from producing account statements to paying accountants to audit the fund. Operating expenses are expressed as a percentage of a fund's average net assets for the year. For most funds, this expense ratio will fall between 0.25% ($2.50 per $1,000 of assets) and 2.5% ($25 per $1,000 of assets), although a few funds charge expenses outside of those two extremes.

In general, the level of fund expenses is related to the investment objective of the fund. For example, advisory expenses usually are highest for aggressive small-company stock funds and international funds; they are generally lowest for funds that do not require significant investment research, such as money market funds. Surprisingly, however, even among funds with the same investment objectives, expenses often vary significantly.

Portfolio Transaction Costs

Transaction costs are incurred in the buying and selling of securities and include brokerage commissions as well as the market impact of a transaction. These costs are not reflected in the expense ratio or sales commission reported by a fund. Instead, transaction costs are paid directly from fund assets and have the effect of reducing the fund's investment return. The greater the volume of buying and selling by the fund, the greater the drag on its investment return from brokerage commissions and other transaction costs. This is why you should review a fund's rate of annual portfolio turnover for an indication of the potential impact of transaction costs on future returns.

Table 6–4
Mutual Fund Fee Table

	Fund A	Fund B	Fund C
Shareholder Transaction Expenses			
Sales load imposed on purchases	None	None	7.25%
Sales load imposed on reinvested dividends	None	None	7.25%
Redemption fees	None	None	None
Exchange fees	None	None	None
Annual Fund Operating Expenses			
Management expenses	0.13%	0.94%	0.70%
Investment advisory fees	0.20	—	—
Shareholder accounting costs	0.08	—	—
12b-1 fees	—	0.50	—
Distribution costs	0.02	—	—
Other expenses	0.03	0.46	0.25
Total Operating Expenses	0.46%	1.90%	0.95%

The Fee Table

You can compare mutual fund costs easily by looking at the fee table printed in the front of every mutual fund prospectus. This table breaks down all of the fees incurred and shows the fund's total expense ratio. Cumulative expenses are expressed in terms of dollars paid on a hypothetical investment of $1,000 at the end of one-, three-, five-, and 10-year periods.

Table 6–4 is a sample fee table showing all expenses and fees that shareholders of three hypothetical mutual funds would incur. Its purpose is to help you to understand how costs and expenses affect investment returns. Table 6–5 illustrates the expenses that a shareholder would incur on a $1,000 investment in each of these funds over various periods, assuming (1) a 5% annual rate of return, and (2) full account redemption at the end of each period.

Table 6–5
Expenses Incurred on a $1,000 Investment

Holding Period	Fund A	Fund B	Fund C
1 year	$ 5	$ 19	$ 81
3 years	15	60	101
5 years	26	103	121
10 years	58	222	181

Mutual Funds and Taxes

It is beyond the scope of this section to delve deeply into all the tax issues that affect mutual fund investors. But you should be aware of some basic tax rules so that you can avoid some common tax pitfalls that fund investors encounter. For a more in-depth source of tax information, ask for the free Publication 564, "Mutual Fund Distributions," from the Internal Revenue Service. You can reach the IRS toll-free at 1-800-829-3676. When in doubt about a tax issue, consult an accountant, lawyer, or other qualified tax professional for expert help.

You should also understand that there is one set of tax rules for taxable fund accounts and a different set for tax-deferred accounts, depending on the type of tax-deferred plan. There is one set of rules for IRAs, another for employer "qualified" retirement plans such as 401(k) plans, and still others for nonprofit 403(b) plans, 457 government plans, annuities, and so on. Although this guide will cover some of the tax aspects of these plans, the tax rules are complex, and you may need expert assistance in dealing with them. In contrast, the rules governing taxable mutual fund accounts are fairly straightforward.

Reporting Your Fund's Taxable Income

Reporting the taxable income distributed by your fund is probably the easiest aspect of mutual fund taxation. The taxable income will be reported to you on IRS Form 1099-DIV, issued in late January. You are responsible for reporting this income on your federal income tax return (as well as any state or local returns) by the appropriate filing deadline.

Taxable distributions by mutual funds come from two sources: (1) dividends, which represent income earned on the fund's underlying securities; and (2) net realized capital gains, which the fund accrues when it sells securities that are worth more than they cost. Capital gains that are designated as "short-term" (from the sale of securities held less than one year) are treated as ordinary dividend income for tax purposes. Long-term capital gains (gains on the sale of securities held for at least one year) were formerly taxed at a maximum rate of 28%. For securities sold after July 28, 1997, long-term capital gains (gains on the sale of securities held more than 18 months) are taxed at a maximum rate of 20%. The procedures for reporting dividends and capital gains are described in the IRS instructions that come with your tax return.

Calculating Your Gains or Losses

While it is relatively easy to report your fund's taxable distributions, calculating your own capital gains or losses from selling shares of your fund can be frustrating. Whenever you sell shares of a fund (except money market funds), you may realize a capital gain or loss. It is up to you to determine the amount of any gains or losses and to report the figure on your tax return. The IRS allows you to choose one of four options for determining the cost basis of your fund shares: (1) first-in, first-out (FIFO); (2) specific identification; (3) average cost single category; or (4) average cost double category. The four approaches are explained in IRS Publication 564.

Using one of these four methods, you first must calculate how much it cost you to buy the fund shares that you sold. In tax terms, this is the "cost basis" of your investment. The cost basis is deducted from the proceeds that you received from selling your fund shares, and the net result is your capital gain or loss. This figure must be reported on Schedule D of your federal income tax return and on your state and local tax returns.

Many mutual fund companies now offer tax cost services to calculate your gains and losses for you; they typically use the "average cost single" method. These services can save you time and possibly accounting fees. Before investing in a fund, ask whether the fund sponsor offers such a service.

Tax-Exempt Funds

For taxpayers in the highest tax brackets, the potentially higher after-tax yields of municipal money market funds and municipal bond funds may make them appropriate alternatives to taxable funds. Municipal funds typically pay lower pretax yields than taxable funds, but their tax-adjusted yields generally are higher for investors in high tax brackets.

Interest income from municipal bond funds is generally exempt from federal income taxes. If a fund invests primarily in the debt obligations of the state in which you reside, the fund's dividend income is also exempt from state and local taxes. Some municipal bond funds also generate "tax preference items," which may affect high-income taxpayers who are subject to the federal alternative minimum tax. Note that while dividend income from municipal funds escapes federal taxation, capital gains distributions by the funds do not. They are fully taxable at the federal level and may be subject to state and local taxes as well.

One final tax exemption worth noting applies to funds that invest in U.S. Treasury securities. Interest income from U.S. Treasury obligations is exempt from state and local taxes in every state. The rules governing the tax exemption vary somewhat from state to state, so check with your state tax authority for details. Of course, federal income taxes still apply to income from U.S. Treasury securities or funds, but in states with high income tax rates, the tax exemption on Treasury income may be quite valuable.

In addition to tax-exempt funds, a new type of mutual fund called the *tax-managed* fund is available. This type of fund uses specific strategies to minimize an investor's tax liability. For example, it holds portfolio turnover to very low levels to avoid triggering capital gains distributions and it tries to offset realized gains with realized losses. There also is a tax-managed balanced fund, which holds only municipal bonds for its fixed-income component.

Avoid the Year-End "Tax Trap"

At the end of each year, mutual funds generally distribute to investors all of the net capital gains that they have realized on the sale of securities during the year. If you are a taxable investor buying shares in a fund just before these year-end distributions, you may find yourself with a substantial tax liability.

For example, suppose you invest $10,000 in a fund at $10 per share and receive 1,000 shares. The day after you invest, the fund declares a $2 per share capital gains distribution. You must now report $2,000 in taxable income for the year ($2 per share in capital gains, times your 1,000 shares), even though you were invested in the fund for just one day. (Of course, if you are investing in a tax-deferred retirement plan, this is not an issue.) To avoid this potential tax bill, you may want to delay your investment until after any large year-end distributions.

Selecting a Financial Adviser

If you feel you need a financial adviser to help you manage your retirement assets, you might start by asking your attorney or accountant to recommend a financial planner knowledgeable about retirement issues. Or you could contact one of several national professional groups for the names of members in your area who are financial planners.

Be aware that financial planners are not covered by uniform state or federal regulations, so their qualifications and business practices vary considerably. More than 21,000 firms have registered as investment advisers with the SEC. Many stockbrokers and insurance agents now shun those titles and call themselves financial advisers, planners, or consultants.

The best financial planners are highly trained, with knowledge of accounting, tax and estate laws, pension planning, and investment management. They also have a certification from at least one of the recognized professional financial planning organizations. At the other end of the spectrum are outright crooks operating under the guise of financial planners. Be wary of individuals who claim to be financial planners but who do not have appropriate training or certification. There are a wide variety of certifications, which can lead to confusion for those unfamiliar with the planning profession. Here is a summary of the relevant certifications:

Certified Financial Planner (CFP). This designation, now held by about 31,000 people, is issued by the International Board of Standards and Practices for Certified Financial Planners in Denver, Colorado. Recipients must pass a 10-hour examination and take continuing education courses.

Chartered Financial Consultant (ChFC). Most of the 27,000 holders of the ChFC designation are insurance agents or have a background in the insurance industry. The ChFC is awarded by The American College in Bryn Mawr, Pennsylvania, to those with at least three years' experience in financial services who have passed 10 two-hour tests.

Chartered Financial Analyst (CFA). The CFA designation, held by about 19,000 individuals, is issued by the Association for Investment Management and Research in Charlottesville, Virginia. Financial planners who are CFAs often have a background as stock market analysts and professional money managers.

IAFP Registry. About 1,000 planners who belong to the International Association for Financial Planning are listed in the group's registry. To be listed, an IAFP member must have at least one financial planner designation, three years' experience as a financial planner, and references from five clients.

Personal Financial Specialist (PFS). This designation is awarded by the American Institute of Certified Public Accountants in New York City to CPAs who meet certain qualifications. More than 13,000 accountants have the PFS designation. Financial planners with the PFS designation often have a background as tax specialists.

Two trade groups for financial planners are the National Association of Personal Financial Advisors (NAPFA), which represents planners who are paid strictly by fees, not sales commissions, and the International Association for Financial Planning (IAFP), whose members include planners paid by fees and those paid by commission.

Fee-Based Planners versus Commission-Based Planners

Financial planners are paid in two basic ways: through fees or commissions. Fee-only planners often charge by the assignment. They typically assess a minimum charge for preparing a comprehensive financial plan, with an escalating scale of higher fees for clients with substantial wealth or complex financial circumstances. They may also charge hourly rates for financial consultation or charge for investment advice with a percentage fee assessed on the dollar value of your investment portfolio.

"Our difficulty is that anyone giving us financial/tax advice seems to be selling something. It's getting hard to trust anyone's advice."

California

Commission-only financial planners expect you to purchase insurance or investment products from them so they can be compensated for their services with commissions on the sale of those products. Some planners charge a combination of fees and commissions, in some cases agreeing to reduce or offset their fees by the amount of any commissions they earn from you. Before hiring a financial planner, you should understand how the planner will be compensated. Ask for full disclosure, in writing, of all fees and commissions, and for information about incentives, bonuses, or anything else of value that the planner is eligible to receive if a client buys a particular product. Do not hire a financial planner who is reluctant to provide in advance full disclosure of all compensation.

After you check a prospective financial planner's references, professional credentials, and compensation, be sure that you are personally comfortable with this person. Can he or she explain complex tax or investment issues in terms that you understand? Do you feel you are talking to a professional adviser, not a salesperson? A good financial planner will approach your assignment by looking at the whole of your personal life, financial circumstances, and investment goals, and will provide objective advice based on your particular needs.

Final Thoughts

In selecting particular mutual funds for your portfolio, you should do enough homework so that you understand the investment objectives and policies, the risks of the funds, and the costs you will incur by investing. When you compare funds, do so carefully, making certain that you are comparing apples with apples. And when evaluating fund performance, do not be so dazzled by past returns that you are blinded to other important considerations, particularly the risk characteristics of the fund. Remember that past performance is not a reliable predictor of future results from a fund.

As you grapple with the decision of which funds to choose for your retirement portfolio, keep in mind that the long-term success of your portfolio will be determined not so much by the specific funds that you select, but on how you choose to allocate your money among the three asset classes. The next chapter will assist you in this crucial task of asset allocation. It provides guidance, tailored to the retired investor, on finding the appropriate mix of assets to meet your needs. You'll be able to combine this information with what you've learned about fund selection to create a personalized investment portfolio. Before moving to the subject of asset allocation, however, here is a quick review of some common sense "rules" of mutual fund investing.

Be skeptical of past performance. No one can predict the future performance of a mutual fund based on its past performance, although funds that have been consistently poor performers over extended periods do tend to repeat their sub-par performance. Also, be sure to evaluate a fund's performance record in the context of the performance of other funds with the same investment objectives and policies, and in the context of the overall financial markets.

Pay attention to costs. Over the long run, costs will have a dramatic impact on the investment return you earn from your funds. Low costs should be almost your only consideration in selecting a money market fund or index fund. Costs should be the overriding consideration within each category of bond fund (long-term, short-term, etc.), but other factors, such as credit quality, may also influence your selections. The cost argument is not as compelling for stock funds, but costs should still be a strong consideration. All other factors held equal, you should always choose a low-cost fund over a high-cost fund.

Avoid "hot" funds. A recipe for failure in fund investing starts with the selection of funds based on the best performance over the last month, quarter, or year. Many top-ranking funds over short periods got their spectacular returns because of temporary market movements or because they invested in narrow segments of the stock market. These hot investments invariably cool off and are replaced by another group of short-term stars.

Don't pay a sales commission. Never pay a sales commission to buy a mutual fund unless you receive enough advice and guidance from the salesperson to justify the commission. Remember, paying a sales load does not mean that you have invested in a better-performing fund. On the contrary, the load will make it harder for the fund to match the return of a similar no-load fund. In short, if you don't need the services of a salesperson or adviser, don't pay a sales commission.

Don't accept cold calls. If a sales pitch sounds too good to be true, you can bet that it is. Your decision to buy a mutual fund—or any other investment—should come only after thoughtful consideration on your part. Be aware that retired investors are specially targeted by con artists.

Allocating Your Financial Assets: What's the Right Mix for You?

Chapter 7

Far too many authors, newsletter publishers, and financial advisers profit handsomely by convincing the public that they have a "system" for investing success. Some of these systems aim to pinpoint the next hot stock, mutual fund, or industrial sector; others recommend strategies for "timing" financial markets, advising their followers to switch among the various asset classes at the drop of a hat, according to a secret formula based on some set of financial or economic indicators.

"I have a mutual fund, a 401(k), an annuity, IRAs, and savings. I'm trying to figure out how to put all of these together."

Illinois

Although one objective study after another has found that such methods are rarely (if ever) effective, hope springs eternal that there is some magic way to identify the next winning investment strategy or the right time to get into or out of the different financial markets. Unfortunately, these strategies typically offer more hype than hope. The plain truth is that the key to investment success is based largely on how you allocate your assets among stocks, bonds, and short-term reserves; market timing and specific investment choices play only a marginal role. Indeed, studies of the performance of corporate pension plans suggest that 90% or more of your long-term investment return will be determined by the asset allocation you select. Less than 10% will be determined by your choice of individual investments. In other words, most of your investment analysis should be dedicated to arriving at an asset allocation that will meet your future spending needs, but still allow you to sleep soundly each night.

This chapter focuses on this crucial question: What mix of stocks, bonds, and short-term reserves is appropriate for you, given your retirement needs and your tolerance for risk? It provides some model retirement portfolios as a framework for you to customize your own investment portfolio, depending on your investment objectives, your financial resources, and your tolerance for fluctuations in the value of your investment principal and in the stream of income you receive from your investments. The chapter concludes with a discussion of issues to consider in fine-tuning your investment portfolio to achieve the right balance between risk and return.

The Asset Allocation Decision

"The best-informed investor is the one who knows himself."

Mark J. Appleman

Many retired investors mistakenly consider just one objective for their portfolio: to produce maximum current income from the assets they've accumulated through a lifetime of work, saving, and investment. This is an obsolete and costly notion that is ill-suited to the dynamic needs of the vast majority of retirees. Given the pervasiveness of inflation, an overemphasis on current income virtually dooms the retiree to a steadily declining standard of living.

Retirees today will be in retirement for many years longer than past generations, both because they are typically retiring at younger ages and because they are living longer. While inflation has been relatively subdued in recent years, it remains an obstacle to a financially secure retirement. The combination of inflation and a longer retirement period means that a retired investor must balance the objective of current income with the need for capital growth. Determining the right balance for you involves several considerations, including your age, your health, your financial circumstances, and your tolerance for risk. Still, it's safe to say that the vast majority of retirees needs both current income to meet daily living expenses and long-term capital growth to offset the effects of inflation. To achieve these objectives while simultaneously controlling the risk from fluctuating securities prices, an investor needs a balanced portfolio consisting of stocks, bonds, and in most cases, short-term reserves.

Although there is no single "retirement age," more than half of all Social Security beneficiaries choose to start receiving retirement benefits within a few months after reaching age 62, as shown in Figure 7–1. Of course, a good many Americans retire even earlier, while others continue to work for years beyond the typical retirement age. Whatever the starting point, you should expect to spend a long time in retirement.

Given the differences in launch dates among retirees—not to mention differences in lifestyles—it probably won't surprise you that no single portfolio allocation is appropriate for all retired investors. Indeed, there are many combinations of financial assets that a retiree might select. Over the next few pages, you will read about three model portfolios that broadly fit the three stages of retirement.

Figure 7–1
When Retirees Start to Receive Social Security Benefits

Retirement Age	62	63	64	65	66+
Percent	58%	8%	11%	17%	6%

Source: 1995 Data, 1996 Social Security Bulletin, Annual Statistical Supplement.

The first portfolio is designed for the young retiree, someone who retires before age 60. The second portfolio is designed for retired investors from 60 to 74 years of age, the "early years" of retirement. The third portfolio is designed for retired investors age 75 and over, who may want to emphasize generating income from their investments at the expense of long-term capital growth.

Each model portfolio has different risk and return characteristics, and you may well wish to tailor the recommended allocations to fit your personal situation by increasing or reducing the riskiness of the different portfolios. In this regard, remember that there is an inescapable trade-off between risk and return. Generally, you can achieve higher investment returns only by incurring higher risks. (The historical returns presented here should be used primarily to gauge the relative risks and returns of the portfolios, not as predictors of actual future performance.)

In calculating the past performance figures for these model portfolios, we have used the Standard & Poor's 500 Composite Stock Price Index as a proxy for the returns on common stocks. Long-term U.S. government bonds serve as a proxy for the returns on long-term bonds, and the 30-day U.S. Treasury bill is used as a benchmark for the returns on short-term reserves. In Figure 7–2, results from the model portfolios

Figure 7–2
Average Annual Returns on Model Retirement Portfolios

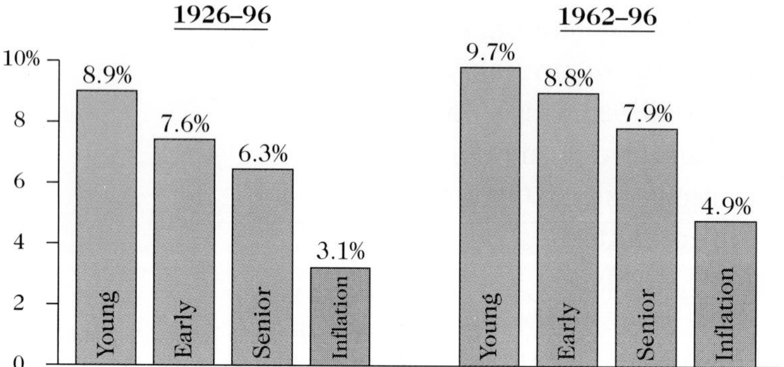

Source: ©*Stocks, Bonds, Bills, and Inflation 1997 Yearbook*™, Ibbotson Associates, Chicago. (Annually updates work by Roger G. Ibbotson and Rex A. Sinquefield.) Used with permission. All rights reserved.

are presented for two extended periods: the 35 years from January 1, 1962, through December 31, 1996, and the 70 years from 1926 through 1996.

The 35-year span is probably the more appropriate historical reference because it omits a lengthy period (1935–49) when the Federal Reserve Board kept short-term interest rates at fixed, and often artificially low, levels. Nonetheless, the period encompasses a variety of market environments and economic conditions, including a period of sharply rising inflation and interest rates (1973–80), a period of disinflation and falling interest rates (1982–93), and periods of relatively low and stable inflation (the 1960s and the early 1990s). Of course, historical returns tell us only about the past, not what will be achieved in the future. Unpredictability is a hallmark of the financial markets, so all we know for certain about future returns on stocks, bonds, and short-term reserves is that they will fluctuate.

An Aside about the Role of Short-Term Reserves

Before we address the model portfolios, it may help to address the question of how much retired investors should keep in "cash"—money invested in short-term savings to cover emergencies. A common rule of thumb for the working years is to have an emergency fund equal to three to six months' worth of living expenses. But many retirees find that this rule makes little sense for them. The financial emergency that a working person typically fears most is the loss of income from a layoff or disabling accident or illness. A retiree receiving income from Social Security, an employer's pension plan, and personal investments has relatively little reason to fear an interruption of income. It's reasonable to assume that the Social Security system will continue to regularly pay benefits (at least for the foreseeable future), and monthly defined benefit pension benefits are insured by a federal agency (up to $2,761 in 1997). Investment income can fluctuate, of course, but the fluctuations from a diversified, balanced portfolio should not be severe.

Because most of their income is derived from secure sources, many retired investors regard one month's living expenses as a sufficient "emergency" reserve. Others feel more comfortable with a larger reserve, equal to three, six, or even 12 months' worth of living expenses. Whatever your preference, you should consider this emergency reserve separately from the short-term reserves included in two of the three model portfolios. The role of short-term reserves in the recommended allocations is not to serve as an emergency fund; it is to stabilize the value of the portfolio and "tone down" the portfolio's risk characteristics.

Young Retiree Portfolio (Before Age 60)

Because their retirement portfolios must provide income for 30 years or longer—making them especially vulnerable to the ravages of inflation—investors in this group have perhaps the toughest task of all. What's more, the "young retiree" may be even more dependent than normal on investment income, since eligibility for Social Security retirement benefits does not begin until age 62. But this desire for current income must be balanced against the need to provide long-term growth in capital to offset inflation.

"I am retiring shortly. I can't decide how to invest, because I've never retired before."

Washington

As might be expected, this portfolio has the heaviest concentration of assets in common stocks. In theory, the extra risk of price fluctuations associated with a large allocation in stocks should be more bearable for younger retirees, who may be able to wait out the storm of a severe downturn in the

Figure 7–3
Young Retiree Portfolio

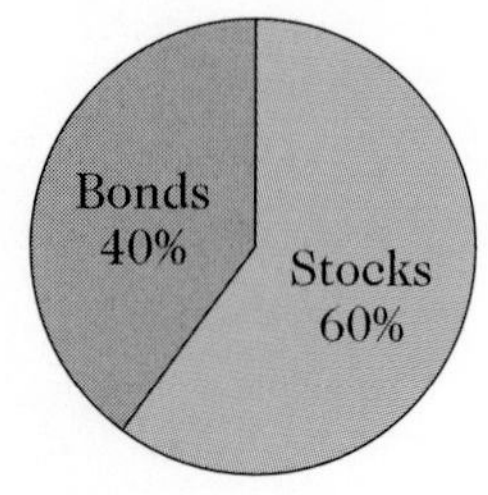

1962–96	
Stock/bond/reserves mix	60/40/0
Average annual return	9.7%
Years with losses (out of 35)	8
Average loss	−6%
Worst annual loss (1974)	−14%
Bear market (1973–74)	−22%

1926–96	
Stock/bond/reserves mix	60/40/0
Average annual return	8.9%
Years with losses (out of 71)	16
Average loss	−8%
Worst annual loss (1931)	−28%

Source: ©*Stocks, Bonds, Bills, and Inflation 1997 Yearbook*™, Ibbotson Associates, Chicago. (Annually updates work by Roger G. Ibbotson and Rex A. Sinquefield.) Used with permission.

financial markets. In the extreme, early retirees also may have the option of returning to work if their investment results are disappointing. The baseline portfolio consists of 60% common stocks and 40% bonds. It is an aggressive portfolio for retirement and is subject to fairly wide year-to-year fluctuations in market value.

As you can see in Figure 7–3, a portfolio allocated in this manner would have produced an average annual total return of 9.7% from 1962 through 1996, a period when inflation averaged 4.9% annually. The income yield on such a portfolio would have averaged 5.6% per year. The hypothetical portfolio would have incurred losses in eight of the 35 years during the period, or roughly one year out of every four. The average loss in the eight down years was −6%, with the steepest annual loss coming in 1974, when the portfolio's value fell by −14%. During the 1973–74 "bear market" for stocks, this portfolio's value fell −22%; it took about 18 months to recoup the loss, assuming the reinvestment of all dividends and interest income.

"It's not the bears and bulls that get you in the stock market. It's the bum steers."

Milton Berle

Over a very long period—1926 through 1996—this asset mix would have produced a slightly lower average annual total return of 8.9% a year, easily beating the average inflation rate of 3.1% a year. Over this 70-year span, this portfolio would have suffered losses in 16 years, or once every four years or so. In the average down year, the portfolio would have declined by −8%, with the worst loss coming in 1931, when the portfolio slumped −28%.

Early Retiree Portfolio (Ages 60 through 74)

If you are a retiree between the ages of 60 and 74, you still have a long-term investing horizon, since your average life expectancy ranges from about 21 years if you are age 60 down to 11 years if you are age 74. (Keep in mind that roughly half of those attaining any particular age will exceed the average life expectancy for that age group.) To protect your assets against inflation, you'll still need to maintain a significant commitment to common stocks, as well as a hefty holding of bonds for current income. You'll also want to hold some short-term reserves, which will provide welcome interest income and stability of principal during periods when the financial markets turn unfriendly for bonds and common stocks. Accordingly, the early retiree portfolio has a mix of 40% common stocks, 40% bonds, and 20% short-term reserves. This recommended mix holds a relatively larger proportion of assets in bonds and short-term reserves to increase the portfolio's current income and reduce its vulnerability to price fluctuations.

Historically, this asset mix has outpaced inflation while providing a solid level of income. What's more, it has declined only modestly during major market downturns. During the 35 years ended December 31, 1996, as shown in Figure 7–4, this allocation would have produced an average annual total return of 8.8%, compared with an average annual inflation rate of 4.9%. On average for the 35 years, this asset mix provided an annual income return of 6%.

The portfolio would have declined in seven of the 35 years, or an average of once every five years. During these down years, the portfolio's value would have fallen an average of −3%—half the average decline experienced by the more aggressive portfolio—with the worst year (1974) resulting in a decline of −7%. During the 1973–74 bear market, this

Figure 7–4
Early Retiree Portfolio

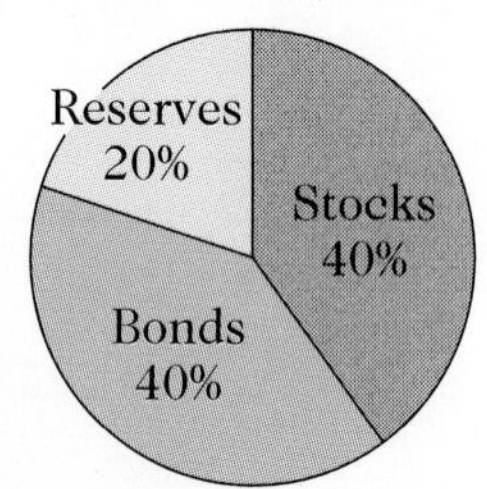

1962–96	
Stock/bond/reserves mix	40/40/20
Average annual return	8.8%
Years with losses (out of 35)	7
Average loss	−3%
Worst annual loss (1974)	−7%
Bear market (1973–74)	−12%

1926–96	
Stock/bond/reserves mix	40/40/20
Average annual return	7.6%
Years with losses (out of 71)	15
Average loss	−5%
Worst annual loss (1931)	−19%

Source: ©*Stocks, Bonds, Bills, and Inflation 1997 Yearbook*™, Ibbotson Associates, Chicago. (Annually updates work by Roger G. Ibbotson and Rex A. Sinquefield.) Used with permission.

"My goal is a little different—it is to have my savings appreciate in value so that I'll have a worthwhile estate for my children. I am doing that by investing in equities. I am switching, where I can, from bonds into equities. For a while, I had too much in bonds."

Maryland

portfolio's value would have declined by −12%. Finally, from the bottom of the market downturn in November 1974, it would have taken roughly six months for the portfolio to recoup its pre-slump value (assuming all distributions had been reinvested).

During the 71-year period from 1926 through 1996, the 40/40/20 portfolio allocation would have achieved an average annual return of 7.6%, versus an average annual inflation rate of 3.1%. The portfolio would have incurred losses in 15 of the 71 years, with an average loss of −5% in those down years. Its worst annual loss would have been −19% in the Great Depression year of 1931.

Senior Retiree Portfolio (Age 75+)

If you are in this stage of retirement, you are probably interested in earning the maximum level of current income reasonably possible. Your actuarial investing time horizon has shortened to less than 20 years, which may not be long enough to ride out a particularly rough period for stocks. By shifting a portion of your assets from common stocks to longer-term bonds, you can boost your current income while decreasing your stock market exposure. Although fluctuations in bond prices will cause some volatility in your principal, these fluctuations can generally be ignored, since your income payments will be undisturbed. In fact, if interest rates rise (causing a "paper" decline in the prices of your bonds), the income from your short-term reserves and bonds will also rise, boosting your current income. During periods of falling interest rates, income from this portfolio will gradually decline, though the decline will be accompanied by a rise in the market value of the portfolio's bonds.

Despite their inherent price volatility, common stocks will continue to make up a portion of your assets, primarily for two reasons. First, your retirement may last a good while longer than you think—about half of 75-year-olds will live for another decade or longer—so you'll need some capital growth as protection against inflation. Second, a small allocation in stocks can actually *reduce* the price fluctuations of your overall portfolio compared with a portfolio consisting only of bonds and short-term reserves, because stock prices do not always move in lockstep with bond prices.

As shown in Figure 7–5, the model portfolio for the late stage of retirement comprises 20% stocks, 60% bonds, and 20% short-term reserves. From 1962 through 1996, this conservative mix of assets would have produced an average annual total return of 7.9%, nearly two percentage points below that of the most aggressive portfolio. Not surprisingly,

Figure 7–5
Senior Retiree Portfolio

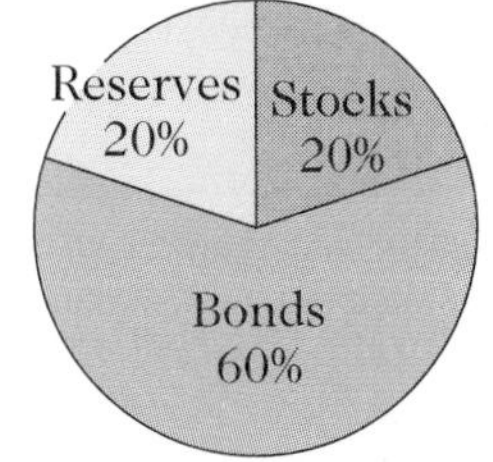

1962–96	
Stock/bond/reserves mix	20/60/20
Average annual return	7.9%
Years with losses (out of 35)	5
Average loss	−2%
Worst annual loss (1994)	−4%
Bear market (1973–74)	−3%

1926–96	
Stock/bond/reserves mix	20/60/20
Average annual return	6.3%
Years with losses (out of 71)	12
Average loss	−3%
Worst annual loss (1931)	−12%

Source: ©*Stocks, Bonds, Bills, and Inflation 1997 Yearbook*™, Ibbotson Associates, Chicago. (Annually updates work by Roger G. Ibbotson and Rex A. Sinquefield.) Used with permission.

virtually all of that 7.9% return would have been received in the form of interest and dividend income; the average income return for this portfolio during the period was 6.8% a year, with the remainder accounted for by capital appreciation.

The heavy weighting of bonds in the portfolio would have helped to mitigate the year-to-year fluctuations in total return in comparison to the early retirement portfolio. This lower volatility is a desirable trait for older retirees, many of whom are liquidating some of their investments during this period and thus can ill afford dramatic fluctuations in the market value of their holdings. However, even the late retirement portfolio is not immune to the perils of the financial markets: it would have fallen in value in five of the 35 years from 1962 through 1996. Not surprisingly, the portfolio's occasional losses would have been muted, with an average drop in the five down years of −2%, and a worst loss of −4% in 1994. The portfolio's light holdings of common stocks would have helped it to withstand the 1973–74 bear market, suffering a mere −3% loss, which was recouped within two months after the downturn ended.

Over the 1926–96 period, the senior retiree portfolio would have produced an average annual return of 6.3%. The portfolio would have suffered losses in 12 of the 71 years, with an average loss of −3% in the down years and a worst-ever decline of −12% in 1931. You can see that, if you plan to pass assets on to your heirs and do not expect to tap into your investment principal during retirement, the senior retiree portfolio is probably too conservative. In such circumstances, you may wish to hold a larger proportion of common stocks to maximize the growth in the estate that you will leave behind you.

As noted earlier, the historical return figures for the three model portfolios are based on returns for the unmanaged Standard & Poor's 500 Index of common stocks, long-term U.S. government bonds, and short-term U.S. Treasury bills. They do not take into account the real-world costs of investing in and maintaining a portfolio of securities. Nor do these returns consider any income taxes that would ordinarily be incurred by an investor in a nonretirement–related account. Taking into account transaction costs, operating expenses, and any taxes on your earnings, your long-term returns are quite likely to fall short of the historical returns of the model portfolios.

On the other hand, your investment choices are considerably more diverse than the three benchmark investments used here. If you decide to allocate 50% or more of your portfolio to common stocks, you might put some of the equity investments in small-company stock funds, which historically have provided higher returns—and greater risk of price fluctuations—than the large-capitalization stocks in the S&P 500 Index. If stocks compose 40% or less of your portfolio, you'll probably want to stick with large-company U.S. stock funds.

If 40% or more of your portfolio is allocated to bonds, you should strongly consider holding both U.S. Treasury bonds and high-quality corporate bonds. Many retirees limit themselves to Treasury bonds and other government securities, overlooking the exceptional diversification and higher yields provided by most corporate bond funds. Remember that a broadly diversified corporate bond fund substantially reduces the impact of a default by a single company. What's more, the risk of interest-rate fluctuations affects Treasury and corporate bonds equally.

One popular inclusion in the portfolios of many retirees is mortgage-backed bond funds, such as GNMA funds. While it certainly makes sense to own a mortgage-backed bond fund for the relatively higher yield it can provide, it should probably not be the centerpiece of your bond portfolio. Although GNMA funds are of exceptionally high quality, the ability of mortgage holders to prepay their mortgage loans adds an element of unpredictability not found in any other bond fund. Likewise, high-yield (junk) bonds are a reasonable investment for even cautious investors *provided* that holdings of these risky bonds are limited to a modest portion—say, no more than 10% to 15% of your total retirement portfolio.

A Few Words about Diversification

"If you're too heavy in one thing, then you should balance it out by getting out of things that you're too heavy in. That's my idea of how to invest."

New Jersey

Some investors, seeing the astonishing historical record of common stocks versus long-term bonds and cash reserves, might reasonably wonder why they shouldn't forgo bonds and cash reserves entirely and hold only common stocks. Indeed, a few well-known commentators and investment managers have advocated just such an approach. Their reasoning is that an investor owning only stocks will, most of the time, enjoy higher returns than an investor who holds a mix of stocks, bonds, and cash reserves. As the argument goes, even if a downturn in stock prices forces the aggressive investor to liquidate some of his or her stock holdings at low prices, stock prices eventually will rebound and reward the aggressive investor.

There are two fundamental problems with this philosophy. First, despite the dominance of common stocks in the past, there is no guarantee that they will continue to outperform either bonds or cash reserves. At the very least, it seems likely that any outperformance by common stocks in the future, particularly over the coming decade, will be nowhere near as large as suggested by the historical record. In short, the past is not always a prologue. The second problem with an all-stock portfolio is that it presupposes a steely nerve and a considerable tolerance for risk. It seems unlikely that most investors could calmly watch as a severe bear market lopped off 30% or more of the value of their retirement portfolio. While such sharp declines are hardly the norm in the equity market, they do occur. It may be reassuring to know that, over sufficiently long periods, stocks have always outperformed bonds, but not all of us can afford to wait the 20 years or more it might take for this long-term outperformance to manifest itself. In other words, the danger for most investors is that they surrender to their fears—or financial needs—and sell stocks following a big market decline.

There is also general agreement among financial experts that short-term reserves will provide the lowest returns of the three major asset classes. So why do two of our three model portfolios include some allocation to reserves? The rationale is that short-term reserves will cushion the overall value of your portfolio from the inevitable fluctuations in the prices of bonds and stocks, providing some welcome stability during financial market duress. At such times, you can tap your reserves to help meet your living expenses without having to sell bonds or stocks at the bottom of a market cycle.

As you'll see in the next section, particular investors need not slavishly adhere to the allocations laid out thus far. Some may elect to hold no reserves; others may hold even more than the model portfolios suggest. Depending on your personal circumstances, you will want to use the model portfolios as a guideline for customizing an investment plan that meets your specific needs.

Fine-Tuning Your Portfolio Allocation

The three model portfolios, then, are intended as starting points in developing your personal portfolio. Just as a garment is tailored to fit your measurements and tastes, your portfolio should fit your individual needs. This section describes how you might alter the mix of assets in the recommended portfolios to provide the best possible fit, taking into account your financial resources, your investing time horizon, your tolerance for risk, and your expectations about the financial markets.

Financial Resources

The adequacy of the income you receive from Social Security and employer pensions may strongly influence the investment mix you select. For instance, if you can get by at first mainly on retirement benefits and thus need relatively modest current income from your investments, you can probably afford to take more risk in pursuit of higher long-term returns. Conversely, if your combined pension benefits and Social Security payments are not sufficient to meet your daily living expenses, you may need to boost your allocation to longer-term bonds and reduce your commitment to common stocks.

"I'm in a transition stage right now. My investments are highly diversified, but I'm gradually moving them more into fixed income."

California

Of course, this kind of trade-off will reduce the long-term growth potential of your investment portfolio, but it is precisely these kinds of difficult real-world decisions that you will need to make as you plan for an extended retirement period.

One particularly important issue to consider with regard to your financial resources is whether you intend to work during your retirement years. As long as you continue to generate current income from your job, you can probably minimize the use of income-oriented investments in your portfolio. If you haven't already paid off the mortgage on your home, you might consider using a portion of the "extra" wages you earn to pay down the remaining principal on your home loan. This will dramatically reduce the baseline income you need to meet your living expenses once you are fully retired, which will let you continue to allocate a relatively large proportion of your assets to lower-yielding, but higher growth potential, common stocks.

Time Horizon

In general, the older you are and the shorter your time horizon for investing, the more conservative your investment portfolio should become. In other words, the proportion of assets you hold in common stocks should decline, and the proportion in bonds and short-term reserves should rise. Common stocks historically have had the widest fluctuations in price of the three major asset classes, which makes stocks a risky proposition if you intend to liquidate your holdings within five years or so.

While the three model portfolios are targeted to specific age ranges, within each model you may wish to alter the asset mix to reflect where you fall within each range. For instance, a 90-year-old investor may wish to hold no common stocks; such a stance would probably be too conservative for a 76-year-old investor who may reasonably expect retirement to last another 15 years. Your health and family history may also affect your allocations. If your health is excellent and your family history suggests a longer-than-average life span, inflation may be more of a concern, and you will want to be more aggressive in your investment mix, boosting your holdings in common stocks.

Risk Tolerance

Regardless of anyone's recommendation, your investment portfolio must pass the "sleep test." That is, you should be comfortable enough with your asset mix that you are not losing sleep because of the inevitable fluctuations that occur in financial markets. No one else can tell you how you should feel about the risk of losing some portion of *your money.* If the thought of your nest egg losing 20% or more of its value during a single year makes you queasy, you'll probably want to place only a token portion of your retirement assets in common stocks. It may be worth the trade-off—a lower potential long-term return and a higher risk of inflation eroding the buying power of your income—for the improvement in your peace of mind. On the other hand, your greatest worry may be that your portfolio won't keep up with inflation. In this case, you may be willing to accept the risk of interim downturns in the stock market in exchange for potentially higher returns.

"Chance favors the prepared mind."

Louis Pasteur

Market Conditions

In general, the most successful investors are those who decide on an investment mix that is appropriate to their situation and then stay the course through the ups and downs of the financial markets. Nonetheless, there may be occasions when the valuations of financial assets seem extraordinarily high or low and you are tempted to alter your strategic allocations. If you must yield to such temptations, it is best to do so only grudgingly. Few investors (even those with considerable experience and the best analytical tools) can predict with any degree of accuracy or consistency the movements of the stock and bond markets.

The problems with market timing are twofold. First, even if you are "right" in thinking that stock prices or interest rates have reached unusually low or unusually high levels, you may well be "wrong" in your timing. Periods of extreme optimism or pessimism in the financial markets often last longer and reach greater heights or depths than anyone expects. Second, even if your odds of guessing correctly on when to get out of stocks were as high as, say, one in three (an extraordinary success ratio), you'd also have to guess correctly on when to get back into the stock market. Assuming that your odds of successfully guessing when to get back in were also as high as one in three, your odds of being right on the full round trip would fall to one chance in nine.

Given the slim odds that you will guess correctly both times, if you feel compelled to change your asset mix based on what you believe is in store for the financial markets, limit yourself to marginal changes. For example, if you think that stock prices are either too high or low on a valuation basis, you might trim or boost your allocation to stocks by no more than 10 to 15 percentage points. Thus, if your basic strategic allocation is 45% stocks, limit any alterations to your stock holdings to a range of 35% to 55%.

Ongoing Asset Allocation Issues

Once you decide on an overall allocation for your retirement portfolio, the "heavy lifting" is done. However, there are a few more issues to consider. First is whether and how often you should adjust your portfolio to keep the balance of assets you desire. You'll also want to consider whether the fixed-income portion of your portfolio should be invested in taxable or tax-exempt bonds. A third matter to consider is whether you want to use an "active" approach to investing or rely on indexing, an investment management approach that relies on low cost and simplicity to produce above-average results over the long term. Finally, consider some techniques for improving your investment results without incurring significantly higher risks.

Rebalancing Your Portfolio

Whatever your asset mix, you can reduce the risk level of your portfolio by rebalancing periodically to maintain your strategic allocation among stocks, bonds, and short-term reserves. Suppose, for example, that you begin with a portfolio valued at $100,000, with 60% invested in common stocks, 30% in bonds, and 10% in reserves. Over the next year, the value of your stock holdings increases by 24%, your bond holdings increase by 8%, and your money market fund increases by 5%. Under these circumstances, the new allocation of your assets at the end of the year is shown in Table 7–1.

Table 7–1
Portfolio Allocation

	Investment Value	Percent of Portfolio
Stocks	$ 74,400	63%
Bonds	32,400	28
Reserves	10,500	9
Total	$117,300	100%

You're happy, of course, that your total portfolio has grown by 17.3%. Unfortunately, the growth has also increased the risk level of your overall portfolio, since stocks performed so much better than bonds and reserves. If your risk tolerance, financial situation, and time horizon have not changed, you may want to shift some of your assets to get back to your original portfolio allocation. To return to your strategic asset mix, you could shift $4,000 out of your stock funds, putting $2,800 into your bond funds and $1,200 into your money market fund. Your adjusted portfolio allocation would be as shown in Table 7–2.

If your assets are not invested in some kind of tax-deferred retirement account, this rebalancing act has one major consequence: taxes. (You may also incur commission costs and/or transaction fees.) If you hold substantial assets in non-retirement accounts, you should probably take a different approach to rebalancing. For instance, if you are adding to your holdings each year, you may be able to rebalance your portfolio by allocating your new investments to the lagging asset classes. Using the earlier example, suppose you intend to contribute

Table 7–2
Portfolio Allocation

	Investment Value	Percent of Portfolio
Stocks	$ 70,400	60%
Bonds	35,200	30
Reserves	11,700	10
Total	$117,300	100%

an additional $5,000 during the coming year. This additional contribution would automatically bring the total value of your portfolio to $122,300 ($117,300 + $5,000). Since your desired allocation to bonds is 30%, the balance of your total bond investments should be $36,690 ($122,300 × 0.30). In order to reach this figure, you would need to contribute $4,290 ($36,690 – $32,400) to your bond investments. The remaining $710 of your $5,000 additional investment would be invested in your cash reserves account, bringing this balance to $11,210 ($10,500 + $710).

Table 7–3
Portfolio Allocation

	Investment Value	Percent of Portfolio
Stocks	$ 74,400	61%
Bonds	36,690	30
Reserves	11,210	9
Total	$122,300	100%

Your new portfolio allocation at the beginning of the year would now be as shown in Table 7–3. While this method does not perfectly rebalance your portfolio, it does avoid the tax liability that would result from selling shares. (As noted earlier, the tax consequences of rebalancing are not a consideration for investors in retirement-related accounts.)

If you intend to *withdraw* $5,000 of your assets during the second year rather than make an additional contribution, the same strategy could be applied. In this case, you could move back toward your target asset allocation by withdrawing the entire $5,000 from your stock holdings. Doing so would reduce your total portfolio value to $112,300 and your stock component to $69,400. Your portfolio allocation at the start of the second year would now be as shown in Table 7–4. Again, the allocation would not precisely reflect your desired mix, but you would at least have moved close to your target.

Table 7–4
Portfolio Allocation

	Investment Value	Percent of Portfolio
Stocks	$ 69,400	62%
Bonds	32,400	29
Reserves	10,500	9
Total	$112,300	100%

Taking the example in Table 7–4 a step further, suppose that in year two your stock funds decline by −10%, your bond funds again provide an 8% return, and your cash reserves provide a 5.5% return. At the end of year two, your portfolio would be allocated as shown in Table 7–5. If you plan to again withdraw

$5,000 to help cover your living expenses during the coming year (reducing your portfolio value from $108,530 to $103,530), you could take $360 from your stock funds, $3,920 from your bond funds, and $720 from your reserves. Your rebalanced portfolio is shown in Table 7–6.

Table 7–5
Portfolio Allocation

	Investment Value	Percent of Portfolio
Stocks	$ 62,460	58%
Bonds	34,990	32
Reserves	11,080	10
Total	$108,530	100%

You can see that by rebalancing your portfolio, you automatically reap some of the gains from your best-performing investments and add to the asset class or classes that have underperformed. This strategy reduces the risk of losses during market downturns, especially severe downturns in the stock market. Of course, if stocks are always the top-performing asset class, year after year, a rebalancing strategy will reduce your gains compared with a "let it ride" approach. But the basis for rebalancing your portfolio is to keep your risk exposure in line with your original strategy. Thus, for most retired investors, a strategy of locking in gains seems a prudent approach.

That said, there is no set rule for how often a portfolio should be rebalanced, although once a year is probably more than sufficient for most investors. More important than the time period you select is that you are disciplined in your approach to rebalancing, and don't allow market psychology to overrule your best intentions. If once-a-year rebalancing seems too problematic to execute, you might follow a less stringent strategy. For instance, some financial advisers advocate rebalancing only when one asset class deviates by a certain percentage—say, five percentage points—from your target. If your target allocation for stocks is 40% and a rising stock market pushes your allocation in stocks to 45%, you could rebalance by taking some of your profits in stocks or by directing any additional contributions to bonds and reserves.

Table 7–6
Portfolio Allocation

	Investment Value	Percent of Portfolio
Stocks	$ 62,100	60%
Bonds	31,070	30
Reserves	10,360	10
Total	$103,530	100%

Taxable Bonds versus Tax-Exempt Bonds

For the bond portion of your portfolio, you must decide whether to hold taxable bonds or tax-exempt bonds. If you are investing in any kind of tax-deferred retirement account, you should *never own tax-exempt bonds* in it, since the interest income on "regular" bonds will not be taxed in your retirement account. What's more, by putting tax-exempt bonds in a tax-advantaged account, you would pay income tax on money withdrawn from the account, including interest that otherwise would have been exempt from income tax. If you are investing in a regular taxable account, your decision whether to hold taxable or tax-exempt bonds will depend on two factors: (1) your marginal tax rate and (2) the differential between yields on taxable bonds and yields on similar tax-exempt bonds.

Because the interest paid on municipal bonds is exempt from federal income taxes (and from state and local income taxes, if the bonds are issued in your home state), yields on municipal bonds will be lower than yields on taxable bonds with similar credit quality and maturities. But, after a taxable bond yield is adjusted for taxes, it may turn out that municipal bonds will provide you with more income on an after-tax basis.

In comparing the yields on taxable and tax-exempt bonds, consider your "marginal" tax rate—the rate of tax you pay on each additional dollar of investment income. Your marginal rate is important, because the federal tax system and most states' tax systems do not treat all income equally. You pay a lower tax rate on your first dollar of income than on your last dollar of income. As you can see in Table 7–7, federal tax rates rise on taxable income above certain levels (the rates are shown for single taxpayers and for married couples filing joint returns).

Table 7–7
1997 Federal Income Tax Rates

Taxable Income		Tax Rate
Single	Married	
Up to $24,650	Up to $41,200	15.0%
$24,651 to $59,750	$41,201 to $99,600	28.0
$59,751 to $124,650	$99,601 to $151,750	31.0
$124,651 to $271,050	$151,751 to $271,050	36.0
$271,051 and up	$271,051 and up	39.6

Table 7–8
Equivalent Tax-Exempt Yields for Taxable Bonds

Marginal Tax Bracket	Yield on Taxable Bond or Bond Fund										
	3%	3.5%	4%	4.5%	5%	5.5%	6%	6.5%	7%	7.5%	8%
15.0%	2.6%	3.0%	3.4%	3.8%	4.3%	4.7%	5.1%	5.5%	6.0%	6.4%	6.8%
28.0	2.2	2.5	2.9	3.2	3.6	4.0	4.3	4.7	5.0	5.4	5.8
31.0	2.1	2.4	2.8	3.1	3.5	3.8	4.1	4.5	4.8	5.2	5.5
36.0	1.9	2.2	2.6	2.9	3.2	3.5	3.8	4.2	4.5	4.8	5.1
39.6	1.8	2.1	2.4	2.7	3.0	3.3	3.6	3.9	4.2	4.5	4.8

There's a straightforward calculation to determine whether tax-exempt bonds would be advantageous for you relative to taxable bonds. First, use Table 7–7 to find the marginal tax rate that applies to you. To calculate the after-tax yield of a taxable bond, multiply its yield by one minus your tax bracket. For example, assume you are considering a taxable bond or bond mutual fund with a yield of, say, 7%. If your marginal federal income tax rate is 28%, multiply 7% by 0.72 (1 − 0.28). The result, 5.04%, is the after-tax yield of the taxable bond. In this case, if you can find a municipal bond or bond fund—of comparable maturity and credit quality—that pays more than 5.04%, you'd be better off with the municipal bond. Table 7–8 shows, for various tax brackets, the after-tax yields provided by taxable bonds at different yield levels. Or if you know the yield on a tax-exempt municipal bond, you can use Table 7–9 to see the taxable-bond equivalent yield, based on your marginal tax rate.

Table 7–9
Taxable Bond Equivalent Yields for Tax-Exempt Bonds

Marginal Tax Bracket	Yield on Tax-Exempt Bond or Bond Fund										
	3%	3.5%	4%	4.5%	5%	5.5%	6%	6.5%	7%	7.5%	8%
15.0%	3.5%	4.1%	4.7%	5.3%	5.9%	6.5%	7.1%	7.6%	8.2%	8.8%	9.4%
28.0	4.2	4.9	5.6	6.3	6.9	7.6	8.3	9.0	9.7	10.4	11.1
31.0	4.3	5.1	5.8	6.5	7.2	8.0	8.7	9.4	10.1	10.9	11.6
36.0	4.7	5.5	6.3	7.0	7.8	8.6	9.4	10.2	10.9	11.7	12.5
39.6	5.0	5.8	6.6	7.5	8.3	9.1	9.9	10.8	11.6	12.4	13.2

Retirees who live in states with high income tax rates, such as New York, Massachusetts, and California, might be further advantaged by holding a state tax-exempt bond fund that holds tax-exempt bonds issued within their state. Keep in mind that bond funds that hold only securities issued within a particular state generally entail a higher level of credit risk due to their concentrated exposure to discrete regions of the country. Thus, investors should probably focus their attention on *insured* state bond funds.

If you owned municipal bonds or municipal bond funds before retirement, you should run through the yield comparison to make sure the tax-exempt bonds still make sense for you. In many cases, a retiree's tax rate will be lower than it was during her or his working years. If you've dropped into the 28% or 15% tax bracket, you may be better off holding taxable bonds rather than municipals. U.S. Treasury statistics indicate that many municipal bonds are held by taxpayers in the 15% tax bracket, even though these investors almost certainly would be better off holding taxable bonds.

Index Funds: The Simple Path to Asset Allocation

Indexing, or "passive" management, is an investment management approach based entirely on quantitative methods. An index fund manager generally holds all of the securities that are included in a particular stock or bond market index in the same proportion as they are represented in the index. Index funds that track very broad markets may hold a representative sample of the securities in their benchmark indexes.

Traditional active fund managers select their investments based on analytical research, judgment, and experience. These active fund managers endeavor to outperform the broad-based market indexes that are emulated by the index funds. (Perhaps more importantly, active fund managers also strive to exceed the performance results of other fund managers.) From the perspective of active fund managers, the financial markets are "inefficient," and it is therefore possible to find undervalued securities that will provide higher returns than the broad market averages.

To get a sense of the difficulty professional investment managers face in achieving their objectives, begin with the fact that all fund managers simply cannot be right since all investors, in the aggregate, can perform no better than the market itself. Thus, for every investor who beats the market index by a given amount, there is another investor who must underperform the index by a like amount. The catch is that all investors in the aggregate must match the return of the market *before expenses*. When fund expenses, sales loads, and portfolio transaction costs are taken into account, all investors in the aggregate actually *underperform* the market indexes, which incur none of the real-world costs of investing. Since these costs—estimated at a total of roughly 2% per year for the typical stock mutual fund—directly reduce a fund's performance, it is easy to see the difficulty that active fund managers face in trying to beat the stock market with any consistency.

Index investors, on the other hand, believe that the financial markets are relatively efficient, at least in the long run. They observe that each professional investment manager constantly seeks to gain a competitive edge over other managers. However, once a manager discovers an "inefficiency" that results in superior performance, the market quickly adjusts to this inefficiency and eliminates any advantage that may have existed. Thus, while a particular money manager may beat the market average over a short period of time, it is extremely difficult to sustain a long-term performance advantage.

Of course, there are a handful of star managers (for example, Warren Buffett and John Neff) who have beaten the market over very long periods. And there will surely be others who will do so in the future. But it is impossible to know in advance who this next generation of top-performing investment managers will be. More often than not, today's top-rated funds will regress to the mean (become average) over some subsequent period. You have to decide whether it is worthwhile risking below-average performance for the slim chance of selecting one of the few truly gifted (or lucky) professional investment managers.

In short, the case for selecting an index fund rests entirely on indexing's inherent cost advantage. There is no magic formula or secret strategy. Because index funds employ no high-cost advisers, they have minimal operating expenses and very low brokerage transaction costs (since they buy and sell securities infrequently). A typical low-cost index fund might incur total operating expenses and transaction costs of as little as 0.2% annually. In contrast, the typical actively managed stock mutual fund incurs operating and advisory expenses totaling 1.4% and transaction costs totaling another 0.6% annually. Thus, the index funds enjoy an annual advantage of 1.8%. This annual expense differential makes it extremely difficult for active fund managers to beat an index fund. In fact, academic studies have shown that only about one out of every four equity mutual funds beats the stock market average over time. The odds may be as low as one out of every five when fund sales charges are taken into account.

This index advantage can mean an enormous difference in performance over time. For example, as shown in Figure 7–6, over the past 20 years the Wilshire 5000 Index, an index that tracks the performance of all U.S. common stocks, outperformed about two-thirds of all actively managed stock funds in six years and failed to outperform at least one-third only once (in 1982). The same general trend can be observed in a comparison of bond fund returns versus the returns of the Lehman Aggregate Bond Index, a

Figure 7–6
Percent of General Equity Funds Outperformed by the Wilshire 5000 Index, 1977–96

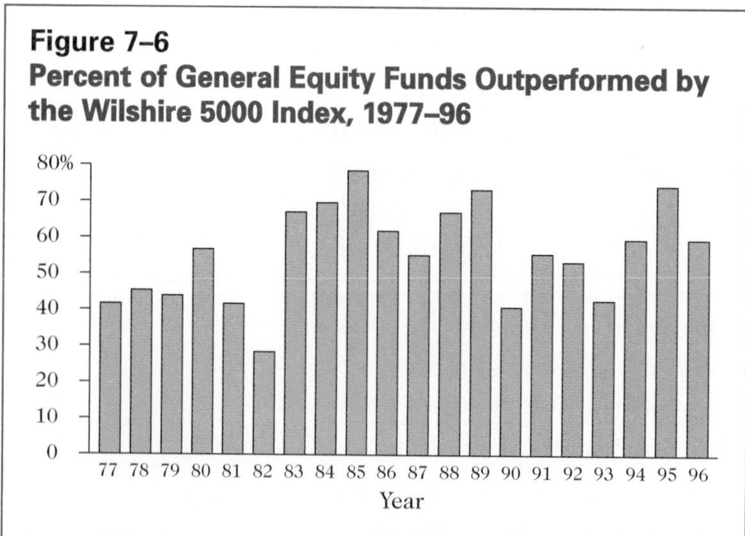

Note: The returns of the Wilshire 5000 Index have been reduced by 0.2% per year to reflect fund costs.
Source: Wilshire Associates.

broad index of investment-grade U.S. bonds. While indexing can never promise the highest returns in any given year, by being consistently above average the index builds a formidable long-term record compared to the average active fund manager.

Given the natural competitive spirit of wanting to beat the market, many first-time investors seem to favor traditional active management. On the other hand, more experienced investors, who presumably understand the difficulty of identifying in advance those fund managers who will provide superior investment returns over the long run, tend to choose an index fund for at least a portion of their total investment portfolio. Implicitly, large corporate and government pension plans also seem to recognize the fallibility of active investment management, as evidenced by their $400 billion commitment to index strategies.

When it comes down to choosing an active fund versus an index fund, most investors seem to favor one of three strategies, as outlined below.

All-Active Strategy You may elect to use active management for your entire retirement portfolio. In taking an all-active approach, you incur the risk that a fund may underperform the market average, but you also have the opportunity to earn above-average returns. In any event, you should be prepared to spend considerable time learning about the many types of active funds that are available and examining their long-term records, expenses, management styles, and the like.

All-Index Strategy In adopting an all-index approach, you should expect to be rewarded with above-average returns over time because of indexing's sustainable low-cost advantage. However, you'll probably forfeit the opportunity to own one of the very best-performing mutual funds.

Core Strategy With a core strategy (employed by many large pension funds), a major component of your investment portfolio is indexed, with the remainder invested in actively managed funds. For example, you might invest half of your retirement savings in index funds and the rest in actively managed stock and bond funds that you believe have the potential to outperform the market over time. The main consideration here is what percentage of your savings to invest in indexed versus active accounts.

Low-Risk Strategies for Boosting Your Returns

A low-risk investment with high returns is the proverbial Holy Grail of investing. While your search for such an investment will surely be in vain, there are techniques you can use to get *somewhat* higher returns while taking little or, in some cases, no additional risk. You can cut your costs, cut out the middleman, check your checking account, and add a dollop of risk. None of these techniques will, by itself, make a huge difference in your investment results, but taken together, they can help to improve your "fiscal fitness."

Cut Your Costs Surprisingly, many investors do not even know how much they're paying for investment services. Yet cost is one of the three critical components (risk and return are the others) of the eternal triangle that determines your investment success. Once you decide on the allocation of assets that provides the right balance of risk and return for your situation, the performances of the financial markets will determine the gross returns you earn on your portfolio. However, your net returns will depend on the costs that you incur on your investments.

The difference between low-cost funds and high-cost funds can be staggering: an expense ratio of 0.30% of assets ($30 a year per $10,000 invested) for a typical low-cost fund compared with 2.5% ($250 a year per $10,000) or more for a high-cost fund. Unfortunately, the presence of high fees or expenses does not imply better returns. Indeed, according to William Sharpe, recipient of the Nobel Prize for economics for his work in finance, "There is virtually no evidence to suggest that funds with higher expense ratios do better, before expenses. Which therefore suggests they will do worse, after expenses."

Cut Out the Middleman If you want to invest in Treasury securities because of their unparalleled credit quality and steady interest payments, and you're confident that you will hold them until they mature, consider buying them yourself directly. You may buy Treasury securities through the Federal Reserve Board at the regular auctions of Treasury bills, notes, and bonds. In doing so, you'll incur no purchase fees or ongoing expenses, and payments of interest and principal are made directly to your bank account by the U.S. Treasury. To learn how to make direct purchases, write to the Federal Reserve Bank of Philadelphia, Publications, 100 N. Sixth St., Philadelphia, PA 19105, and ask for the pamphlet "Buying Treasury Securities."

Check Your Checking Account Many investors keep far too much cash idling in their checking accounts or in low-yielding savings accounts. If you have $5,000 of excess cash in a typical interest-bearing checking account, you're probably earning 2% or less in interest. Even with such modest sums, you could earn an extra $150 or more each year by moving the cash to a money market mutual fund. Although money market funds are not covered by federal deposit insurance, your cash remains easily accessible, since most money market funds offer checkwriting privileges. Also, shop around occasionally to make sure you aren't overpaying in service fees on your checking account or your credit cards, insurance premiums, or other financial services. Over the course of a year, a careful shopper can save hundreds of dollars in service and account maintenance fees, interest charges, and insurance premiums.

Add a Dollop of Risk Many investors could prudently boost their returns by taking a small amount of additional risk. For example, investors willing to give up the advantage of federal deposit insurance usually can receive more interest income from money market mutual funds than from bank savings accounts or short-term bank CDs. Likewise, you may be able to keep a portion of your cash reserves in higher-yielding short-term bond funds (with average maturities of roughly two years) rather than in bank accounts or money market mutual funds. The short-term bond fund is subject to a modest amount of interest-rate risk, but you are rewarded for this extra risk with yields that have typically averaged one to two percentage points higher than yields on money market funds. On $10,000, that amounts to a difference of $100 to $150 each year.

You might also consider tiptoeing into the foreign markets. Adding a small stake (equal to no more than 10% or 20% of your total equity holdings) in foreign stocks has, in recent decades, boosted the overall returns of a portfolio of common stocks while reducing the fluctuations in returns from the portfolio. Other ways to take on a bit more risk in the search for higher returns are to slightly increase your allocation to common stocks and to shift some of your bond holdings from intermediate-term maturities to longer maturities.

Final Thoughts

You've probably figured out by now that successful investing need not be complicated. Indeed, simplicity can be a virtue in investing, as it is in many other facets of life. You can simplify your investing chores and still get good results by concentrating your efforts on choosing an appropriate mix of retirement assets that will meet your long-term spending needs. Remember that portfolio allocation will be a much more important determinant of your investment success than your individual stock or mutual fund selections, so make sure you are taking enough risk to achieve your long-term objectives.

Once you've decided on the appropriate allocation for your portfolio, you need do little more than an occasional tweaking of your assets to keep your portfolio allocations in balance. It is possible to make the selection of individual securities and mutual funds a full-time pursuit, if that's how you wish to spend your time in retirement. But there is a simpler alternative that will almost surely prove more rewarding:

use broad stock and bond index funds as the core portion of your retirement portfolio and round out your holdings with low-cost, mainstream bond and stock funds. With a solid foundation of index funds, your portfolio will perform in line with the stock and bond markets, which means that, over time, you'll probably earn better returns than most professional money managers. In the race between the tortoise and the hare, the steady, dependable tortoise wins every time.

"Investing is not nearly as difficult as it seems."

John C. Bogle

YOUR RETIREMENT ROADMAP: INCOME, HEALTH CARE, AND ESTATE PLANNING

Part 3

Withdrawing Your Retirement Assets

Chapter 8

Your investment strategy is only one ingredient in the formula for successfully managing your retirement assets. While a balanced investment portfolio should provide solid returns that will augment your Social Security and pension income, you must prudently manage the withdrawals from your savings and investments to be certain that you do not outlive your assets.

"Do I have enough assets to cover my life span?"

Pennsylvania

This chapter provides guidance for developing a personalized strategy for withdrawing funds from your retirement portfolio. It begins with an examination of perhaps the most crucial concern for the retired person: Will your investments provide sufficient income throughout your entire retirement? A worksheet will help you to estimate not only how long your retirement investments will last, given different assumptions about your spending and the returns on your investments, but also whether you have sufficient assets to meet the level of investment income called for in your retirement spending plans. Once you have determined a realistic spending level, you'll receive guidance on the most appropriate methods to tap your investments for income during retirement, with particular emphasis on the tax rules that govern retirement plan distributions. The chapter concludes with some convenient strategies for using mutual funds to implement your retirement spending plan.

How Long Will Your Savings Last?

By completing the budgeting and net worth worksheets discussed in Chapter 2, you took the first step toward developing a realistic spending plan for your retirement. The net worth worksheet tells you what level of savings and investments you have to work with. The income and expense worksheets tell you how much income you'll need from your investment portfolio to supplement your pension and Social Security benefits.

This information, of course, is merely the baseline for your analysis. You can't simply withdraw from your retirement savings whatever amount of cash is needed to close the yearly gap between your spending requirements and your Social Security and pension benefits. If you do that, you'll have no way of knowing whether your savings and investments are sufficient to see you (and, of course, your spouse) through retirement. Of course, since you don't know in advance how long you and your spouse will live, the future returns on your investments, or the future rate of inflation, you can never be absolutely certain that your nest egg is large enough to meet your retirement income needs. But if you use reasonable assumptions, perhaps a bit on the conservative side, you will have a fairly good idea of whether you can support the retirement lifestyle you have in mind. The general idea is to reduce your risk of being too far off the mark with your withdrawal program.

To get a quick idea of how long your savings and investments are likely to last, take a look at the estimates presented in Table 8–1. This simple chart shows, for various rates of return and withdrawal rates, the number of years you can expect your assets to last. To use Table 8–1, first determine the annual dollar amount that you're currently withdrawing (or planning to withdraw) as a percentage of your current total retirement savings and investments. For example, if you have $200,000 saved and expect to receive $1,000 a month from your investments, your withdrawal rate is 6% [($1,000 × 12 months) ÷ $200,000 = 6%]. Most retired investors will have balanced portfolios that have earned average annual returns in the range of 5% to 8%. If so, as Table 8–1 shows, you can't spend more than 6% to 8% of your retirement assets each year if you want your assets to last for more than 20 years. With a nest egg of $100,000, your spending from investments would be limited to $6,000 to $8,000 annually ($500 to $667 monthly).

Table 8–1 has an important limitation. It assumes there is no increase in the level of your withdrawals over the years. Since, in the real world, living costs have risen steadily over time, this isn't a very realistic assumption for most retired investors.

Nonetheless, the table sends a clear message that the retired investor must be careful in setting a withdrawal schedule. If you want to finance 30 years of retirement and your investments earn an average return of 7% a year, you will have to limit your annual withdrawals to no more than 8% of your initial nest egg. Even that withdrawal rate will be

Table 8–1
How Long Will Your Retirement Assets Last?

Annual Withdrawal Rate	Average Annual Total Return									
	1%	2%	3%	4%	5%	6%	7%	8%	9%	10%
15%	6	7	7	7	8	8	9	9	10	11
14	7	7	8	8	9	9	10	11	11	13
13	8	8	8	9	9	10	11	12	13	15
12	8	9	9	10	11	11	12	14	16	18
11	9	10	10	11	12	13	14	16	19	25
10	10	11	12	13	14	15	17	20	26	
9	11	12	13	14	16	18	22	28		
8	13	14	15	17	20	23	30			
7	15	16	18	21	25	33				
6	18	20	23	28	36					
5	22	25	30	41						
	Years Your Assets Will Last									

too high if you want to allow for some increases in your investment withdrawals during the later years to compensate for rising prices.

Rising versus Level Withdrawals

Before moving on to the actual withdrawal worksheet, take a few moments to consider whether you want the withdrawals from your investment portfolio to be flat or to rise over time to compensate for inflation. Many retirees underestimate the impact of inflation and make little or no provision for increased withdrawals from their investments. These investors have a false sense of security because the current income from their investments is covering their current spending needs.

Unfortunately, if the future looks anything like the past half century, inflation will steadily erode the buying power of each dollar that you earn. If you don't plan for a steadily rising withdrawal from your investments, you can be certain that your standard of living will gradually decline, as price increases force you to—at the very least—sacrifice some of the extras to which you may have become accustomed, such as travel, recreation, and dining out. At worst, over an extended period, you may not be able to withdraw enough to meet your most basic living expenses.

Figure 8–1
Two Withdrawal Methods: Level and Rising Payments

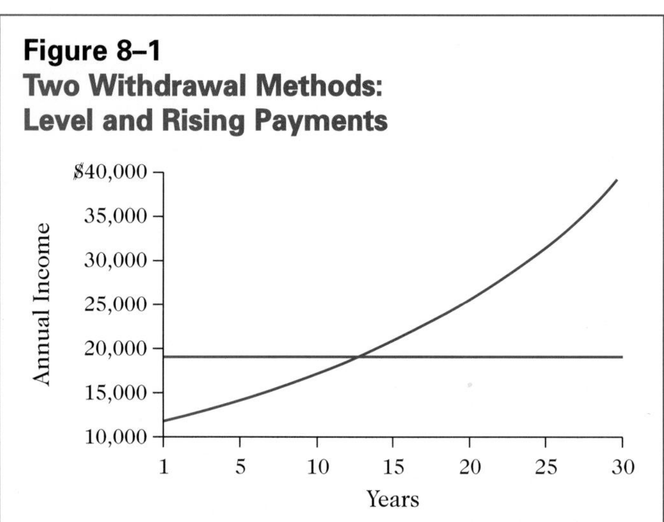

The implications of the two withdrawal strategies of level or rising payments are illustrated in Figure 8–1. Each example assumes a 7% annual return on an investment portfolio of $250,000 over a 30-year retirement period, during which inflation averages 4% annually. Under these assumptions, you could receive 30 annual payments of $18,825 (or $1,570 a month) if you wanted a level stream of payments. However, by year 30, the $18,825 annual amount would have purchasing power equivalent to only $5,762 in today's dollars, a shocking reduction in purchasing power of nearly 70%. If you wanted your income to rise 4% per year to offset this inflation effect, you could receive $12,200 in the first year (or $1,020 per month), with your annual withdrawal amount gradually rising to $38,100 ($3,175 per month) in year 30.

Obviously, either choice—level payments or rising payments—will involve some trade-offs on your part. If you choose level payments to get more income in your early retirement years, you'll have to sacrifice later in retirement, as higher prices for basic living expenses consume an ever-larger portion of your retirement income. If you plan for rising payments from your retirement assets, you are, in effect, making sacrifices in the early stages of retirement by reducing the amount of income you draw from your nest egg.

Most financial planners recommend that you plan for rising withdrawals from your retirement investments, especially if you will not be receiving an employer-sponsored pension or if your employer's pension payments are not adjusted for inflation. Nonetheless, your need for current income at the time that you retire may mean that you simply cannot afford to accept less income now in order to receive a rising stream of income later. You may also have reason to believe that your own "personal" inflation rate will not rise as fast as consumer prices in general, or you may expect your living costs to decline in later years, perhaps because you plan to reduce over time the amounts you spend on travel and entertainment. You should know, however, that economic research into inflation suggests that the *overall* living costs of older Americans tend to rise at roughly the same pace as those of younger Americans.

Whichever option you choose, the worksheet allows you to calculate available distributions based on your accumulated retirement investments. In each case, the amount you will be able to withdraw for any particular retirement period is based on the amount of money you have accumulated and on the rate of return you assume for your investments. Under the rising-payment alternative, the worksheet assumes that your withdrawals will increase by 4% a year to offset inflation. As noted earlier, there is no way to know whether actual inflation rates in the future will be higher or lower than this 4% figure. But, all things considered, making this assumption is a safer alternative than simply ignoring any potential inflation impact.

Withdrawal Worksheet

Using the withdrawal worksheet presented over the next few pages, you will begin to piece together a strategic withdrawal plan. (A complete copy of the worksheet may be found in Appendix A.) Keep in mind as you prepare the worksheet that it does not take into account the effect that taxes will have on your investment earnings or on your withdrawals from retirement savings. Later in this chapter, the tax rules governing distributions from retirement plans and retirement savings will be covered in more detail.

In general, withdrawals from tax-deferred accounts, such as IRAs or 401(k) plans, are considered by the federal government to be taxable as regular income; however, the investment earnings of these tax-deferred accounts are not taxed each year. If your retirement savings are invested in both taxable accounts and tax-deferred accounts, all the withdrawals from your tax-deferred accounts will be taxable as ordinary income, while only part of the money you spend from your taxable accounts will be taxable.

(Vanguard's companion computer software program for retired investors features greater flexibility than the printed worksheets. The software's worksheets allow you to quickly test a wide variety of assumptions, including different lengths for your retirement, various rates of investment return, and varying withdrawal rates. If the worksheets in this chapter are inadequate for your situation, you may find the software helpful.)

Part 1: Retirement Income Summary

You should use this first section of the worksheet, shown in Table 8–2, to summarize all the major sources of retirement income at your disposal other than your retirement investments. If you completed the income section in Chapter 2 on page 24, you should already have these figures. An example of a hypothetical retired couple, Alice and Ralph, is included to demonstrate how to complete the worksheet.

Table 8–2
Part 1: Income Summary

	Alice and Ralph	Your Situation
Use this section to summarize your monthly retirement income from the following sources:		
1. Social Security	$1,250	
2. Pension	800	
3. Other income (e.g., rental payments, part-time job)	425	
4. Total income (Line 1 + Line 2 + Line 3)	2,475	

Line 1: Enter your monthly Social Security benefit payment. If you haven't started receiving benefits, contact your local Social Security office to obtain an estimate. Alice and Ralph receive combined benefits of $1,250 a month.

Line 2: Enter any monthly payments you receive (or expect to receive) from employer-provided pensions. The pension benefits our hypothetical couple receive total $800 a month.

Line 3: Enter any other retirement income that you expect to receive (part-time work, rental payments, etc.) Take-home pay from Alice's part-time job amounts to about $425 a month.

Line 4: Add Lines 1 through 3 to calculate your total monthly retirement income, outside of your investment portfolio. The total in our example is $2,475 a month.

Part 2: Your Retirement Assumptions

Before you begin to analyze how much you can withdraw from your nest egg, you must derive estimates for two key variables during your retirement: your investment return and the number of years you expect to be drawing on your investments.

Line 5: Enter your assumed investment return in Table 8–3. This figure reflects the average annual total return that you expect to earn on your accumulated assets during your retirement. Remember that total return consists of the income (interest and dividends) on your invested assets as well as any rise or fall in the market value of your investments.

When it comes to estimating future investment returns, it is especially dangerous to rely on averages from the recent past. The period from year-end 1982 through 1996 was an extraordinary one for investors: inflation averaged just 3.7% per year; short-term reserves provided average returns of 6.5% per year; long-term bonds provided average returns of 13.3% per year; and common stocks provided average returns of 16.8% per year. It seems highly unlikely that investment returns will be so generous in the coming decade.

Before deciding on your assumed investment returns, you should probably review Chapter 4 for its discussion on forecasting long-term returns from bonds and stocks. Most importantly, try various assumptions in your worksheet to see how lower and higher returns will affect your retirement plans. Your best bet might be to estimate a rate of return for each asset class and then weight these returns according to your portfolio allocation. For instance, suppose your portfolio has 60% in stocks and 40% in bonds, and you expect average annual returns of 8% from stocks and 6% from bonds. The weighted, or blended, return for your portfolio would be 7.2% (0.60 × 8% = 4.8%, plus 0.40 × 6% = 2.4%). Our hypothetical retired couple has a portfolio invested 40% in common stocks, 40% in bonds, and 20% in cash reserves. They assume average annual returns of 8% on their stocks, 6.5% on their bonds, and 5% on their cash reserves. The weighted average annual return expected from their portfolio is 6.8% (0.40 × 8% = 3.2%, plus 0.40 × 6.5% = 2.6%, plus 0.20 × 5% = 1.0%).

One caveat about these calculations: they imply more precision than is realistic. Although the return estimates are calculated to the tenth of a percentage point, do not expect such exactitude from your own estimates. Investment returns will vary considerably from year to year, and even the best methodology for predicting annual average returns over the

Table 8–3
Part 2: Your Retirement Assumptions

	Alice and Ralph	Your Situation
5. Investment return	7%	
6. Retirement period (in years)	30	

long term would do extraordinarily well to be accurate within a percentage point or two. For the example on our worksheet, we'll round off the return estimate of 6.8% to 7%.

Line 6: Enter your assumed retirement period in Table 8–3. This figure should be the number of years that you (and your spouse) expect to be making withdrawals from your retirement savings. To make sure that you don't run out of money, it is best to make conservative assumptions about the length of your retirement. Be mindful that the life expectancy data on page 5 in Chapter 1 are *averages* and that roughly half of those at any particular age are likely to live beyond the average life expectancy. It is particularly important to assume a longer-than-average retirement if you are in good health and you have a family history of long life spans. Our couple, Ralph, age 66, and Alice, age 64, assume a retirement period of 30 years.

Part 3: Rising versus Level Payments

Line 7: If you elect to receive a level stream of withdrawals from your investments, you should enter on Table 8–4 the

Table 8–4
Part 3: Withdrawal Factors

	Alice and Ralph	Your Situation
7. Level income factor (Table 8–5)	0	
8. Rising income factor (Table 8–5)	0.0489	

Table 8–5
Factors for Worksheet

Level Income Factor

Retirement Period	Annual Investment Return						
	6%	7%	8%	9%	10%	11%	12%
15	0.0971	0.1026	0.1082	0.1138	0.1195	0.1253	0.1311
20	0.0822	0.0882	0.0943	0.1005	0.1068	0.1131	0.1195
25	0.0738	0.0802	0.0867	0.0934	0.1002	0.1070	0.1138
30	0.0685	0.0753	0.0822	0.0893	0.0964	0.1036	0.1108
35	0.0651	0.0722	0.0794	0.0868	0.0943	0.1017	0.1092
40	0.0627	0.0701	0.0776	0.0853	0.0930	0.1006	0.1083

Rising Income Factor*

Retirement Period	Annual Investment Return						
	6%	7%	8%	9%	10%	11%	12%
15	0.0759	0.0807	0.0857	0.0907	0.0959	0.1011	0.1065
20	0.0596	0.0646	0.0699	0.0753	0.0809	0.0866	0.0924
25	0.0498	0.0551	0.0606	0.0664	0.0723	0.0785	0.0847
30	0.0433	0.0489	0.0547	0.0607	0.0670	0.0735	0.0801
35	0.0388	0.0445	0.0505	0.0569	0.0635	0.0702	0.0772
40	0.0354	0.0413	0.0475	0.0541	0.0610	0.0681	0.0753

*Assumes a 4% annual distribution growth rate.

appropriate withdrawal factor found in Table 8–5. (If you do not wish to receive level payments, enter 0.) To find the withdrawal factor, move down the appropriate investment return column in the upper section of Table 8–5 until you reach the row representing the number of years for your assumed retirement period. The withdrawal factor is the spot where the column and the row intersect. For example, assuming a 7% return and a 30-year retirement period, the level payment income factor would be 0.0753, or 7.53%. In our example, Alice and Ralph want to plan for rising payments, so they enter 0 on Line 7.

Line 8: If you elect to receive a rising stream of withdrawals from your investments, find the appropriate rising payment income factor from the lower section of Table 8–5 and enter it on Line 8 in Table 8–4. Again assuming a 7% annual return and a 30-year retirement period, the rising payment income factor from Table 8–5 would be 0.0489, or 4.89%. Our hypothetical retirees expect a return slightly lower than 7%, but for ease, they use a factor of 0.0489.

Part 4: How Much Can You Withdraw?

Line 9: To estimate how much you can withdraw from your portfolio over the years, you need to know how much you have to work with. Take into account the total current market value of your savings and investment accounts, including money invested in IRAs, employer-sponsored savings plans such as 401(k) or profit-sharing plans, bank and brokerage accounts, and so on. You should be able to retrieve these figures easily from the net worth worksheet you prepared on page 13. After totaling all these asset figures, enter the aggregate amount on Line 9 in Table 8–6. In our example, the couple have $150,000 in savings and investments.

Line 10: If you have decided to take level withdrawals, determine the annual level of income you can withdraw (given your earlier assumptions) by multiplying Line 9 by Line 7. Enter this result on Line 10 of Table 8–6. If you withdraw this sum each year from your investment portfolio, your retirement savings should last for the number of years you specified in Line 2, provided that you earn the rate of return you assumed on Line 5. If they had chosen to receive level payments, our hypothetical couple could anticipate spending $11,300 from their investment portfolio each year throughout

Table 8–6
Part 4: How Much Can You Withdraw from Your Investments?

	Alice and Ralph	Your Situation
9. Retirement lump-sum savings	$150,000	
10. Level income, annual (Line 9 × Line 7)	0	
11. Level income, monthly (Line 10 ÷ 12)	0	
12. Rising income, annual (Line 9 × Line 8)	7,330	
13. Rising income, monthly (Line 8 ÷ 12)	610	

retirement, given the assumptions for their investment returns and retirement period. Since Alice and Ralph have chosen rising payments, they enter 0 on Line 10.

Line 11: To convert the annual fixed withdrawal amount into a monthly income figure, divide the figure on Line 10 by 12 months and enter the result. Again, our hypothetical couple enter 0 since they have chosen a rising payment.

Line 12: If you have decided to take rising withdrawals, determine the annual level of income you can withdraw in the first year of retirement (given your earlier assumptions) by multiplying Line 9 by Line 8. The rising payment factor on Line 8 assumes a 4% annual rise in your withdrawals. For our couple, this calculation results in income of $7,330 (0.0489 × $150,000) for the first year of retirement. The amount is expected to rise by 4% to $7,620 in the second year, and so on.

Line 13: To convert your annual withdrawal amount for the first year of retirement into a monthly income figure, divide Line 12 by 12 months and enter the result. This calculation produces monthly income of $610 for the first year of the 30-year retirement expected by our hypothetical couple. In year two, the withdrawals would rise by $20 a month to $630. In the thirtieth year of retirement, the rising payment method would allow for monthly income of $2,000, assuming that the investment return averaged 7% a year.

Part 5: The Reality Check

Your next step is to determine whether the withdrawals you can realistically expect to receive from your investments are sufficient to meet your retirement spending plans.

Line 14: Calculate your total monthly retirement income by adding Line 4 and either Line 11 (if you are taking level payments from your investment portfolio) or Line 13 (if you elect

Table 8–7
Part 5: The Reality Check

	Alice and Ralph	Your Situation
14. Total monthly retirement income (Line 4 + Line 11 or Line 13)	$3,085	
15. Your monthly retirement budget	3,000	
16. Monthly surplus (shortfall)	85	

to take rising withdrawals). Enter the total on Line 14 in Table 8–7. For our couple, the total of Line 4 and Line 13 is $3,085 a month.

Line 15: Enter your monthly retirement expenditures from your budget worksheet on pages 16–17 in Chapter 2. Alice and Ralph have budgeted $3,000 a month in spending.

Line 16: Subtract Line 15 from Line 14, and enter the result here. If Line 14 is larger than Line 15, this is the monthly *surplus* you should have after paying all your bills. If Line 14 is smaller than Line 15, this is the monthly *shortfall* in your retirement budget. Alice and Ralph have a surplus of $85.

Analyzing Your Results

If your estimated surplus or shortfall is a small percentage, say one or two percentage points of your projected budget, your needs and expectations are essentially in balance. However, if your projections show a large shortfall or surplus, you may want to go through the exercise again just to make sure you haven't overlooked some detail or made some math error.

"Don't sweat it out, just squeezing by so you can leave money for your heirs. Enjoy the money—you earned it."

Connecticut

If you find no error and still have a large surplus, you can sleep well knowing that you have the ability to substantially increase your annual spending. To be safe, however, you should redo the worksheet assuming lower investment returns—even if you were conservative the first time. This further analysis gives you an indication of how sensitive your spending ability is to changes in the returns on financial assets. As you analyze the surplus of $85 a month for the hypothetical couple, this margin is actually quite thin, given that they receive $425 monthly from part-time employment. Presumably this extra income will cease at some point in the future, so a real-life couple in this situation might want to tighten up on spending to achieve a bigger surplus that could augment their savings for later years, when the income from part-time work is no longer coming in.

Obviously, if your figures produce a significant budget shortfall, you should consider whether to change your assumptions. Perhaps you can curtail your spending to get your retirement plan back in balance. It's possible, of course, that your projected investment returns are overly conservative and that higher return assumptions will close the gap. However, before "fixing" your budget shortfall by assuming higher investment returns, finish reading this chapter so that you have a fuller appreciation of the unpredictability and variability of investment returns.

Coping with a Market Misfortune

In retirement planning, it's important to realize that investment returns in any one year—or even over periods as long as a decade—can vary substantially from the historical averages. While the averages are nice to consider, the returns that you will earn during your retirement will depend exclusively on how the financial markets perform during the specific period that your money is invested. Consider, for example, the case of two investors, each retired at age 65, each with a $300,000 portfolio allocated in exactly the same manner: 40% stocks, 40% bonds, and 20% short-term reserves. Each retiree planned for 25 years of retirement, each decided on rising withdrawals from his investment portfolio, each assumed his investments would return 8% a year, and each decided to rebalance his portfolio once a year. Using a worksheet much like the one in this chapter, each investor calculated that he could withdraw 6% of his investment principal, or $18,000 ($1,500 a month), in the first year of retirement.

While these two retirees seem to have identical circumstances going into retirement, there is one very important difference: Investor A retired at the end of 1972 and Investor B retired exactly two years later, at the end of 1974. Figure 8–2 shows how changing investment conditions can make a dramatic difference in the outcome of your retirement spending plans. Investor B had the good fortune to miss the 1973–74 bear market, when the Standard & Poor's 500 Composite Stock Price Index lost −37% (including the dividend income), an accident of timing that made all the difference in the world. You can see that Investor A's assets were exhausted in less than 15 years, while Investor B's nest egg was still in good shape after 20 years of retirement. Amazingly, at year-end 1995, Investor B had $520,000 remaining in retirement savings; Investor A had depleted his entire nest egg by the end of 1987.

The point of this comparison is to reinforce the importance of making conservative initial assumptions about your investment returns and then regularly reassessing all of your assumptions about returns on financial assets, inflation, and your retirement period. After a period of poor results in the financial markets, you may need to trim back your withdrawals rather than make major changes in the mix of your investments. In general, most investors tend to avoid a particular asset class after it has done poorly and shift money into an asset class following a period of strong relative performance. This strategy inevitably leads them to sell stocks or bonds *after* their prices have declined significantly, although this may prove to be the best time to be shifting cash into

Figure 8–2
The Impact of Investment Timing

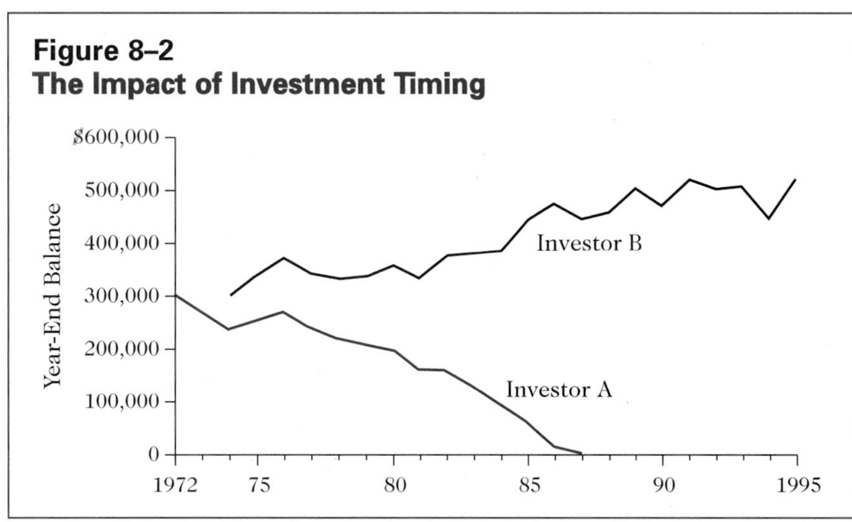

stocks or bonds. Conversely, the worst time to invest in a particular asset class is after the "easy money" has been made. To avoid falling into this trap, hold steadily to your long-term plan for allocating your assets.

Just Take the Income: A Dangerous Approach

Some retired investors may regard worksheets and withdrawal factors as more trouble than they're worth. They argue that if they simply limit their withdrawals to the income generated by their investments, they are certain never to run out of money. After all, if you're not touching your principal, how can you get into trouble?

While this approach seems attractive—particularly when you run the numbers and find that, given your current budget, you can make ends meet by drawing only on the current income from your investment portfolio—it entails considerable hazards. The main problem is that investors who plan to live solely on their investment income will likely focus on investments that provide high current income, such as bonds, annuities, and CDs. These investors reason that, since they are getting enough income from these "safe" investments, there is no reason to take the risk of price fluctuations that go hand in hand with common stock ownership.

Sadly, no investment provides a high level of current income that can be sustained for an extended period, while also protecting you against wide price fluctuations. For instance, it is certainly true that longer-term bonds, with their relatively high current yields, may provide more than sufficient income in the early years of your retirement. Unfortunately, as discussed in Chapter 4, a fixed-income investment is precisely what the name implies: an investment whose income is fixed for some particular period. As a result, these investments do not provide any long-term growth to offset the effects of inflation. What's more, longer-term bonds are susceptible to wide swings in principal value as interest rates fluctuate.

Of course, a fixed-income investor could avoid this price volatility by holding shorter-term bonds, CDs, or money market funds. In this case, however, the loss of purchasing power due to inflation is accelerated during periods of declining interest rates. As shorter-term investments such as CDs mature, they must be rolled over into lower-yielding investments, reducing your income even though prices continue to increase. Millions of retired investors lived through exactly this scenario in the late 1980s and early 1990s. Their living standards were squeezed from two directions. Each dollar of income bought a little less each year because of inflation even though inflation was fairly "tame"; then income began to fall sharply as bonds and CDs carrying double-digit yields matured and had to be replaced by investments with yields several percentage points lower.

When all is said and done, there are only two ways to achieve growth in income from your retirement savings. One is to reinvest some of the income generated by your fixed-income investments, building up your assets so they can produce more income in future years. The second way is to invest in common stocks, which historically have provided growth in income and, over long periods, growth in capital.

Another danger of the "spend the income" approach is that it may unnecessarily squeeze the retired investor's budget. By dipping into your principal judiciously, you can maintain a higher standard of living during retirement than if you only draw on the income from your investments. Remember that any nest egg you leave to your heirs will be worth considerably less in real dollars than you think, even if you manage to hold on to your entire investment portfolio.

Retirement Plans and Taxes

Taxes are an inescapable consideration when it comes to tapping your retirement plan assets. In general, there is a basic trade-off. In exchange for letting your capital grow within your retirement plans free of income tax, the government will tax the money as ordinary income when you begin to withdraw it. The tax rules—enforced with some severe tax penalties—are designed to discourage "early" withdrawals from tax-advantaged retirement plans. The rules are also intended to prevent the use of retirement plans to permanently shelter investments from income tax—except in the case of Roth IRAs.

The following section explains the basic tax rules governing retirement plans. However, because the penalties for violating the tax rules on retirement distributions are so severe, you may wish to seek professional guidance from an accountant or lawyer who specializes in tax matters. Also, it's important to note that the tax treatment of withdrawals from retirement plans varies widely from state to state. In a handful of states, income from pension plans is exempt from state income tax; other states allow partial exemptions for pension income.

The Required Minimum Distribution

You can't let the money in your retirement plans grow tax-deferred indefinitely. You must start to withdraw money from a traditional IRA by April 1 of the year after you turn age 70½. Withdrawals from a qualified employer retirement plan must also begin by April 1 of the year after you turn age 70½ or by April 1 of the year after you retire—whichever is later. For both traditional IRAs and qualified plans, you must continue to take withdrawals at least annually. If you fail to take the money out in a timely manner, or if you take out less than is required by the rules, you'll pay a 50% penalty tax on the amount that should have been withdrawn. And you must still withdraw the correct amount and pay the appropriate taxes. It is relatively easy to run afoul of the rules dictating required minimum distributions, since the minimums can be difficult to calculate.

Your *required minimum distribution* from your retirement assets includes assets held in IRAs (except Roth IRAs), SIMPLEs, Keogh accounts, 401(k), 403(b), and other plans.

Roth IRAs are not subject to required minimum distribution rules. You may withdraw more than the minimum in any given year, but you get no "credit" in future years for additional amounts taken in earlier years. The minimum distribution that you must take is based on your life expectancy or, if you choose, on the joint life expectancy (officially the "joint life and last survivor expectancy") of you and your beneficiary. The younger your beneficiary, the longer the joint life expectancy and the less you will be required to take from your retirement plans. (However, to prevent you from skirting the minimum distribution rules, there are limits to the life expectancy you can use for a beneficiary other than your spouse.)

Using a joint life expectancy can substantially reduce the amount of the required minimum distribution from your retirement plans. For example, consider the case of a 70-year-old retiree who has a single life expectancy, under IRS tables, of 16.0 years. This person would be required to withdraw a minimum of 6.25% of her retirement plan assets for the year. On the other hand, a 70-year-old with a 66-year-old spouse who has been designated primary beneficiary of the retirement assets would have a joint life expectancy of 22.5 years, and would have to withdraw only 4.44% of the retirement plan assets. The joint life expectancy guidelines and tables are contained in IRS Publication 590, "Individual Retirement Arrangements," which you can order at no charge by calling the IRS at 1-800-829-3676.

To calculate your required minimum distribution on your own, follow the five steps follow the five steps below. (This does not apply to Roth IRAs.)

1. Determine your age on December 31 of the year in which you reach 70½. That is, if you were born on April 10, 1927, you will reach age 70½ in 1997 and will still be age 70 at the end of 1997. (If you were born on August 31, 1926, you will also reach age 70½ in 1997, but you will be age 71 at the end of 1997.)

2. Determine the age of the primary beneficiary of your IRA account at year-end. In this example, assume that your spouse is your primary beneficiary and will be 66 years old on December 31, 1997.
3. Find the joint life expectancy figure for you and your beneficiary in the life expectancy tables of Publication 590. In this example, your joint life expectancy is 22.5 years, based on year-end ages of 70 for you and 66 for your beneficiary.
4. Determine the total balance of your IRAs as of December 31 of the prior year (1996, in this case). For this example, assume that you have a total balance of $200,000 at year-end 1996.
5. Calculate your required minimum distribution for 1997 by dividing your year-end 1996 asset balance by your life expectancy factor. In this case, $200,000 divided by 22.5 equals $8,889, or 4.4% of your total retirement plan balance.

Under IRS regulations, you would be required to withdraw at least $8,889 from your IRA by April 1, 1998. Remember, even though you would not be required to take this distribution until April 1, 1998, it represents your required minimum distribution for *1997.* Your required minimum distribution for 1998 will have to be made by December 31, 1998, so you could wind up taking two taxable distributions for tax year 1998.

As you calculate your required minimum distributions in subsequent years, you have two choices. First, you may simply subtract a year from the previous year's life expectancy figure. In our example, at the end of 1998 you could simply divide your account balance as of December 31, 1997, by 21.5. Alternatively, you could recalculate your life expectancy each year, which would minimize the amount of your required distribution. In the example above, you would check the IRS life expectancy tables for a 71-year-old with a

67-year-old beneficiary and find a joint life expectancy figure of 21.7 years. Once you choose to recalculate or not to recalculate your life expectancy, you must continue to use that method for the rest of your life.

These examples are of simple required minimum distribution calculations. In many cases, the calculations are more complex. For a more detailed explanation of the minimum distribution rules, refer to IRS Publication 590. If you need assistance, the bank, mutual fund, or other institution serving as the trustee for your retirement plan should be able to assist you in the required minimum distribution calculations.

Other Rules on Minimum Distributions

Multiple Beneficiaries If you have designated more than one beneficiary for a traditional IRA, the beneficiary with the shortest life expectancy must be used to determine the period over which you must take withdrawals from that account.

Installments You may take required minimum distributions in installments (weekly, monthly, or quarterly), so long as the total distributions for the year equal at least the minimum distributions required for the year.

Multiple IRAs If you have more than one traditional IRA (not counting Roth IRAs), you must calculate the required minimum distribution for each account. However, you may total the required distributions from each separate account and take the entire amount from any one traditional IRA or from a combination of them. Suppose, for example, that you had two traditional IRAs, one containing $25,000 and the other holding $40,000. If your joint life expectancy were 22.5 years, the distribution from the first account would be $1,111 ($25,000 divided by 22.5), and the distribution from the second would be $1,778 ($40,000 divided by 22.5). You could withdraw the total required distribution—$2,889—from either traditional IRA.

Premature Withdrawals

You may not withdraw money from a tax-advantaged plan until you reach age 59½. If you violate this rule, your withdrawal is subject to a 10% penalty tax *in addition to* the usual income tax due on retirement plan withdrawals. There are several notable exceptions to this rule:

1. Distributions made because of death or disability are not subject to penalty, even for people under age 59½.
2. You can avoid the penalty tax, even if you are under age 59½, if you take a series of "substantially equal" withdrawals based on your life expectancy. To use this "annuity exception," you must take at least one withdrawal each year until you reach age 59½ or for at least five years, whichever is the longer period.
3. If you are between the ages 55 and 59½ and have retired or been laid off, you may take distributions without penalty from any qualified retirement plan or 403(b) plan (but not an IRA).

Estimated Tax Payments

You can see that retirement brings with it a tangle of new tax considerations that you did not have to face during your working years. For many taxpayers, the need to make estimated tax payments first arises after retirement, when they are getting substantial income from their investments combined with distributions from their pensions. Estimated tax payments are due to the IRS on certain levels of income that are not subject to withholding tax. Sources of such income include interest, dividends, capital gains from the sale of assets, income from self-employment, rent, and alimony. In general, you're required to make tax payments—through withholding or quarterly estimated tax payments—equal to at least 90% of your final income tax owed for the year.

The general rule is that you must make estimated tax payments if you expect to owe at least $500 in tax (for the 1997 tax year; amount rises to $1,000 in subsequent tax years) *after* you subtract any tax credits or taxes already withheld *and* if you expect that the combined total of your withholding and credits will be less than: (1) 90% of the tax you'll owe on your tax return for the year; or (2) 100% of the tax shown on your tax return from the previous year. (For those with adjusted gross incomes over $150,000, the figure is 105% if the previous tax year began in 1998, 1999, or 2000; 112% if previous tax year began in 2001; and 110% if previous tax year began in 2002 or later.) Put another way, you *won't* owe estimated tax payments as long as any withholding and estimated tax payments cover at least 90% of the tax you'll owe or equal the amount you owed in taxes for the previous year. (You don't have to pay estimated tax in the current year if you had no income tax liability for the previous year or did not have to file a tax return for the previous year.)

To calculate and pay estimated tax, you'll need IRS Form 1040-ES, "Estimated Tax for Individuals." You don't have to make estimated tax payments until you have income on which you'll owe the tax. Estimated tax payments are generally due in equal installments payable by mid-April, mid-June, mid-September, and mid-January. Most states also require estimated tax payments, though state rules vary on the amount of tax that triggers the requirement and on due dates for the tax.

Managing Your Assets During Retirement

In general, in order to take full advantage of your tax-deferred investments, it is advisable to first draw down any savings and investments from your taxable accounts. For example, assume you want to receive $10,000 this year from your investment portfolio, which comprises $100,000 in taxable accounts and $100,000 in tax-deferred accounts. You'd like your withdrawals to increase each year to offset the effects of inflation,

"For us, it's a balancing act. We want to keep up our living standard, but we don't want to run out of money."

Georgia

which you estimate will average 4% a year. Assume that you earn an annual average return of 7% a year, before taxes, on your investments both inside and outside your retirement accounts. Finally, assume that you pay combined state and federal income taxes of 31% on your investment income.

Under this scenario, you might be surprised at the dramatic advantage of tapping your taxable accounts first. If you were to take your withdrawals at the start of each year from your taxable accounts, you would withdraw a total of $54,165 over five years, including the adjustments for inflation. During this same period, the earnings on your taxable accounts would have amounted to $26,748, on which you would have paid $8,293 in taxes. At the end of the five-year period, the total value of your taxable accounts would be $64,294. Your tax-deferred accounts, on the other hand, would have grown from $100,000 to $140,255. The combined value of your taxable and tax-deferred accounts at the end of the five-year period, then, would be $204,545.

Conversely, if you had tapped your tax-deferred accounts for your annual withdrawals, you would have had to withdraw a larger sum each year to get the same level of income, since withdrawals from tax-deferred accounts are taxed as ordinary income. Thus, in the first year, you would have had to withdraw $14,492 from your traditional IRA and pay taxes of $4,492, which would leave you with a *net* withdrawal of $10,000. Meanwhile, your taxable accounts would have earned $7,000 in the first year, on which you would owe $2,170 in taxes. After five years, the after-tax value of your taxable accounts would have been $126,600. The value of your remaining tax-deferred IRA accounts would have been $44,160, taking into account withdrawals of $78,500 and investment earnings of $22,660. Your combined nest egg would have been $170,760, or $33,785 less than if the withdrawals had been made solely from your taxable accounts. This $33,785 is nearly 17% of the $200,000 investment with which you started.

Of course, eventually you must begin to take withdrawals from your tax-deferred accounts. As mentioned earlier, required minimum distributions from retirement plans (except for Roth IRAs) must begin by April 1 of the year after you attain age 70½. On those withdrawals, you will have to "pay the piper" by paying income tax on the entire sum withdrawn each year. However, until that day of reckoning arrives, you will have enjoyed the benefits of tax-deferred compounding of your investment earnings.

If you have a Roth IRA, your withdrawals will not be taxed provided you owned the account for five years and you are over age 59½ (or in the case of death, disability, or you are using a distribution of up to $10,000 to buy a first home). Roth IRAs are not subject to required minimum distribution rules. Contributions to a Roth IRA are not deductible, and income limits restrict who may contribute to a Roth IRA.

Also, if you expect to leave assets to your children or other heirs and you have unusually large capital gains on certain stocks or mutual funds held outside retirement accounts, you may wish to hold on to these securities instead of selling them and then having to pay taxes on the realized capital gain. The reason is that, upon your death, the cost basis of your investments will be "stepped up" to their then-current market value before they are transferred to your heirs. (Beneficiaries do *not* get a "stepped up" cost basis in your retirement plans.) This will erase the capital gains and the built-up tax liability. (The current market value of the securities will, however, be counted as part of your estate for purposes of the federal estate tax.)

Withdrawals and Rebalancing Your Portfolio

As discussed in some detail in Chapter 7, you can reduce the risks of your investment program by periodically rebalancing your retirement portfolio. Because the relative returns from stocks, bonds, and short-term reserves vary considerably from period to period, the mix of assets in your portfolio will, over time, deviate from your target allocation. By regularly rebalancing your portfolio, you automatically lock in the gains on the best-performing portion of your investments and shift money toward the lagging asset class. While this practice runs

My biggest problem is that having set up an asset allocation, what should I do next to get income? Do I sell an equal amount from each asset? Only from stock funds? Bond funds? Only from those doing well? Or just the opposite?

Kansas

counter to any desire to let your winners ride and sell your losers, there is a danger in letting a strong bull market in stocks or bonds increase your exposure to either asset class without limits. When the inevitable downturn comes, your portfolio will suffer disproportionately. What's more, by underweighting the "downtrodden" part of your portfolio, you will miss out on gains if that sector of the financial market rebounds.

Although rebalancing will entail some effort on your part, you can use your periodic withdrawals from your savings and investments to accomplish it. For convenience, you may choose to make monthly withdrawals from any short-term reserves held in your bank account or money market mutual fund. If so, you might choose to rebalance once a year, perhaps at tax time in mid-April, at year-end, on your birthday, or on some other significant anniversary. Alternatively, you could take a more proactive approach and rebalance as you remove money each month or quarter.

As you move through various stages of retirement, you may wish to change the makeup of your portfolio. You can use the regular withdrawals from your investment portfolio to accomplish these transitions. For instance, people in the later years of retirement may wish to emphasize bonds or other fixed-income investments and reduce the proportion of their assets invested in common stocks. Such a transition can boost the current income from their portfolio and reduce their exposure to a severe downdraft in stock prices. You could engineer such a transition for your portfolio gradually by taking a larger part of your regular withdrawal from stocks or stock funds than from other portions of the portfolio.

Planning Withdrawals for Big-Ticket Purchases

With typical retirement periods now stretching past two decades, retired investors need to plan for the occasional "big-ticket" purchase: a vacation home, a new car, a roof for their home. How you prepare for such purchases will depend on how much time you have until you need the money and, to some degree, on your investing temperament.

If you know when the expense will occur, you might invest the estimated sum in a Treasury security of the appropriate maturity. You would receive regular interest income and be assured of having the cash on hand when you need it to make the purchase. If you can't be certain when you'll need to make the purchase, you may want more liquidity so that you'll be able to withdraw the funds quickly and easily when the time arrives. For an expense that may occur within a year, a money market mutual fund or regular savings account provides liquidity and certainty that your principal will not decline. If the expense is two to four years in the future, you might invest in a short-term bond fund, which generally provides higher yields than a money market fund and carries only a modest risk of a decline in your principal. You might plan for the prospective purchase by making regular "installment payments" into a separate account set aside for that purpose.

"Money has gotten tighter. I'm getting by, but I can't afford to travel like I used to."

California

It goes without saying that the potential for precipitous price fluctuations makes stocks or long-term bonds a risky parking place for money that you are likely to need for a purchase in less than five years. While you increase your chance of earning higher returns, you also incur the considerable risk of having to liquidate your investment at a loss during a sudden downturn in the financial markets.

Using Mutual Funds to Get the Income You Need

One of the primary advantages of mutual funds, as outlined in Chapter 5, is their liquidity. Fund shares are priced daily, and you may liquidate them—convert them to cash—by merely picking up a telephone and requesting a redemption of all or a portion of your shares in a fund. This attribute makes it easy to tap your mutual fund investments for regular income during your retirement. Most mutual funds offer several options for getting access to the money you have invested.

- You can receive—by check or electronic funds transfer to a bank account or money market fund—regular distributions of interest or dividend income earned by a mutual fund. Money market funds and bond funds typically pay out their dividends on a monthly basis, while most stock funds pay dividends quarterly, semiannually, or annually. Distributions of capital gains realized by a fund, typically made once a year, can be received in cash or reinvested in additional shares of your fund.
- You can set up scheduled, automatic exchanges or withdrawals of any amount from your fund. You can have shares exchanged from a bond or stock fund into your money market fund, or have proceeds of automatic withdrawals sent to you by check or deposited in your bank by electronic funds transfer. If your budget calls for $1,000 a month from your investments, you can arrange to have that sum exchanged or deposited automatically in your money market fund or bank account each month.
- You can call a toll-free telephone number to redeem shares, with the proceeds sent to you by check or electronic transfer.
- Checkwriting is available on virtually all money market funds and bond funds, so you can redeem shares simply by writing a check. (Checkwriting is not allowed on funds held within IRAs.)

Final Thoughts

You have seen throughout this guide that planning is a crucial factor in an investor's success in accumulating retirement assets. Such planning is equally important when it comes time to retire and begin drawing on your retirement savings. Without planning, it is easy to underestimate the retirement investing challenge and to withdraw too much, too soon, from your investments, putting you in a severe bind in your later retirement years. At the other extreme, some retired investors are so fearful of running out of money that they needlessly forgo a more comfortable standard of living. A thoughtful withdrawal plan will allow you to steer a middle course that will see you safely through retirement.

Remember that a good withdrawal strategy takes into account several critical factors: the need for long-term growth in your income stream, the need to keep the mix of your investment assets in good balance as you tap your portfolio, and the tax consequences of various withdrawal options. You should balance these needs against the benefits of keeping your withdrawal strategy reasonably simple and convenient, so you don't spend an inordinate amount of your time managing the process.

Finally, take the time to review your withdrawal plan periodically to see whether your actual results are in line with the assumptions you made at the outset. You may find that your estimates were overly conservative and that you can increase the withdrawal rate from your investments without endangering your security in later years. On the other hand, you may find that your assumptions were optimistic compared to your investment results or spending patterns and that you'll have to "trim your sails" a bit to get back on course. The earlier you find out that you're off course, the less severe any change will have to be.

At the end of the day, you should have a healthy respect for the uncertainty that lies ahead as you step into retirement, but retirement need not be a period of anxiety and worry. If you craft a spending strategy that fits your budget, make reasonable assumptions about your life expectancy and the returns you will earn on your investments, and monitor your progress on a yearly basis, you're likely to enjoy a fulfilling and worry-free retirement.

Social Security and Medicare

Chapter 9

Retirement in the United States has been profoundly shaped by the Social Security system, which was created just six decades ago. Before the Social Security Act was passed in 1935, relatively few Americans stopped working for reasons other than illness, infirmity, or economic downturns that wiped out their jobs.

Ida Mae Fuller, a legal secretary from Vermont, was Social Security's first recipient. She and her employer paid $44 in Social Security taxes. By the time of her death at age 100, she had received $20,944 in Social Security benefits.

Thomas G. Donlan, Don't Count On It!

There was no generally recognized "retirement age" until Social Security took effect on January 1, 1937, when the normal retirement age was set at 65. (Reduced benefits for early retirement at age 62 became available for women in 1957 and for men in 1962.) According to historians of the system, the choice of age 65 was arbitrary. But after Social Security was established, many private employers adopted 62 or 65 as the normal retirement age for their own retirement plans. Over the years, Social Security benefits increased, the Medicare health insurance system was added (in 1965), and private retirement plans became more widespread. The result is the modern pattern of longer and relatively more secure retirements. Indeed, at today's typical retirement age of 62, the average American has about 20 years to live.

The primary goal of Social Security and Medicare is to provide a floor for the financial and medical needs of retirees. In that respect, the programs have been a success, as the proportion of Americans age 65 or older with incomes below the poverty line has declined from 35% in 1959 to 10% in 1996. Today, 63% of beneficiaries 65 or older receive more than half of their annual income from Social Security. This heavy dependence on Social Security is why older Americans are especially concerned about the system's financial health, concerns that are not unfounded. Unless changes are made, many experts believe that the Social Security trust funds will be exhausted in 32 years (21 years, under pessimistic assumptions).

Trustees of Social Security forecast that under current rules, using moderate estimates, benefit payments will outstrip tax revenue by the year 2012, and Social Security's trust funds will be exhausted by the year 2029. If retirees live longer than the trustees' estimates, and if other conditions such as inflation, interest rates, and unemployment also exceed estimates, Social Security could run out of money by the year 2018. By then, moderate estimates are that just 2.7 workers will be paying into the system for each person receiving Social Security benefits (including dependents and survivors), compared with 8.6 workers per beneficiary in 1955 and 3.3 workers per beneficiary in 1996.

Although there is no near-term danger of insolvency for Social Security, the system's long-range problems are serious. However, given that these problems are well documented, there is ample time for steps to be taken to shore up the finances of Social Security. To get the system into balance, it is likely that some combination of benefit reductions and tax increases will be enacted. While major changes in Social Security benefits will primarily affect those who are many years away from retiring, people who are in or near retirement should consider the possibility that taxes on Social Security benefits could rise, as they have in the past, or that cost-of-living adjustments to Social Security benefits could be modified.

For those who are a decade or more from retirement, experts recommend that personal investment plans be designed not only to supplement the level of benefits currently being promised, but to make up for the reduction in benefit levels that may have to take place for the Social Security system to remain solvent. One such reduction is already built into the system. Social Security's "normal" retirement age—the age at which full benefits can be drawn—is 65 for those born before 1938, but it gradually rises for those born in 1938 and beyond. For Americans born in 1960 or later, normal retirement age is 67, as Table 9–1 shows.

This chapter focuses on the two most critical issues for retirees: (1) Social Security monthly retirement benefits and (2) Medicare health care coverage. The first section reviews the rules on retirement benefits and the financial implications of retiring either before or after the normal retirement age. It also covers the effect that continuing to work past age 65 can have on your Social Security retirement benefits. A worksheet will explain how much, if any, of your Social Security benefits may be subject to income tax. The second section covers the health care benefits available under the Medicare program and explains the coverage limitations that you will face. The chapter concludes with a brief description of supplemental health care insurance that you may need.

Table 9–1
Normal Retirement Age Increases

Year of Birth	Normal Retirement Age
1937 and earlier	65
1938	65 and 2 months
1939	65 and 4 months
1940	65 and 6 months
1941	65 and 8 months
1942	65 and 10 months
1943–54	66
1955	66 and 2 months
1956	66 and 4 months
1957	66 and 6 months
1958	66 and 8 months
1959	66 and 10 months
1960 and after	67

Source: William M. Mercer, Inc., 1997. Reprinted with permission.

What You Should Know about Your Social Security Retirement Benefits

You are entitled to Social Security retirement income if you paid into the system through payroll deductions or self-employment taxes and had sufficient earnings over a minimum number of years to reach "insured status." For most people, attaining insured status requires the accumulation of 40 earnings credits. (You can earn up to four credits each year.) The amount of earnings needed to get one credit rises each year with inflation. In 1998, a person had to earn $700 to chalk up one credit, or $2,800 to get the maximum of four credits.

While most of us earn far more credits than needed to qualify for Social Security, these extra credits do not increase the amount of your retirement benefit. However, the monthly retirement benefit does rise as your earnings increase. Part of the benefits formula is the average monthly earnings (indexed for wage inflation) you received during your working years.

For those born after 1928, the highest 35 years of earnings are used in the calculation. In 1998, the maximum Social Security benefit for someone at the normal retirement age of 65 was $1,342 a month, or $16,104 a year. Your spouse is entitled to benefits based on his or her own earnings, up to the maximum of $1,342 a month. If both of you qualify for the maximum benefits, you could receive a total of $32,208.

If your spouse has not worked outside the home or hasn't worked enough to qualify for Social Security benefits, he or she is entitled to receive a benefit based on your earnings. A spouse who had enough earnings to qualify for a benefit will receive either that benefit or the spousal benefit, whichever is larger. The spousal benefit ranges from 37.5% to 50% of your normal retirement age benefit, depending on the age of your spouse when you retire. The maximum combined benefit for such a married couple, both attaining age 65 in 1998, is $2,013 per month, or $24,156 a year.

Social Security benefits are adjusted each year for inflation. The inflation adjustment is added to benefit checks in January, based on changes in the Consumer Price Index. Because there is some concern that the Consumer Price Index overstates inflation, there is some sentiment in Congress for changing the Index or the way it is used to adjust Social Security and other government benefits. Such a step could reduce future inflation adjustments to Social Security benefits.

It is critical to remember that Social Security benefits are designed to replace only a fraction of each individual's preretirement income. The benefits formula is progressive, meaning that the retirement benefit for lower-income workers is a higher percentage of their earnings than the benefit received by higher-income workers. As a result, if your pay over the years has consistently been at or above the maximum Social Security wage base ($68,400 in 1998), your retirement benefit will equal only about 24% of your preretirement pay. At lower income levels, benefits will represent a bigger proportion of your preretirement wages.

How to Apply for Benefits

Being eligible to receive Social Security benefits doesn't mean that you automatically receive the monthly checks. You can't start receiving your benefits until you file an application. Happily, applications generally can be taken over the phone at Social Security's toll-free number, 1-800-772-1213. It is advisable to contact Social Security in January of the year that you want to begin receiving your benefits.

For example, at age 65, a single retiree whose annual income at retirement in 1997 was about $24,000 will get Social Security benefits of roughly $10,400 a year, equal to about 43% of preretirement income. In either case, employer pensions or personal savings are needed to boost retirement income to allow retirees to maintain something close to their preretirement living standards.

The amount of your benefit will be affected by the age at which you choose to begin receiving benefits. The monthly benefit payment is permanently lower if you choose to get benefits before the normal retirement age, and permanently higher if you choose to defer payments until after the normal retirement age. It's wise to consider carefully your decision to start getting benefits, because the financial implications are so important. However, the retirement decision is not irrevocable. If you quit work, begin to draw Social Security, and then go back to work, you can simply stop getting your benefits. If you tell Social Security to suspend your benefits, your monthly benefit will be recalculated when you elect to retire again and the benefit will be increased to reflect the additional time that you were working and not drawing benefits.

Retiring Early

If your normal retirement age is 65 and you choose to collect benefits before then, the amount of the benefit is reduced by $\frac{5}{9}$ of 1% for each month before you turn 65. So if you start getting benefits at age 62, the current reduction from the normal benefit is 20% ($\frac{5}{9} \times 36$ months). Of course, these lower payments are approximately offset by the longer payment period. In essence, you start ahead of a later retiree by thousands of dollars, but you receive a smaller monthly benefit for life. Figure 9–1 illustrates the early retirement "penalty."

What is the break-even point? Under the current formula, the beneficiary who takes a lower payment earlier is better off for up to 15 years, relative to someone who defers. Consider, for example, two people of the same age and with the same earnings histories. If one retires at age 62 and the other retires at age 65, it will take 12 years for the later retiree to catch up to the earlier retiree in total Social Security benefits received. From that point on, the later retiree will have received more in total benefits.

Figure 9–1
Early Retirement Penalty
(Reduction in Social Security Benefits)

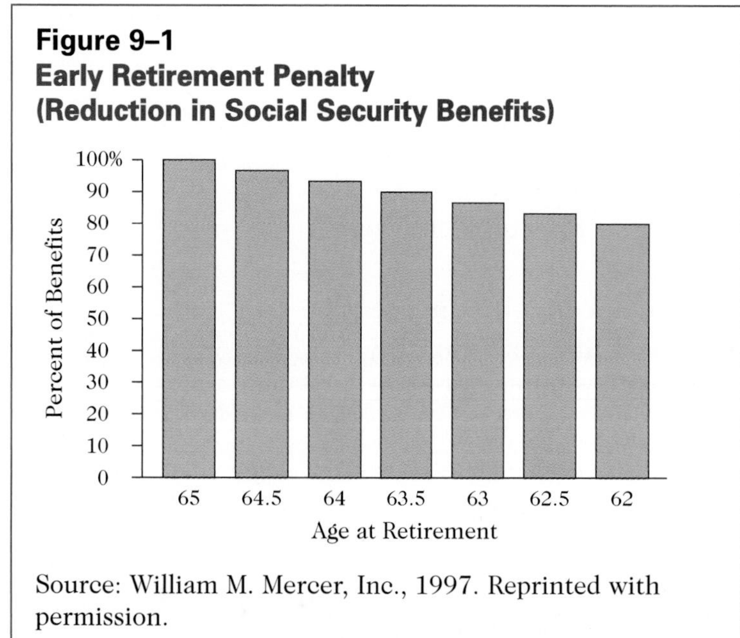

Source: William M. Mercer, Inc., 1997. Reprinted with permission.

Of course, if the early retiree is able to invest some of her Social Security benefits and pile up some investment income or gains, it will take the later retiree even more time to catch up. On the other hand, by continuing to work and deferring retirement, the later retiree probably will boost the size of his monthly benefit by increasing the average earnings that Social Security uses to determine the benefit. This is often the case, since many workers earn the most in the later years of their careers.

Deferring Social Security Benefits

Just as retiring before Social Security's normal retirement age cuts the monthly benefit you'll receive, waiting until after age 65 will increase your monthly benefit. If you turn age 65 in

1997 or 1998, Social Security raises your benefit by 5% for each year until age 70 (actually prorated by months) that you postpone taking full benefits. The delayed retirement credit does not increase the benefit to your spouse, but it does increase the benefit paid to your widow or widower. As Table 9–2 shows, the annual increase you get for delaying retirement benefits will rise by one-half a percentage point every two years until it reaches 8% for those born in 1943 or later.

Table 9–2
How Social Security Benefits Rise for Each Year You Delay Retirement

Year of Birth	Delayed Retirement Credit
1931–32	5.0%
1933–34	5.5
1935–36	6.0
1937–38	6.5
1939–40	7.0
1941–42	7.5
1943 or later	8.0

Source: William M. Mercer, Inc., 1997. Reprinted with permission.

If delaying retirement seems especially attractive, consider that it may take 20 years for your larger monthly check to make up for the benefits you missed. Suppose you turn 65 in 1997 and delay your retirement for one year. Your benefit will be 5% higher because you deferred retirement by one year. Nonetheless, it will take 20 years, until age 86, for you to receive the same total amount of benefits that you would have received by retiring at age 65. For those who turn 65 in later years, the break-even point is shorter because the increase in benefits for deferring retirement gets bigger, as shown in Table 9–2.

In deciding when to start receiving benefits, you may want to consider several issues. If you are eager to retire and will need the Social Security checks in order to stop working, then you have little choice but to start receiving benefits immediately. If you are quite healthy and your family history suggests a long life span, you may be better off deferring the receipt of benefits and collecting a larger monthly payment in the future. Your work plans are also an extremely important factor to consider. If you continue working after you start to receive Social Security, your benefits will be reduced if your earnings exceed certain levels. Thus, if you continue to work past age 62, you may be better off waiting to receive Social Security benefits until you actually retire, since your employment earnings may reduce your benefits.

Working During Retirement

The combination of Social Security limitations on earnings and the income taxation of benefits creates strong disincentives for full-time employment past age 62. For Social Security recipients below age 65, the benefit is reduced by $1 for each $2 you earn above the earnings limitation. This limitation, $9,120 in 1998, rises each year based on the change in average wages for all employees. If you are age 65 to age 69, your Social Security benefit is cut by $1 for each $3 earned above the limitation ($14,500 in 1998). Those 70 or older are not subject to any earnings limitation. The limitation applies only to earnings from work or net profit from self-employment, not to income from pensions, annuities, investments, Social Security, or veterans' benefits. If your benefits are reduced because of earnings above the limitation, future benefits will be increased.

How Social Security Benefits Are Taxed

Social Security benefits are free of federal income taxes for most retirees. But for those with incomes above certain levels ($25,000 for single people or $32,000 for married couples filing joint returns), up to half of their Social Security benefits received are subject to income tax. For those with incomes above a second threshold ($34,000 for single taxpayers or $44,000 for a couple), up to 85% of Social Security benefits are subject to federal income tax.

Not surprisingly, figuring the tax on Social Security benefits is anything but simple. The taxation of Social Security benefits is based on three factors:

1. Your adjusted gross income (AGI), including wages, dividends, interest, and pension benefits.
2. Any tax-exempt income, such as interest from a municipal bond or dividends from a municipal bond mutual fund.
3. Half of the Social Security benefits that you (and your spouse, if you file a joint return) receive during the year.

The amount of your Social Security benefits subject to tax is based on your income as it relates to the two-step rate thresholds mentioned before: $25,000 and $34,000 for single taxpayers, or $32,000 and $44,000 for couples filing a joint return.

Table 9–3 is an example of how the tax would be figured for a typical retired couple, Mr. and Mrs. Jones. (You can use the right-hand column to determine the projected taxes on your Social Security income.) The Joneses have adjusted gross income totaling $36,000 from a company pension plan, taxable investment income, and wages from part-time work. They also get $4,000 in tax-exempt interest from municipal bonds. They add to that half of their $12,000 Social Security benefits, for a total of $46,000. The Joneses subtract from this amount the $32,000 amount of the first tax threshold. That leaves an excess of $14,000 over the threshold. Next, the Joneses subtract the $44,000 second threshold amount from the total income figure of $46,000. That results in an excess of $2,000.

Table 9–3
How Your Social Security Income Is Taxed

	The Joneses	Your Figures
A. Adjusted gross income (income from wages, dividends, interest, pensions)	$36,000	______
B. Tax-exempt interest	4,000	______
C. 50% of Social Security benefits	6,000	______
D. Total of Lines A, B, and C (modified AGI)	46,000	______
E. Excess of Line D over first threshold ($32,000)	14,000	______
F. Excess of Line D over second threshold ($44,000)	2,000	______
G. 50% of Line E, plus 35% of Line F	7,700	______
H. 85% of Social Security benefits	10,200	______
I. 50% of benefits, plus 85% of Line F	7,700	______
J. Add smallest of Lines G, H, I to Line A (AGI)	43,700	______

Finally, the Joneses have to calculate three numbers. First, they add 50% of the excess over the first threshold ($7,000, or 50% of $14,000) to 35% of the excess over the second threshold ($700, or 35% of $2,000). That gives them the first number, $7,700. Next, they calculate 85% of their annual Social Security benefits (85% of $12,000 equals $10,200). These two figures—$7,700 and $10,200—are compared to a third number, which is equal to 50% of their annual Social Security benefits plus 85% of the excess over the second threshold (50% of $12,000, or $6,000, *plus* 85% of $2,000, or $1,700, equals $7,700). They take the lowest of the three numbers—$7,700—and add it to their adjusted gross income of $36,000 for a total of $43,700 in taxable income. In this example, 64% of the Joneses' annual Social Security benefits are taxable.

The income thresholds for taxation of Social Security benefits are not indexed for inflation under current law, so as incomes rise in future years, more Social Security recipients will be hit by income tax on a larger share of their benefits. It would not be surprising if all Social Security benefits eventually became subject to income tax, just as most other pension benefits are.

Other Social Security Benefits

Although Social Security is synonymous with retirement, the program provides other important benefits, including survivors' benefits and disability insurance.

Survivors' Benefits

Survivors' benefits may be paid by Social Security to family members of a breadwinner. Those eligible for survivors' benefits are a widow or widower who is 60 or older; a widow or widower who is disabled and 50 or older; a widow or widower of any age with a child under 16 or caring for a disabled child who is receiving Social Security benefits; unmarried children under 18 (under 19 if a full-time high school student, or any age if disabled before age 22); or the parents age 62 or older of the deceased, if the parents depended on the deceased for at least half of their financial support.

The amount of survivors' benefits depends on the earnings record of the deceased. If you are a widow or widower receiving survivors' benefits, you may switch to your own retirement benefits (assuming that you are eligible for such benefits and that they would be higher than the survivors'

Have You Checked Your Benefits Lately?

If you're nearing retirement and haven't checked your Social Security records within the past few years, do so right away. Employers and the Social Security Administration sometimes make errors that keep workers from being credited with all the earnings on which they paid Social Security taxes. At best, such errors can require you to engage in a lengthy effort to get the proper credits to your record. At worst, errors can result in a lower benefit than you actually earned or even the denial of benefits.

To check your Social Security records, all you have to do is fill out a request form, which you can order by calling 1-800-772-1213. After submitting the request, you'll get a statement showing your past earnings and a projection of your retirement benefits. Check the statement for errors; if you find one, report it at once to your local Social Security office. If you're 60 or older and aren't yet receiving benefits, Social Security will automatically send you an annual statement of earnings and projected benefits. In 1999, the Social Security Administration plans to begin sending annual statements to all Americans age 25 or older.

benefits you currently receive). The rules for making this switch can be complicated; thus, it is wise to check with a Social Security representative first to make sure you choose the option that is best for you.

Disability Benefits and Retirement

Disability benefits are available to people who become severely disabled after having worked long enough and recently enough under Social Security to qualify. To be considered disabled, a person must be so severely impaired in mental or physical ability that he or she cannot perform any substantial gainful work. The disability must be expected—based on medical evidence—to last for at least 12 months or to result in an earlier death. The amount of disability benefits depends on your earnings before becoming disabled and your age at the onset of disability. When you reach normal retirement age, disability benefit payments stop and are replaced by a Social Security retirement benefit of an equal amount.

Medicare Benefits

The federal Medicare program provides important benefits for people age 65 and older and for Americans with long-term disabilities. For its 37 million enrollees, Medicare covers a large portion of approved charges for physicians' bills, hospital stays of up to 150 days, and skilled nursing care after a hospital stay.

Because of rapidly rising medical costs, Medicare is approaching a financial crisis. Trustees of the system estimate that the Medicare Hospital Insurance Trust Fund will be out of money no later than 2002 unless ways are found to significantly restrain the growth in spending or to provide more revenue. Medicare is a target for elected officials seeking ways to restrain the growth in federal spending, and retirees should expect that premiums and copayments may rise and that some services may be restricted.

Medicare is a two-part system. Part A covers hospital care and skilled nursing care (after you pay an up-front deductible of $764 in 1998). Part A is financed primarily by payroll taxes on workers, employers, and the self-employed. The Medicare payroll tax is 2.9% of payroll; half of that, or 1.45% is withheld from a worker's pay, and a matching amount is paid by the employer.

Part B of the Medicare program covers the cost of physicians' bills and outpatient services provided by hospitals. Medicare Part B is paid for by a combination of general tax revenue, which covers about 75% of the cost, and monthly premiums charged to Medicare participants, which cover the remaining 25%. The monthly premium charged for Part B ($43.80 in 1998) is taken out of your Social Security check. The premium usually rises each year to cover rising medical costs. In addition, Medicare participants are required to pay a deductible of $100 a year for Part B services.

Everyone who is eligible for Social Security benefits is also eligible for Medicare upon reaching age 65. If you retire early—at, say, age 63—you must wait until age 65 to enroll in Medicare. If you begin getting Social Security benefits at age 65, you probably will enroll in Medicare when you apply for

Social Security. If you plan to keep working past age 65, you may still apply for Medicare as soon as you reach age 65.

When you enroll in Part A of Medicare, you are automatically enrolled in Part B, unless you decline such coverage. Premiums for Part B are deducted from your Social Security benefit or billed to you quarterly if you are not getting Social Security benefits because of continued employment.

What Medicare Covers

Part A generally covers your hospital bills for 60 days, except for an initial deductible. The deductible is $764 in 1998 and rises each year. After a full 60 days in the hospital, you must pay part of your bill. This co-insurance amount, $191 per day in 1998, also rises each year. After 90 days in the hospital, your co-insurance payment doubles (to $382 per day in 1998). Medicare does not pay anything toward hospital care after 150 days in a benefit period.

Part A also pays the full cost of preapproved coverage at a skilled-nursing-care facility for the first 20 days after a hospital stay. For the next 80 days, you must pay a co-insurance premium ($95.50 per day in 1998), while Medicare covers the rest of the allowable charge. After 100 days in a benefit period, Medicare pays nothing toward the cost of nursing care. If your doctor prescribes certain approved home care services, such as physical therapy, intermittent skilled-nursing care, or rehabilitation equipment, Medicare will pay the full cost. Medicare will also pay most of the cost of hospice care for terminally ill patients for up to 210 days. Finally, after you pay the $100 deductible, Medicare Part B pays for 80% of approved charges for doctor bills, medical supplies, diagnostic tests, and outpatient hospital care.

Keep in mind that, although Medicare pays for many types of health care, it is not a complete health insurance program. On average, Americans 65 and older spend more than $2,800 a year from their own pockets for health care, counting Medicare deductibles and services not covered by Medicare. Among the items Medicare does not cover are:

- Treatment or services that Medicare does not deem to be medically necessary or reasonable.
- Routine physical examinations, dental care, cosmetic surgery, foot care, eyeglasses, or hearing aids.
- Most prescription drugs and medicines taken outside of a hospital.
- Private-duty nursing or extra costs for a private hospital room, telephone, or television.
- Skilled-nursing care after 100 days in a benefit period.
- Custodial nursing care.
- Health care provided outside the United States, other than certain limited exceptions in Canada and Mexico.

Because of these and other gaps in Medicare coverage, many retirees buy long-term care insurance policies and Medicare supplement insurance, known as "medigap" insurance. Medicare supplement insurance pays some of the expenses not covered by Medicare. If you expect to rely on Medicare alone during retirement and will have no other health care coverage, you should consider buying a medigap policy.

Since 1992, federal law has required insurers to offer medigap policies in 10 standardized formats, which must be categorized as A through J. The Plan A policy covers co-insurance for doctor bills and copayments for hospital stays of more than 60 days. The full-featured policy, Category J, is designed to meet virtually the entire range of expenses and deductibles that are not covered by Medicare, including outpatient prescription drugs, at-home care, co-insurance for skilled nursing care, health care outside the United States, and preventive care such as physical exams. The other types of policies, B through I, offer varying mixes of coverage options. Table 9–4 provides an overview of the basic features of each medigap option.

Once you reach age 65, you are automatically eligible to buy Medicare supplement insurance if you apply within six

Table 9–4
The 10 Standard Medigap Policies (A–J)

Policy Type	A	B	C	D	E	F	G	H	I	J
Basic benefits	●	●	●	●	●	●	●	●	●	●
Part A—hospital deductible	○	●	●	●	●	●	●	●	●	●
Part B—doctor deductible	○	○	●	○	○	●	○	○	○	●
Part B—% of excess doctor bill	0%	0%	0%	0%	0%	100%	80%	0%	100%	100%
Skilled nursing co-insurance	○	○	●	●	●	●	●	●	●	●
At-home care	○	○	○	●	○	○	●	○	●	●
Prescription drugs	○	○	○	○	○	○	○	●	●	●
Preventive care	○	○	○	○	●	○	○	○	○	●
Health care abroad	○	○	●	●	●	●	●	●	●	●

● Policy offers this benefit. ○ Policy does not offer this benefit.

Source: William M. Mercer, Inc., 1997. Reprinted with permission.

months of enrolling in Medicare Part B. During this six-month open enrollment period, you cannot be rejected for medigap insurance because of illness, an existing medical condition, or your medical claims history on earlier policies. Naturally, the more services and coverage your medigap policy pays for, the more expensive the premium will be. It's best to buy only the features you need, so you're not paying for unnecessary coverage.

The standardization requirement makes it easier for you to compare different insurance companies' medigap policies and to buy the right mix of benefits for you. Although the policies are standard from company to company, the prices they charge can vary considerably. It pays to shop around to make sure you get the best deal possible. If your income and assets are low enough, you may qualify for Medicaid, the joint federal–state program that provides medical care to financially needy people.

For detailed descriptions of the 10 medigap insurance plans, read *The Guide to Health Insurance for People with Medicare*, published by the U.S. Department of Health and Human Services. To order a free copy, call 1-800-772-1213.

For $3, you may obtain two booklets from the Medicare Rights Center: *Medicare Basics, 1997,* and *Your Medicare Options, 1997.* To order the two booklets, send $3 to Medicare Rights Center, Box 95, 160 Broadway, 8th Floor, New York, NY 10036.

Medicare Terminology

Medicare has its own lingo that you should know as you consider the two parts of Medicare and the features of the 10 medigap plans. Following are some important terms to understand.

Accepting assignment An agreement by a doctor or other service provider to accept the Medicare-approved amount as the entire fee and to receive payment directly from Medicare.

Approved amount The amount that Medicare will pay for a particular treatment or service. Sometimes called the allowable amount or the recognized amount.

Benefit period The benefit period begins on the first day you are hospitalized and ends after you have been out of the hospital or skilled-nursing facility for 60 days. When the benefit period ends, you must pay a new deductible if you need more hospital treatment.

Co-insurance The share of expenses you must continue to pay after you have paid any deductibles. Co-insurance may be a fixed dollar amount or a percentage of the expenses. For example, under Part B of the Medicare program, you pay 20% of approved physician charges as co-insurance.

Deductible The amount of expenses you must pay up front before any Medicare benefit payments begin.

Nonparticipating provider A physician or other health care provider who may not accept assignment and who may charge more than the approved amount. You must pay the difference between the provider's bill and the approved Medicare payment for the service. Since 1993, it has been illegal for a nonparticipating provider to charge you more than 15% over the approved amount.

Participating provider A physician or other service provider who agrees to accept the Medicare-approved amount as full payment for services.

Long-Term Care Insurance

"The problem with a policy is that the big print giveth and the small print taketh away."

Milton Berle

One of the big limitations of Medicare coverage is that it excludes coverage for basic nursing-home care, the cost of which now averages some $30,000 a year. To prepare for this possibility, many people buy long-term care insurance. Rather than reimbursing you or paying for expenses that you actually incur, these policies pay daily benefits that range from $30 to $250. You should be sure that the level of reimbursement your policy provides will cover the cost of care in the area where you live, since nursing care costs vary considerably from one part of the country to another.

Also, although premium rates vary depending on the level of benefits you select, such coverage is generally more expensive if you wait until after you retire to sign up. For example, long-term care premiums for a 70-year-old are roughly four times as high as the premiums that a 55-year-old would pay for comparable coverage. Premiums for someone who buys a policy at age 65 can range from about $1,000 a year to more than $2,200.

As a rule, you should avoid long-term care insurance policies that require a hospital stay before you can qualify for benefits. Also, it's important to check on the financial strength of the insurance company that issues your policy. The company should carry a top rating from at least one of the independent rating agencies, such as A. M. Best Co. (A+ or better), Standard & Poor's Corp. (AA or better), Moody's Investors Service (Aa or better), or Duff & Phelps Inc. (AA or better).

What to Look for in a Long-Term Care Policy

In general, you should consider six main factors when you shop for long-term care insurance:

1. The policy should be guaranteed renewable for life. This means that your coverage cannot be canceled by the insurance company.
2. The policy should pay benefits regardless of the level of care. In other words, be sure that you are covered not only for care at a nursing home, but also for home care and adult day care.
3. Don't buy more coverage than you need. You can save money by choosing a shorter coverage period. The term of coverage is the number of years for which your policy will pay benefits. The options for this term range from one year to your lifetime. You can pay less in premiums and still cover the likely length of a nursing home stay by choosing a three-year or five-year term of coverage instead of a lifetime policy.
4. The longer the waiting period, or deductible period, the lower your premium. The waiting period is the time between the day that you start to need long-term care and the day that the policy starts to pay benefits. Waiting periods range from 21 days to 365 days. If your own savings are sufficient, buy a policy with a 60-day or 90-day waiting period. This will lower your premiums considerably compared with a 21-day or 30-day period.
5. Benefits should be paid at any time in which you are unable to perform without assistance two of the activities of daily living (such as eating, dressing, or bathing) or if you become mentally impaired. Coverage should specifically include Parkinson's disease and Alzheimer's disease.
6. Inflation protection can help your insurance benefits keep pace with rising costs for health care. Many policies offer the option of increasing your benefits (and, of course, your premiums) each year to match increases in the Consumer Price Index.

Final Thoughts

The Social Security system has had a powerful impact on America's economy and on the shape of today's retirement landscape. It has helped to sharply reduce poverty among older Americans and has influenced the design of private retirement plans. However, Social Security was designed only as a safety net for retired Americans; it cannot, by itself, meet all the financial needs of most retirees. Nor is the Medicare program sufficient, by itself, to meet all the health care demands of most retirees. Since both Medicare and Social Security are likely to be affected by government cost-cutting efforts, you will want to stay alert to possible benefit reductions in both programs (such as a smaller cost-of-living adjustment for Social Security benefits) and to increases in co-insurance deductibles and premiums for Medicare.

While it is important that you understand the services and benefits Social Security can provide to you, it is equally important to recognize and prepare for the services and benefits it will not provide. This chapter is designed to help you make the most out of Social Security and Medicare, but it should not be considered a comprehensive source of information on those programs. If you think you need more comprehensive information, consider buying a copy of the *1997 Mercer Guide to Social Security,* a 200-page book that thoroughly describes Social Security and Medicare benefits and eligibility requirements. You can purchase it in many bookstores, or send a check for $12.50 to William M. Mercer, Inc., Social Security Division, 404 S. 4th Ave., #1500, Louisville, KY 40202.

Estate Planning

Chapter 10

Even if you've never consulted a lawyer or drawn up a will, you have an estate plan. How can that be? Well, if you haven't put together an estate plan to direct the manner in which your assets are to be distributed when you're gone, the plan will be laid out for you by the laws of your state. When you die without a will, state law decides who receives your property. Needless to say, the dictates of state law will rarely agree with your wishes.

"I have no desire to die rich. I'd rather be related to people who do."

Martin Mull

For instance, if you die without a will, many states require that your spouse share the estate with your children, so your spouse could get shortchanged. Without a will, you can't specify who gets a particular piece of jewelry or a family heirloom. If you have minor children or other dependents, a court will decide who is appointed their guardian if your will does not name one. Also, if no will is in place, there will probably be significant delays in the settling of your estate, which could slow the distribution of assets to your heirs at a time when they desperately need the money. In short, failure to plan can leave your personal affairs in a tangle, causing distress to your family and resulting in the payment of unnecessary taxes and legal or administrative fees. Sadly, fewer than half of all adults in America have a will.

One reason that so few adults have a will is that estate planning is often viewed as being only for the wealthy. Although opportunities for tax savings increase with wealth, estate planning can benefit nearly everyone. Just as a financial plan helps you to provide for yourself and your family during your life, an estate plan will help you develop the best blueprint to provide for your loved ones after you have passed on. An estate plan can even help you and your family to cope with problems that may occur when you're alive, such as determining who will manage your assets and make financial decisions on your behalf if you should become incapacitated.

While estate planning need not be intricate or expensive, it can get quite complex when a large estate or complicated family issues are involved. Just about every adult—retired or not—should have at least a basic estate plan, even if it consists of only a will. This chapter will highlight some key aspects of estate planning, but it is by no means a complete treatise on the subject. Also, you should be aware that estate laws vary from state to state; this discussion will concern itself mostly with federal taxation of estates. Given the complexity of estate law (and the enormous amounts of money at stake if these laws are not properly accounted for in your planning), estate planning is not a do-it-yourself project. You, of course, must make all the decisions, but to develop your estate plan you should get expert, personalized advice. You may even need a team of specialists, starting with an attorney with expertise in estate planning, and perhaps an accountant or tax adviser, an insurance adviser, an investment adviser or financial planner, and a bank trust officer.

The goal of this chapter, then, is not to make you an expert on estate planning, but to outline some basic planning techniques and to explain the potential benefits of estate planning. If you, like millions of other people, have put off estate planning, it's important that you take steps to begin the process now. It may seem morbid at first, but directing who

Estate Planning Checklist

Do you have a will?
When was the last time you reviewed your will?
Have there been any major changes in your personal or financial situation?
Do you understand the different tax ramifications of holding title (e.g., joint tenancy versus community property) to your assets?
Do your heirs/executor know where to locate important documents?
Are you familiar with the beneficiary designations on your accounts, policies, etc.?
Is it time to revisit your estate plan?

gets what from your property can actually be satisfying. So is the knowledge that you've minimized the anguish and strife that can follow your death.

Getting Started

"I used to think you only needed a will if you were rich. But then I saw the mess left behind when my brother-in-law died without a will."

Florida

If you have a will or estate plan and have not updated it in several years, start by reviewing the will or plan and highlighting anything that you don't understand or that no longer fits your situation or your goals. You should review your will or estate plan anytime a major change in your life may alter your goals or financial situation. For example, a change might be triggered by a death or birth in the family, a marriage, a divorce, a move to another state, or a big change in your financial status or in tax laws. The important thing is to make sure that your instructions still match your current wishes. If you have questions about your will or want to alter it, contact your attorney. If you want to make a small change in your will, it must be done through a codicil, which amends old provisions. You can't simply scratch out the old provision and write the new one over it. Changes in the will must be signed, dated, and witnessed according to the laws of your state.

If you don't have a will, you should contact an attorney as soon as you can to have one drawn up. You will make the job easier, and possibly save legal fees, if you do some preparation before meeting with the attorney. You should:

- Make a list of your assets—real estate, investments, and personal property—and note whether each item is owned

Finding an Estate Lawyer

Not all lawyers are experts on handling estate plans. Your best bet is to get a reference from a friend, relative, or colleague who has drawn up an estate plan. You can get a list of experienced estate lawyers in your state from the American College of Trust and Estate Counsel (ACTEC), 3415 S. Sepulveda Blvd., Suite 330, Los Angeles, CA 90034, or call 1-310-398-1888. To be a member of ACTEC, a lawyer must have practiced trust and estate law for at least 10 years.

in your name, in your spouse's name, or jointly. Be sure to include retirement accounts and any pension benefits you have. The records worksheets in Appendix B and your net worth worksheet on page 13 may help you to organize this information.

- List information about life insurance policies covering you or your spouse. You'll want to note the policy owner, beneficiary, any cash surrender value, and any outstanding loans on the policies.
- Think about who you would want to name as executor for your will, as trustee for any trusts you create, and as guardian for any dependents. Also, designate a potential backup for each position. Consider your beneficiaries. If you have children or grandchildren, do you want to divide your bequests evenly or vary them according to need? Are there specific pieces of property—real estate, family heirlooms, or art—that you want to give to specific family members? Are all your potential beneficiaries temperamentally able to handle an inheritance?

Coping with Incapacity

One unpleasant possibility for which you should prepare is the chance that age or infirmity will someday rob you of the ability to manage your affairs. Suppose an illness or accident temporarily or permanently prevents you from paying bills, managing your investments, or caring for your home. Who will manage these activities for you? Or suppose you suffer from a terminal illness. What medical procedures or treatments do you want performed? Which would you not wish to endure? Confronting such scenarios and making contingency plans are important aspects of estate planning that can relieve family members of emotional burdens and ensure that your wishes are carried out, even if you're unable to express them.

The Power of Attorney A durable power of attorney is a document you can use to designate someone as your

Traits of a Good Executor

As the person who sees to it that the terms of your will are carried out, your executor should be, first, willing to do a job that is time-consuming, tiring, detailed, and thankless.

The executor has to track down all your property, notify your creditors, deal with heirs, lawyers, creditors, bankers, life insurers, property appraisers, and others with some involvement in your estate.

Because it can be a tough job, make sure the executor you name has agreed to do the job. You can assure your executor that legal or financial expertise is not required, since lawyers and financial advisers can be hired. But it does help to select someone who is honest, fair, well-organized, and attentive to the sensitive nature of the job and to your heirs' feelings.

guardian, or *attorney-in-fact,* in the event that you become incompetent to manage your financial and business affairs. Drawing up a power of attorney is an essential step in estate planning, since there is a good chance that you could at some point suffer from a stroke, senility, or some other incapacitating injury or disease.

Because there are standardized forms and rules, a power of attorney is fairly easy and inexpensive to arrange. There is also room for flexibility. You can choose to have the power of attorney take effect immediately upon being signed and legally notarized. Or you can create a "springing" power of attorney, which springs into effect only if and when you become disabled. The powers you grant to the attorney-in-fact to act in your stead can be wide-ranging or limited in scope. You could allow the attorney-in-fact to make health care decisions for you, to make gifts of your property to family members, and to sign contracts in your name. As long as you are competent, you may revoke a power of attorney and set up a new one. Upon your death, the power is revoked automatically and the executor named in your will is in charge of handling your estate according to the specifications of your will. If you own property in more than one state, you may have to have a power of attorney written in each state to comply with its laws.

Rules differ from state to state as to who is eligible to be named attorney-in-fact on your behalf, whether you need to file the document with a particular government office, and so on. It's best to consult a lawyer to learn the rules that apply in your state. Of course, the person you choose as attorney-in-fact must be someone you would trust with your life. This person should have some reasonable level of financial knowledge and, ideally, some idea of your financial goals and wishes. Often a spouse or adult child is chosen as attorney-in-fact. Estate planners recommend that you name an alternate attorney-in-fact in case your first choice is unable or unwilling to take on the responsibility.

Living Wills A living will is a document you can use to specify what sort of medical care you want—and don't want—if you become terminally ill. In a living will, you should clearly outline your wishes about the quality of life you wish to maintain, your religious beliefs about prolonging life, and under what circumstances you would not want medical treatment. For example, state whether you would want artificial feeding and hydration, whether you would want respirators or other mechanical means of sustaining your life to be used, and whether you would want to use medications and other procedures to lessen your pain, even if they might bring death sooner. Of course, a living will need not be focused on *refusing* care. You can state that you want every available procedure to be performed to keep you alive, including mechanical respiration, artificial feeding and hydration, heart resuscitation, and so on.

Many estate planners recommend that you also draw up a separate power of attorney designating someone, perhaps a friend or family member, to make health care decisions for you. This document, also called a health care proxy, can be an alternative or an adjunct to a living will. You should carefully consider this option, because you can't anticipate in your living will every possible ailment or injury that you might contract or every possible treatment that might be available.

Laws covering living wills and health care proxies differ from state to state, so check with an attorney before drawing up one of these documents. Free sample versions of a living will and a durable power of attorney, written with your state's laws in mind, are available from Choice in Dying, a nonprofit group that developed the first living will more than 25 years ago. To order a living will and durable power of attorney, call Choice in Dying at 1-800-989-9455.

Basics of Estate Planning

An estate plan should be flexible enough to cover all sorts of contingencies. You don't know, for example, which partner in a marriage will die first. What would happen if you both died at the same time while traveling? How would a sudden increase or decrease in the value of your assets affect your plans? In thinking about these and other scenarios, it is helpful to understand some of the basic rules and techniques of estate planning. This section will discuss both federal estate taxes and state death taxes, explain what determines the ownership of your property after you die, and outline some fundamental strategies for saving on estate taxes.

The Federal Estate Tax

Many American families have nothing to fear from the federal estate tax, because the tax applies only to the portion of an estate's net value (after debts are paid off) that exceeds a designated exemption figure. If your estate is worth less than $625,000 in 1998 (the figure will gradually increase to $1 million in 2006)—and you're fairly certain that it won't exceed that sum at your death—you will not be subject to federal taxes. A married couple who have properly arranged their affairs can have an estate worth double the exemption figure and pay no federal estate taxes. (State tax is another matter. Each state has its own law on estate or death taxes.)

Before you decide that you're off the hook with regard to estate planning, it's worth noting that many people underestimate the value of their estates. For example, the face value of insurance on your life is included in your estate (if you are the owner of the policy) and can push up the value of your estate substantially. Or, if there is a substantial amount of life insurance on one partner in a marriage and that person dies, the insurance proceeds typically pass to the surviving spouse. The insurance money, combined with the couple's home and other assets, can push the value of the survivor's estate well past the exemption figure threshold for the federal estate tax. The balance sheet information you compiled in Chapter 2 can help you to determine the value of your estate. Remember, the estate tax applies to all your assets, even the value of your furniture, clothing, and other personal property. For married couples, half of all assets owned jointly counts toward each spouse's estate. Also, half of any property that you own jointly with someone else, such as real estate that you own with a brother or sister, counts toward your estate.

If you still think estate planning is more trouble than it's worth, remember that federal estate taxes rise to as high as 55% of an estate's total value. (There are a few deductions allowed from your estate, as shown in Table 10–1.) To diminish your opportunity to evade the estate tax by giving away your assets to your children or other heirs, the federal government also levies a gift tax that is "unified" with the estate tax. The gift tax, which is applied to large sums of money or other assets that you transfer to someone else while you're alive, currently has the same tax rates, deductions, and rules as the estate tax. If you make gifts beyond the allowable limits (generally $10,000 per year per recipient of gifts, although that limit will be indexed to inflation beginning in 1999), the excess amount counts against the exemption figure, which will be indexed in the future based on cost of living. However, some legal loopholes for gift-giving are available, as you'll learn later in the chapter.

State Death Taxes

The federal government is not alone in wanting a slice of your estate. Every state (and the District of Columbia) has a tax on the transfer of assets after death. If you own property in more than one state, your estate may be subject to taxes in each state. In some states, the tax is on the amount of the inheritance received from an estate, and tax rates may vary depending on the relationship of the heir to the deceased. Other states levy a tax, similar to the federal estate tax, on the value of the estate of a deceased person. You can get a credit that reduces your federal estate tax for some or all of the estate tax paid to a state. This federal estate tax credit ranges from 0.8% to 16% of the taxable amount of the estate. On a taxable estate of $1 million, for instance, the maximum federal estate tax credit is $33,200. Some states levy a tax equal to the maximum federal estate tax credit. This is called a "soak-up" tax, since states that charge it soak up the entire estate tax credit allowable under federal law.

Table 10–1
Deductions from Your Taxable Estate

- **Debts** include all financial obligations (e.g., credit card balances, mortgages, liens on property, accrued rent and lease payments).
- **Funeral expenses** (e.g., headstone, cost of post-ceremony meal for guests).
- **Administrative expenses** (e.g., attorney's fees, appraisal fees, probate fees).
- **Casualty losses** (e.g., unreimbursed theft and casualty losses suffered after the decedent's death and before distribution of the estate).
- **Marital deduction** is unlimited if your estate is left to your spouse.
- **Charitable deduction** is unlimited if your estate is left to a qualified charity.

State death taxes may bear little resemblance to the federal estate tax in terms of defining what is taxable or whether your estate gets a full exemption from tax on property that passes to your spouse. If you are considering a move to another state upon or after your retirement, the death tax may be a factor to consider in selecting a new home.

By now you can probably see that the high tax rates on large estates and gifts make estate planning crucial if you want to make sure that the assets you have worked to accumulate go to your loved ones rather than to government coffers.

Property and Your Will

The instructions in your will may not be as complete as you might wish. For example, property that you hold jointly with your spouse—typically your home, bank accounts, mutual funds, stocks, perhaps even your cars—all will pass directly to your surviving spouse after you die, no matter what your will says. Similarly, life insurance proceeds, pension payments, and IRAs pass to the beneficiaries named in the policies or accounts, unless you have named your estate or a trust as the beneficiary. The trouble with these "automatic" transfers is that they may result in the payment of higher estate taxes than necessary. Some tax-saving strategies may require you to take some property out of joint ownership. Other strategies might make it necessary to name your estate or a trust as beneficiary of certain assets. Your estate plan will help you to make sure that your assets are held and titled so that your property goes where you want it to go in the most tax-efficient manner. You should also determine if you live in a "community property" state. If you do, you should check with an attorney to see if any specific rules or laws will apply to your assets upon your death.

Tax-Saving Strategies

There are three main planning techniques available to minimize estate taxes: the unlimited marital deduction; the unified estate tax credit; and the use of gifts and bequests to reduce the estate subject to tax. The tax-saving strategies you may need to employ depend mainly on the size of your estate.

Modest Estates: Assets under the Exemption Figure

Most Americans fall into this category. If the combined value of assets owned by you and your spouse is less than the exemption figure, your estate will be free of federal estate tax. In this case, your estate plan should concentrate on minimizing or avoiding state taxes on estates or inheritances. You'll most likely want to leave the entire estate to your surviving spouse, or to your children if you have no spouse.

Medium-Size Estates: From the Exemption Figure to Double that Amount

Estates of this size can be tricky, since some strategies that are best for purposes of saving taxes may not be practical to execute. To avoid estate taxes, neither spouse should be the sole owner of more than the exemption figure. When the first spouse dies, he or she should leave no more than whatever the exemption figure is in assets to the surviving spouse. To accomplish this, some assets from the deceased may need to go directly to a "bypass" trust operated for the benefit of the surviving spouse. Unfortunately, given the fluctuating value of your home, personal tangible assets, and financial assets, it can be difficult to neatly divide the ownership of a couple's estate. Also, the surviving spouse may be uncomfortable not having direct access to the entire estate.

Figure 10–1 provides a simplified example of how an estate transfer might work for a married couple with an estate valued at $1.2 million in 1997, when the exemption figure is $600,000 per person. After the husband's death, the $600,000 in assets he owned goes into a bypass trust. The money isn't taxed because of the unified tax credit that shelters $600,000 from estate tax. Income from the trust—and even some of the trust's principal—can be directed to his widow. When she dies, the assets in the trust pass on to the couple's heirs. The $600,000 in assets owned by the wife also can pass on to the heirs free of estate tax because of the $600,000 unified tax credit available to her. Unified tax credits are discussed in more detail on page 229.

Large Estates: More Than Double the Exemption Figure

Because estates of this size have the most to lose to estate taxes, most sophisticated estate-planning strategies are designed for such estates. A variety of gift-giving strategies, trusts, and other techniques may be used to reduce the taxable estate. On extremely large estates, planning may involve generation-skipping gifts to pass wealth on to grandchildren or great-grandchildren.

Figure 10–1
How a Bypass Trust Can Reduce Estate Taxes

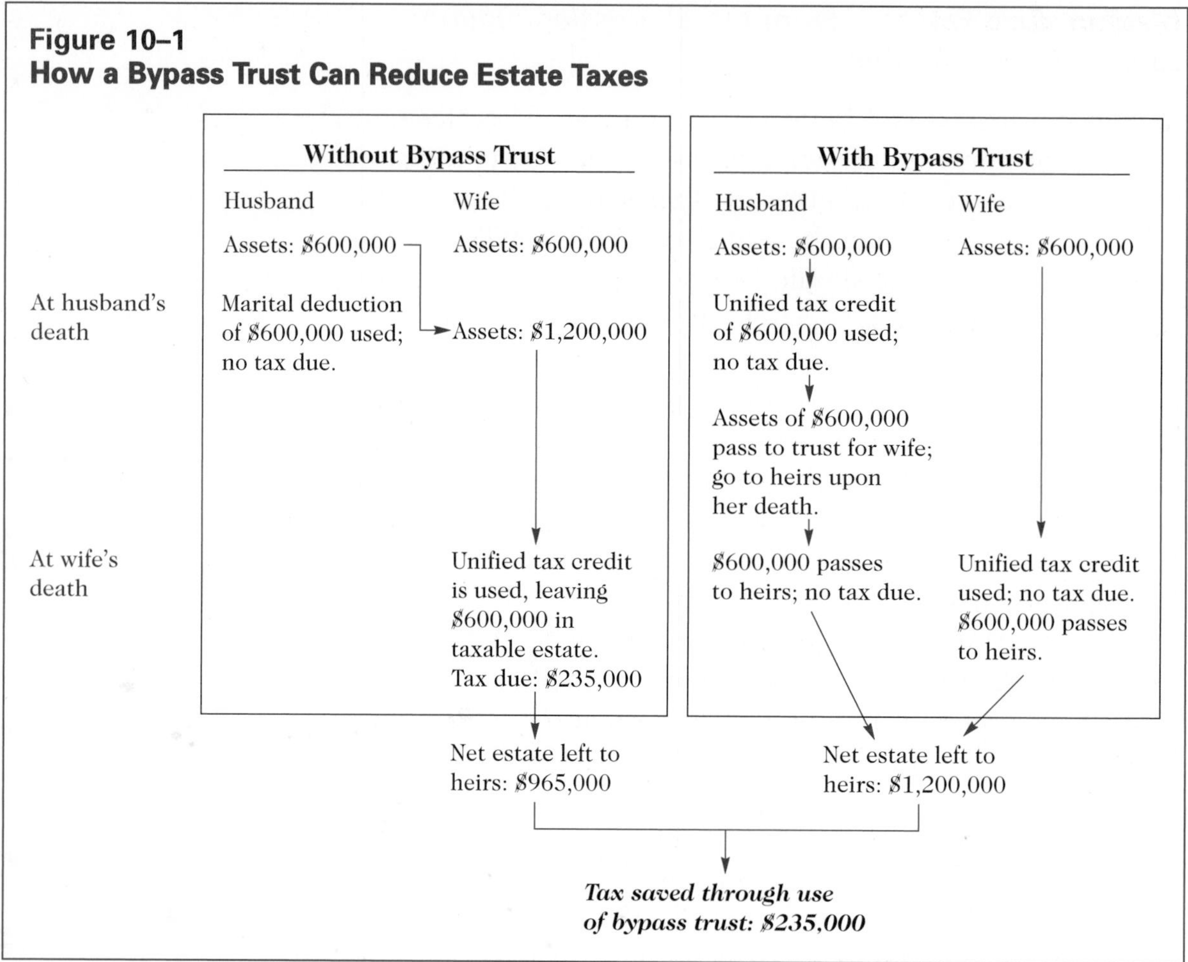

The Marital Deduction

There is no estate tax on assets that are transferred from one spouse to another, no matter how much money and property are involved. This unlimited marital deduction allows one spouse to leave all of the couple's assets to the other and pay no estate tax. While this ruling may seem munificent on the part of the federal government, the tax is merely deferred, not eliminated. When the surviving spouse dies, all of the assets that remain from the first spouse are now part of the second spouse's estate, which is subject to the federal estate tax. Thus, couples with large estates should plan carefully to take advantage of each spouse's unified tax credit.

Unified Tax Credit

Every citizen is entitled to a unified tax credit that is enough to protect an amount equal to the exemption figure from estate or gift tax. If each partner in a marriage has $600,000 (the exemption figure in 1997) in separate assets (not jointly owned at the time of death), the couple will be able to pass along $1.2 million to their heirs free of gift or estate taxes. One of the most common mistakes couples make is failing to take full advantage of the full exemption available to each partner.

Suppose, for example, that Mr. and Mrs. Jones have $2.2 million in assets, all jointly owned. Mr. Jones dies first, leaving everything to Mrs. Jones. His $1.1 million in property passes to Mrs. Jones free of estate tax because of the unlimited marital deduction. However, if Mrs. Jones dies in 1997, she has only her own estate tax credit available, good on $600,000 in assets in that year. The rest of her estate, $1.6 million, is subject to estate tax, which takes a whopping $686,000. That leaves only about $1.5 million for the Jones children to inherit.

As a tax-saving alternative, Mr. Jones could have put $600,000 in assets held in his name into a credit shelter trust, or bypass trust, for the Joneses' children. The trust income and up to 5% of its principal each year would be available to Mrs. Jones during her lifetime. After her death, the money in the trust would go to the Jones children, free of estate tax because of Mr. Jones' $600,000 exclusion. When Mrs. Jones died, her estate would total $1.6 million, and her estate tax credit would shield $600,000 from estate taxes. The tax on the remaining $1 million would be $408,000, a savings of $278,000 compared with the first scenario.

Reducing Your Estate through Gifts

Another way to cut your estate taxes is to leave a smaller estate by making gifts or bequests to your family or to religious or charitable organizations. Some giving strategies can provide both income and income tax benefits to you while you're living and still save estate taxes after your death. In general, it is more tax-efficient to pass money to your heirs through gifts than through bequests from your estate. The reason is that any tax you incur on the gifts that you make while living is removed from your estate and thus isn't around to be subject to the estate tax. Any taxes owed on your estate, on the other hand, will be paid out of the funds that were in your estate and that were, thus, subject to the estate tax. This section provides a quick overview of some gift strategies.

Gifts to Family: The $10,000 Loophole Currently, you may give your children, grandchildren, or others up to $10,000 each year without incurring the federal gift tax and without using up any of your exemption from gift and estate taxes. If you are married, you and your spouse may each give $10,000 to as many different people as you choose. Alternatively, one of you may give $20,000 per year, as long as the other spouse consents and makes no gift to that person.

The advantage of making such gifts is that by transferring the money to others, you have reduced the value of your estate and, ultimately, the amount of estate tax that your estate will pay. The chief disadvantages of this strategy are that you deplete your assets and lose the use and control of the money you've given away. It's possible to be too generous early in your retirement and find out later on that your assets have dwindled to dangerously low levels. Another potential problem is making gifts to irresponsible family members who might fritter away the money. In such instances, you may consider the use of trusts or custodial arrangements to maintain some degree of control over the money. A final caution: If you give more than $10,000 ($20,000 per couple) to any one person in any one year, the excess amount will reduce the estate tax credit available to you.

Educational Gifts Another loophole in the estate tax laws enables you to pay someone's medical expenses or college or private school tuition without it counting against your gift tax limit. For example, you could pay $12,000 in tuition for a grandchild and still make a $10,000 gift to that grandchild without running afoul of the gift tax limits in a given year. Strict rules cover this tax break. For example, a tuition payment must be made directly to the college or school. Also, the gift must be for tuition and not for ancillary costs of school, such as books.

"I wanted to provide for my grandchildren's college. I don't see how my kids can afford to pay all that tuition."

Ohio

Charitable Gifts Gifts to a qualified charity are not subject to estate taxes, whether the gift is made during your lifetime or after your death according to the terms of your will. If you're inclined to make gifts to charities, gifts made during your life provide you with income tax deductions and the satisfaction of seeing your money put to good use. When it comes to really large gifts, however, there are limitations on how much you can deduct for income tax purposes. If you want to keep control of your assets during your life and make your charitable gifts through your will, the gifts will save estate taxes by reducing the size of your taxable estate.

Tax-Saving Trusts

Trusts can be useful devices for saving taxes and carrying out the goals of your estate plan. A trust is not necessarily complicated, and you don't have to have millions of dollars to set one up. It is merely an arrangement under which a trustee (which can be a person or an institution, such as a bank or mutual fund complex) is named the legal owner of assets for the benefit of another person or persons. Terms of the trust are usually outlined in a written trust document that sets out who gets what from the trust and outlines the responsibilities of the trustee. (Although many trust agreements can be adopted using standardized forms that your lawyer or bank has on hand, you have the right to include other provisions in a trust, so long as it is not in violation of state law.) A trustee is usually granted wide leeway in making important decisions, such as whether to invade the principal of the trust, if needed, to provide income to the beneficiaries.

You've already learned about one type of trust—the credit shelter, or bypass, trust, which allows both spouses to take advantage of their full estate tax credit. But this is only one of many different types of trusts that provide tax-saving options to fit a variety of estate-planning situations. Some trusts allow you to give away assets even as you continue to receive income payments; others can help you to minimize taxes, speed up the distribution of your property, and otherwise carry out your estate plans. This section reviews some basic information about trusts and their role in estate planning. It is far from comprehensive, but it may give you a feel for some of the many uses of trusts.

Trusts can be irrevocable or revocable. As the name implies, an *irrevocable trust* may not be revoked or changed after you create it. There are many types of irrevocable trusts. A common reason for setting up irrevocable trusts is to shift assets out of your estate so that the future growth in value of the assets isn't subject to estate tax. An irrevocable trust may be created during your lifetime, or it may be created by the terms of your will. You'll need good advice from an estate planner to set up an irrevocable trust. Since you can't change the terms of the trust once you've created it, you want to carefully think through the decisions you make. Also, depending on the terms of a trust, the IRS may or may not consider the assets you put into it to have been removed from your estate for estate tax purposes.

Living Trusts *Revocable trusts,* on the other hand, can be revoked or altered whenever you choose. A common type of revocable trust is popularly called the *living trust,* and is often touted as a way to avoid probate, the legal process in which a court oversees the executor who carries out the terms of your will.

A living trust allows you to control the assets that you contribute to it while you're still alive. You can reserve the right to make withdrawals from the trust or to add to its assets at any time. You can name yourself or someone else as trustee, and you can name a co-trustee so that either of you can make decisions about the trust's assets if the other is disabled. For example, if you expect to travel a great deal after retirement, you may want to create a living trust and name a co-trustee to handle your financial affairs while you're globe-trotting. The co-trustee can pay your bills, make tax payments for you, or handle other chores.

After you die, the trust becomes irrevocable, and whoever you have named as successor trustee distributes the property to the beneficiaries according to the terms of the trust, without going through probate. In this way, a living trust substitutes for a last will and testament, whose terms are administered under court supervision. If you own property in several states, the living trust can be a way to avoid probate proceedings in each state. A living trust can also minimize the delays in distributing property that can occur during the probate process. And a living trust can provide privacy in the administration of assets before and after your death, since there is no public record created as there is when a will is administered through probate.

Saving probate costs, maintaining privacy, and avoiding delays in distributing your assets are all legitimate reasons to consider a living trust. However, rarely do the costs of probate alone justify the use of a living trust. In some states, probate costs are modest because probate is a relatively simple and inexpensive process. Executors often waive fees, particularly if they are family members or beneficiaries of your will. Outside administrators charge fees, but so would an outside trustee you might hire as successor trustee. Although state laws governing probate generally allow attorneys to receive a fee based on a percentage of an estate's value, you can often reduce legal costs by negotiating hourly rates with estate attorneys.

Living trusts are not without drawbacks of their own, and they are not a solution for all estate planning problems. There is a good deal of paperwork involved in setting up a living trust, since you must change the title to any property that you contribute to it. Also, there are fees for setting up and operating the trust. Creating a living trust does not eliminate the need for a will, since as a practical matter you can't hold all your assets inside the trust. And, contrary to the impression sometimes created by promoters of living trusts, the arrangements do not provide tax savings for you or your estate. Assets in a living trust are subject to estate tax along with the rest of your assets. Income from the trust is taxed as it is received. Also, because the grantor has not irrevocably disposed of assets in the trust, those assets are included in the grantor's estate for estate tax purposes.

You should consider many factors, not just the potential savings in probate costs, before deciding to use a living trust. A living trust should be viewed as part of a comprehensive estate plan, not as a substitute for one.

Charitable Remainder Trust This trust allows you or any other beneficiary that you name to receive income from any assets donated to the trust. The income can continue for a fixed period of time or for the life of the beneficiary. At the end of either period, the balance in the trust passes to the charity. You are allowed an income tax deduction for the present value of the balance, or remainder interest, that will eventually pass to the charity.

Charitable Lead Trust This trust is the opposite of the remainder trust: The income from the trust goes to the charity, while the remaining balance at the end of the trust's term is passed on to the beneficiary you have named. You get a tax deduction for the present value of the income paid to the charity.

Crummey Trust This trust gets its name from a court case. It is used most often by people with very large estates who want to give away some of their assets but who are uncertain about the ability of the recipient to handle the money. It can be used for minors or adults, and the trustee may use his or her discretion in distributing income and principal from the trust. You can set up the trust to continue to any particular age of the recipient, or to dole out the trust principal in stages.

When used correctly, a Crummey Trust can prevent premium payments to an irrevocable life insurance trust from being considered a gift to the trust's beneficiaries. Be sure to consult only experienced estate-planning attorneys when using a Crummey Trust.

QTIP Trust The qualified terminable interest property (QTIP) trust is a type of marital trust set up by one partner to specify what happens to the trust assets when the surviving spouse dies. The surviving spouse cannot name or change beneficiaries of the trust. A QTIP trust is typically used by people who have children from an earlier marriage and who want to make sure those children get their inheritance. The assets in a QTIP trust are not subject to estate taxes when the first spouse dies, but they are included in the estate of the surviving spouse and are subject to tax when that spouse dies.

Estate-Freezing Trusts If you have a large estate, you may consider the use of trusts that allow you to freeze the value of your property for estate tax purposes while retaining the use of the assets for yourself before ultimately passing on the property to your heirs. The rules for these trusts are quite strict, so to use them correctly you'll need expert guidance.

Qualified Personal Residence Trusts This type of irrevocable trust, also known as a personal residence grantor retained interest trust, or GRIT, allows you to shift your primary residence, vacation home, or both out of your estate and into a trust. You set the term of the trust—it can be any number of years. Afterward, ownership of the property passes to your children or other heirs. In the meantime, you keep living in the house. By shifting the home out of your estate and into the trust, you freeze its value for tax purposes. Make certain the trust instrument has language that will prevent the trust from returning the residence back to the control of the grantor or his or her spouse. For gift and estate tax purposes, the value of the home is reduced by the value ascribed to your use of it during the term of the trust. Also, any appreciation in the value of the home while it's in the trust is passed along to your children without being taxed.

If the parent who puts the home in trust dies before the trust's term is over, ownership of the home reverts to the parent's estate and is subject to estate tax at its full value. For this reason, the donor should choose a term for the trust that he or she is reasonably confident of outliving.

Generation-Skipping Transfer Tax

If you have a very large estate, it has doubtless occurred to you that estate taxes are a serious impediment to keeping that wealth in the family. If you leave substantial assets to your children, and they in turn leave large estates to their children, your assets will be taxed twice (once after your death and again after your children die) before they get passed along to your grandchildren. On a large estate, the effect is to take away three-quarters of the assets before they reach your grandchildren.

One way to avoid the double taxation is to leave money in trust for your grandchildren. You thus skip one generation's worth of estate tax. But there is a limit on how much you can transfer to a "skip" generation. That limit is $1 million ($2 million if a couple splits their gifts), no matter how many grandchildren you have. Trusts can be set up to take advantage of the $1 million tax exemption while you're living or by your estate under terms you set forth in your will.

The restrictions and rules governing the $1 million exemption are, to put it mildly, complex. The strategies that can be employed in setting up such trusts are also complex and varied. If you have assets enough to consider this strategy, you'll want an expert estate lawyer to draw up your estate plan. If you run afoul of the rules, you'll pay a generation-skipping transfer tax of 55% *on top of any regular estate tax due* on the assets transferred. Given the draconian nature of this double tax, the cost of expert advice in this area is trivial.

Some advisers recommend against using a generation-skipping transfer trust even if you have the money to do so. Although the strategy can save taxes, it can cause problems for your children. They may have trouble controlling their offspring if your grandchildren know they've got a big bequest coming from you. The natural streak of independence in young people can be strengthened by the knowledge that a large pot of money will soon be theirs, courtesy of grandma and grandpa.

Any part of the $1 million exemption that is not used while you're alive can be used against any assets you leave to grandchildren or great-grandchildren in your will.

Life Insurance and Estate Planning

Life insurance may have a place in your estate plans, even if you no longer need it to substitute for your salary and provide for your spouse and children after your death. Part of your estate planning should be to make sure that you'll have enough cash or liquid assets to handle expenses that will come due within a few months after your death. These include your final living expenses (bills, outstanding debts, property taxes, and final income tax returns), the costs of probating your will, and estate and death taxes. If you have a family business or extensive real estate holdings, this planning is particularly crucial, since you'll want to avoid having assets sold at distress prices because cash is needed to settle your affairs. Providing this sort of liquidity is one role for life insurance.

Life insurance proceeds are not subject to income tax, but they can be subject to estate tax, depending on how the policy is owned. This is where estate-planning advice is needed. Planners say that improperly setting up life insurance policies is one of the more common—and costly—errors related to estate planning. If you are considered to be the owner or controller of the policy, the proceeds are considered part of your taxable estate. If your estate, counting the life insurance proceeds, exceeds the exemption figure, the life insurance adds to the tax bite on your estate. With proper planning, however, you can keep the financial protection of life insurance while avoiding the payment of estate taxes on the proceeds.

The way to accomplish this objective is to remove the proceeds from your estate and your spouse's estate by setting up an irrevocable life insurance trust to own the insurance policy.

When you die, the life insurance proceeds can be distributed by the trust to your heirs free of tax. This technique can be used to provide the available cash to pay estate taxes on large estates, so that your property doesn't have to be sold to come up with the tax payment. A warning: It is easy to run afoul of the strict rules governing ownership in the life insurance policy. If you do so, you may be deemed to be the policy owner, and its proceeds may be included in your estate.

A couple can use a special type of life insurance policy, called survivorship life insurance, to fund the life insurance trust to provide cash for paying estate taxes. Survivorship life insurance covers both partners in a marriage but pays off only after the second spouse dies. Hence, this type of policy is often called "second-to-die" life insurance. This insurance is cheaper to buy than separate policies for each spouse. However, as with all insurance, you should shop carefully, because cost and terms can vary widely from one policy to another. Be wary if a salesperson touts second-to-die policies as a magic solution to estate-planning problems. In some circumstances a regular, single-life insurance policy is the better way to meet estate-planning goals.

Final Thoughts

As you've seen, estate planning should be part of nearly everyone's overall financial plan. After all, decisions about who gets what from your estate are too important to be left to an inflexible set of state laws that may dictate outcomes far different from those you would wish to see. Likewise, the potential impact of estate and death taxes on your heirs is too large to be ignored or left to chance.

It may not be pleasant—either for you or for them—to discuss your estate plans with your children. But such discussions are probably a good idea. Explaining your plans and decisions, even if it's done by letter or on tape to be viewed after your death, may avoid bitterness and bad feeling, especially if you've left unequal shares.

Inertia—the tendency of an object at rest to stay at rest or an object in motion to continue along a path—is a powerful force in human nature as well as in physics. But don't let inertia keep you from getting started on your estate plans.

Contingency Planning for the Retired Investor

Chapter **11**

Most of the material covered in this guide—budgeting, investing, estate planning, Social Security—applies to all or nearly all retirees. But not all retired investors are cut from the same cloth. Although they share quite a bit of common ground, each retiree has individual needs and desires, and each is faced with a different set of financial circumstances.

This chapter attempts to address some of the special circumstances that may confront retired investors. It begins with a discussion of some steps you can take if, like many retirees, you find that your resources simply are not adequate to finance the retirement you desire. You'll discover a number of creative ways that you can tap the equity built up in your home to provide cash for your retirement needs. You'll also learn about some critical factors to consider before relocating for your retirement. Finally, the chapter concludes with some ideas for dealing with the financial implications of the death of a spouse, a divorce, or the unexpected return of a child to your once-empty nest.

When Your Financial Resources Fall Short

It is a sad fact that thousands of retirees each year have trouble making ends meet. Sometimes a severe illness, an accident, or some other calamity unexpectedly boosts expenses or depletes savings. The death of a spouse can result in reduced monthly income from pensions or Social Security, leaving the surviving partner with insufficient resources. Divorce, in addition to being emotionally traumatic, can devastate a couple's finances. A retired couple can be hit with unexpected expenses from having to support a child or

"I've stretched my budget by taking in a roommate to share my house. I had plenty of room after my husband died, and it is nice having someone else around. The extra income sure helps, too."

Florida

grandchild. Some retired investors spend too freely because they underestimate their probable life spans; other retirees fail to anticipate the effects of inflation or the possibility that interest income from their investments may decline sharply. And some retirees simply run out of money because they have beaten the actuarial odds and far surpassed normal life expectancies.

These are just a few of the circumstances that can unexpectedly complicate a comfortable retirement. Whatever the reasons for the financial difficulty, there are several strategies that may help you to address any financial shortfall. While some of these options may not be very appealing, keep in mind that the earlier you diagnose and bolster a weakness in your finances, the easier it will be to get back on an even keel.

Of course, there is no magic solution to a financial shortfall. You must either boost your income, reduce your spending, or achieve some combination of the two. In a sense, cutting your spending is the easiest adjustment to make. But once you've become accustomed to a given lifestyle, it becomes more and more difficult to compromise and make sacrifices. After all, yesterday's luxuries (dining out, cable TV, air travel) have become today's necessities. Nonetheless, if you've completed the budget worksheets in Chapter 2, you'll probably be able to identify some relatively painless ways to trim your budget. The remainder of this section will focus on strategies designed to boost your income.

Returning to Work

At some time or other during their retirement, about 25% of all retirees return to work, either part-time or full-time. About one of every eight Social Security recipients currently receives employment income. Indeed, according to the U.S. Department of Labor, about 3.7 million Americans age 65 or older are employed, and 153,000 are classified as looking for work. While some of these retirees return to work because they want the challenges and social interaction provided in the workplace, many of these "non-retirees" work solely out of necessity.

Returning to work, even to a part-time job at relatively low wages, can be an enormous help in stretching your resources. Here are some of the more obvious ways that returning to work bolsters your financial situation:

- Because of the extra income you earn, you will need to make more modest withdrawals from your retirement savings. You may even earn enough to add to your savings and investments. This boosts the amount of income you'll receive in the future, after you have completely stopped working. If you receive a wage and you're under age 70½, you can continue to contribute to a traditional IRA or a Roth IRA. With a traditional IRA, you may qualify for a tax deduction for your contribution, in addition to enjoying the tax-deferred compounding of your investment. If you are over age 70½ and still working, you can contribute to a Roth IRA (subject to income limits) but those contributions are *not* deductible.
- Employee benefits you receive may enable you to reduce your spending or augment your savings. Employer-provided health insurance, for example, may reduce your out-of-pocket medical expenses. Or you may be able to add to your nest egg through employee stock-purchase plans, thrift plans, or retirement plans.
- You can continue to draw Social Security benefits while drawing a paycheck. If you're 70 or older, you can receive all the Social Security benefits you're entitled to, no matter how much you earn from work. If you are younger than 65, you may earn up to $9,120 a year (for 1998) without losing any Social Security benefits. For each $2 you earn above that limit, your Social Security benefits are cut by $1. If you're age 65 to age 69, you may earn up to $14,500 (again, for 1998) without losing any Social Security benefits, but you lose $1 in benefits for each $3 in earnings above the limit.

- If you want to suspend your Social Security benefits while you return to work, you may do so. You'll be able to "re-retire" at a later time and receive Social Security payments again, but with a higher monthly benefit.

If you need to return to work to boost your income, you may be surprised to find that your services are in demand. Some retirees worry that their skills have become obsolete or that they can't learn to use computers or other new technology. But many employers prize older workers for their work ethic, experience, and communications skills. If you are interested in returning to the workforce, now or later, you might be interested in either of two free booklets available from the American Association of Retired Persons (AARP): "How to Stay Employable: A Guide to the Midlife and Older Worker" and "Returning to the Job Market: A Woman's Guide to Employment Planning." To get either publication, write to the AARP at 601 E. Street N.W., Washington, D.C. 20049 or call 1-800-424-3410.

Let Your Home Pay You

If you're like many retirees, your home is probably one of the biggest assets you own. But your home is a unique financial asset. After all the effort it took to make it *yours*—hundreds of monthly mortgage payments, property taxes, repairs, and upkeep—you probably have some emotional attachment to it. This emotional aspect is one reason many retirees have a difficult time considering their home as a source of retirement income.

This reluctance is certainly understandable. However, many retired investors find themselves "house rich and cash poor." They own a home, perhaps free of debt, but are scraping by from month to month. In this situation, using some of your home equity is a sensible way to help finance your retirement years.

Trading Down Your Home The new federal tax law permits a single taxpayer to shelter up to $250,000 (joint filers can shelter up to $500,000) of capital gains on the sale of a principal residence. To qualify, you must have owned and occupied the home for at least two of the previous five years. This exclusion is available each time a residence is sold, but not more that once every two years.

There are other advantages to trading down beyond the possibility of generating extra cash for investing and financing your retirement. A number of home-related expenses—taxes, homeowners' insurance, utilities, maintenance, and repairs—will probably decline if you move to a smaller, less expensive home. You'll also have less area to keep clean, less lawn and garden to tend, and less sidewalk to keep edged and free from snow. Not surprisingly, there also are potential disadvantages to trading down. The most important risk is that you may not like your new home and neighborhood as much as the old, where you may be leaving behind long-time friends and favorite activities. On balance, if you're happy where you are and you don't need money from your home equity right away, there's no compelling reason to move just yet.

For more information on the mathematics of trading down, refer to IRS Form 2119. Guidance on tax ramifications of a home sale is available in IRS Publication 523, "Selling Your Home," which you can order by calling 1-800-829-3676.

If you plan to trade down to a lower-cost home in another part of the country (or world), there are some important factors to consider before you make a commitment to relocate.

Personal and family feelings Consider how you'll feel about being separated from family, friends, and your community. Obviously, it will be easier to relocate if you have friends or family living near the new location.

Know what you're getting Before you make a major lifestyle change like relocating, visit the proposed area at different times of the year. Ideally, you might rent an apartment for several months to check out the new site. You may love Florida or Arizona in the winter, when the warm weather is a balm to your body and spirit. But you may be less enamored of these areas in mid-August, when the heat and humidity can be intense. Be sure to check out the hospital and other health care facilities in the area, especially if you have a medical condition that may require specialized or emergency care. Investigate the recreational and cultural opportunities to be sure the pursuits you enjoy are available. In retirement, you'll have more time to enjoy movies, the arts, reading, adult classes, and so on. Make certain your interests can be accommodated in the new location.

Consider all taxes, not just income taxes Moving to a state with no income tax may sound wonderfully attractive. But if you're just beginning retirement, keep in mind that you won't be generating much, if any, earned income from wages or salary. Thus, the absence of a state income tax may not save you as much as you thought. Also, states with no income taxes typically have relatively high sales taxes, an important consideration since retirees typically spend a larger proportion of their income on goods and services than working people. States with low or no income tax may also tax both tangible personal property (such as cars and boats) and intangible property (such as stocks, bonds, and mutual funds). Also, states differ in the way they tax income from pensions, estates, and inheritances. In short, you should consider a state's total tax picture in deciding about relocation. "Relocation Tax Guide," a pamphlet on state tax issues that may affect relocation decisions, is available from the AARP. The pamphlet lists the various types of state taxes and gives the addresses and phone numbers of all the state revenue departments so that you can request more detailed information.

Compare costs carefully Try to carefully estimate the costs of living in your new location. Among the items whose cost can vary considerably from one state to another are housing, utilities, taxes, car insurance, and recreation. You may pay lower heating but higher electricity costs for air conditioning. If you move far from family and friends, factor in higher costs for visits.

Be prepared to "disengage" from your old location If you buy a retirement home in another state, the tax authorities from your old home state may try to keep taxing you. To avoid the risk of being taxed as a resident of both states, you must abandon your domicile in the old state. Evidence that you've done so might include the following: (1) getting a new driver's license and relinquishing your old one; (2) moving your bank, brokerage, and mutual fund accounts; (3) changing your voter registration; (4) renting a safe-deposit box at the new location for your valuables; and (5) choosing non-resident status or resigning from business and social organizations at your old home.

Reverse Mortgages Reverse mortgage loans are a relatively new form of mortgage that allow you to convert the equity in your home into installment payments that could provide you with extra monthly income for as long as you live. By taking out a reverse mortgage, you borrow against your property. Ordinarily, a homeowner who takes out a reverse mortgage receives monthly installments instead of a lump sum. Instead of paying off part of your loan balance each month, as with a regular mortgage loan, you add to your loan balance each month as you receive the payment from the lender and as interest accrues on the money loaned to you so far. The payments, or loan advances, that you receive from a reverse mortgage are not taxable as income and do not affect your Social Security benefits or eligibility for Medicare.

As long as you continue to live in the home, you cannot be forced to sell or leave, and you still get your monthly payment. Even if you receive payments for a very long time, the amount owed on your loan is limited to the market value of your home. (Part of the "charge" against your home equity is an insurance premium paid to a reserve fund that compensates the lender for losses incurred when borrowers have unusually long lives.) The most popular reverse mortgages are those insured by the Federal Housing Administration (FHA), which guarantees the annuity payments due to you in case the lender defaults.

For those who feel comfortable and happy in their own homes, a reverse mortgage is a way to have your cake and eat it too. You can stay in your home while receiving income payments from your home equity. Three principal options are available for receiving your loan proceeds: (1) You can receive monthly payments for as long as you're in the home; (2) you can arrange to get monthly payments for a specific period (say, 10 years); or (3) you can choose to get a credit line that you can tap for cash whenever you want it, perhaps to pay for home repairs or a medical bill.

Because you make no monthly payments on the reverse mortgage loan, you do not need to have a salary or other earnings to qualify. There are closing costs and other up-front fees, but lenders typically include these fees in the mortgage amount, so you don't have to come up with much cash to get the loan. Of course, if these closing costs are rolled over into the mortgage, your home equity is diminished by their amount.

When you die, move, or sell your home, the reverse mortgage loan becomes due immediately. Usually the loan is repaid with the proceeds from the sale of your home. But the balance can be paid off with other assets, by money from your heirs if they don't want to sell the home, or even by refinancing the home. As long as your home is worth more than your loan balance, you or your heirs get the difference between the home's value and the amount due on the loan. But you or your heirs *never* owe the lender more than the loan balance or the market value of your home, *whichever is less.*

The amount of monthly income you can get from a reverse mortgage depends on several factors: your age, interest rates at the time of the loan, and the value of your home. Reverse mortgage loans are available for people age 62 or older, but the monthly income paid by the lender gets much higher as the borrowers get older. An 85-year-old taking out a reverse mortgage, for example, might get two or three times the monthly income from the loan that a 65-year-old borrower would get on a property with the same value.

In addition to the interest payments on your reverse mortgage loan, you'll pay an origination fee of 1% to 2% of the loan amount, a one-time insurance premium of 2% of your maximum loan amount, and an insurance premium that adds half a percentage point (0.5%) to the interest rate charged on your loan balance. Other closing costs you will incur include appraisal fees, credit reports, title insurance, a survey of your property, and various recording and notary fees that typically total somewhere between $1,000 and $1,500. Some lenders may also charge a loan-servicing fee of up to $30 a month.

Overall, the fees on reverse mortgage loans tend to be higher than on other loans. New federal rules require lenders to disclose to you the total annual loan cost in a way that makes it easier to compare competing mortgage offers. These rules require lenders to show you a total annual loan cost (or TALC) rate for two points in time: at your life expectancy (based on actuarial tables) and at a point beyond your life expectancy.

Table 11–1 shows the amount of *monthly* income you could receive, assuming various ages, from reverse mortgage loans of varying amounts. The table assumes an 8.5% expected interest rate, $2,000 in closing costs, and a 2% initial insurance premium. The table assumes that the closing costs and insurance premium, as well as an amount needed to pay monthly servicing fees, are financed as part of the loan.

Table 11–1
Monthly Income a Reverse Mortgage Can Provide

	Maximum Loan Amount				
Age	$50,000	$70,000	$90,000	$110,000	$124,875
62	$ 76	$124	$173	$221	$ 257
65	90	145	199	253	294
70	119	184	250	316	365
75	154	235	315	396	456
80	203	303	403	503	578
85	279	401	530	659	754
90	396	576	756	936	1,071
	Monthly Loan Proceeds				

Source: Federal National Mortgage Association.

A reverse mortgage works exactly the opposite of a regular mortgage loan. The lender pays you, adding each payment, plus interest, to your loan balance. A simplified example of how this loan works is provided in Table 11–2. The example shown is based on the same $90,000 reverse mortgage loan at an 8.5% interest rate to an 80-year-old homeowner. As shown in Table 11–1, these assumptions give rise to a monthly loan amount of $403, given insurance and closing costs.

As you can see in Table 11–2, after the first loan advance, the borrower would owe $403. In the next month, the homeowner would receive another $403 and owe $3 in interest on the first month's advance, for a total loan balance of $809. In the second month, the homeowner would again get $403, which would be added to the previous balance along with $6 in interest, bringing the loan balance to $1,218. After a year under this example, the borrower would have received payments of $4,836 and would owe $5,064, including $228 in accrued interest.

The biggest drawback to a reverse mortgage loan is that it reduces the estate that you'll pass along to your heirs after you die. What's more, because of the high up-front costs, these loans are not a practical solution for a modest or short-term financial need. The up-front costs also make reverse mortgages a poor option if you plan to sell your home and move within two or three years. If the closing costs of the mortgage are spread out over only a few years, you will, in effect, have paid a very high interest rate for the loan. In general, reverse

Table 11–2
How a Reverse Mortgage Loan Works

In Month	Last Month's Loan Balance	Interest on Last Month's Balance	Current Month's Advance	Current Amount Owed	Monthly Rise in Amount Owed
0	$ 0	$ 0	$403	$ 403	$403
1	403	3	403	809	406
2	809	6	403	1,218	409
3	1,218	9	403	1,630	412
4	1,630	12	403	2,045	415

mortgage loans work best for older retirees, since the monthly payment amount from a reverse mortgage rises as the age of the borrower increases. If you are relatively young—say, below the age of 70—the income from the mortgage loan may be disappointingly small. Finally, there is a potential psychological drawback to consider: It may bother you to owe money again on a property that you had owned free and clear.

On the other hand, the income from a reverse mortgage loan can help you to maintain or improve your standard of living while enabling you to stay in a home that you enjoy. In this respect, reverse mortgages can be an attractive alternative to trading down to a lower-cost home. In short, you can think of the reverse mortgage as a way to take advantage of the substantial investment you've made in your home.

If you think a reverse mortgage loan might make sense for you, consider the idea in light of your overall financial and estate plans. Your home is a valuable asset, so you don't want to make a quick or uninformed decision. Be sure to check with several lenders to get the best loan terms. You can get a list of lenders in your area by calling the Federal National Mortgage Association (FNMA) at 1-800-732-6643. FNMA also offers a free 84-page guide, "Money from Home," that explains reverse mortgage loans and provides worksheets to help you figure out whether one is likely to meet your needs. Another free guide, a 45-page booklet called "Home-Made Money," is available from the AARP (AARP/Fulfillment, Home Equity Information Center, 601 E. Street N.W., Washington, D.C. 20049).

Sale–Leaseback Arrangements A sale–leaseback transaction is typically arranged between retirees and their children. The parents sell their home to the child (or a partnership of two or more children), and then lease the home from the child and continue to live in it. In a sale–leaseback transaction, the parents can take advantage of the capital gains exclusion (up to $500,000 for joint filers) on the sale of their home, and finance part of the child's purchase by taking back a mortgage on the property. For the transaction to pass muster with the

IRS, the sales price, mortgage interest rate, and monthly rental for the property must be at market rates.

The sale–leaseback arrangement can benefit both you and your child, especially if your child is in a higher tax bracket than you are. The child gets tax deductions (for mortgage interest, depreciation, and property taxes) to offset the rental income she receives from you. She also gets an investment that may increase in value over the years. You'll owe taxes on the interest portion of the mortgage payment that you receive from your child, but if you're in a low tax bracket, the tax on the interest you get will be smaller than the tax deduction your child can take for paying the same interest. Both of you will benefit from lower costs by not having to pay sales commissions to arrange the transaction.

Although the transaction must be done at market prices and rates, there is leeway in determining what constitutes a fair market price, a fair rate of interest, and a fair rental agreement. Obviously, you'll want to arrive at a sales price and mortgage payment that are attractive to you, given the rental rate you negotiate. With your child as the owner, you presumably will have an excellent landlord–tenant relationship and will not have to worry about excessive rental increases or being evicted when your lease is up. Nonetheless, it's best to write into the contract some assurances as to the length of the lease and future rental charges.

Though sale–leaseback arrangements can make sense, they involve important tax and estate planning issues. Consult a qualified attorney or tax adviser to make sure the transaction is appropriate for your situation.

Getting Cash from Your Life Insurance

Another option to consider if you're having trouble making ends meet is to get cash from your life insurance policy by borrowing from it, canceling it, or rolling it over into an annuity. Do you still need the life insurance protection in the first place? If not, consider canceling, or cashing out of, your policy. Money you were paying for premiums on the policy can be used for other expenses.

In general, unless there is a very large estate for which life insurance is needed to pay estate taxes, a retiree needs life insurance coverage only to provide income for dependents after the retiree's death. If your spouse can live comfortably on the Social Security benefits, pension benefits, and investments you will leave behind, there's really no need for ongoing insurance protection. It's possible, of course, that you'd want to keep a policy anyway to leave more money for your heirs or to charity. But if you're having a tough time living from day to day, you should strongly consider getting at the cash value of your insurance. There are three basic ways to get money from an insurance policy: borrow from it, cancel it, or roll the cash value into an annuity.

Borrowing from Your Policy Borrowing against the cash value of your life insurance policy is probably the best option, since you pay no income tax on the money borrowed. The insurance company typically deducts from the loan amount interest for the first year of the loan. Likewise, subsequent interest charges are deducted from your policy's cash value. The cash value of your policy continues to earn interest, though typically at a lower rate than before you borrowed against it. If you continue to make premium payments, your policy's cash value will probably continue to rise, despite the interest charges on your loan. However, the face value of your insurance policy will decline by the amount borrowed, so if you die, the death benefit is reduced by the amount you borrowed plus the interest on the loan.

Canceling Your Policy If you cancel, or surrender, a cash-value life insurance policy, you'll get a check for the cash value, minus any surrender charge or loans outstanding on the policy. You can then spend or invest the proceeds any way you wish. Of course, this action terminates your insurance coverage. Some policies allow "partial surrenders" of the cash value and coverage. If you surrender a policy, you will owe income taxes on the portion of the cash value that exceeds the total amount of premiums you've paid over the years. If the premiums you've paid on the policy exceed the cash value, you cannot deduct the "loss" from your income, as you can with capital losses on investments. But you can take advantage of the loss in another way: a rollover into an annuity, permitted under Section 1035 of the tax law.

A Section 1035 Rollover Suppose you paid a total of $30,000 in premiums on a life insurance policy with a cash value of only $25,000. By doing a Section 1035 rollover, you could assign the old policy to a new insurance company, which then cashes in the old policy to pay for an annuity. The annuity then pays you a monthly distribution (a 70-year-old woman could expect to get more than $200 a month for the remainder of her life from a $25,000 immediate annuity).

Under Section 1035, you can carry over the $30,000 cost basis from the first policy to your annuity. That way, you won't be taxed on the first $5,000 in earnings from the annuity. Of course, an annuity won't work for you if you have a short-term need for a big chunk of cash. If you're in poor health, the annuity may turn out to be a bad deal, since you may not live long enough to collect a fair return on your money. (For more information on annuities, see Chapter 4.)

If you're not sure how much you're earning on a cash-value life insurance policy, there is one independent source for analyzing the policy and its true investment return to you. The Consumer Federation of America (CFA) will evaluate your policy (or a policy proposed by an agent) to calculate the rate of earnings on it. The CFA's Insurance Group charges $40 for an analysis ($30 for each additional analysis that you request at the same time). Do not send in the policy for evaluation. Instead, send an "in-force ledger statement," or "Illustration of Future Values," which your agent can provide, showing the policy values for the next several years, based on current mortality charges and interest rates. If there are any riders on the policy, such as a waiver of premium or accidental death benefit, send a copy of the part of your insurance policy that specifies the price of the riders. Send payment and the policy information to James H. Hunt, CFA/IG, 8 Tahanto St., Concord, NH 03301-3835.

Government Assistance

There are a variety of government programs designed to help older low-income Americans. Following are brief descriptions of three such programs: Supplemental Security Income, food stamps, and Medicaid.

Supplemental Security Income This program is run by the Social Security Administration, though money to run it comes from general tax revenue and not from Social Security payroll taxes. Many older people who are eligible for Supplemental Security Income (SSI) do not participate, often because they are unaware of the program. The Older Women's League, an advocacy group, estimates that one million older women eligible for SSI benefits do not receive them.

SSI makes monthly payments to citizens or legal residents age 65 or older who have low incomes and few assets. Although there is a basic national SSI payment (a maximum of $494 for one person in 1998, $741 for a couple), about half of the states supplement the national payment. The amount a person receives depends on the recipient's income and whether someone helps to pay for food and shelter for the recipient. The maximum income a recipient can have to qualify for SSI also varies from state to state.

The asset limit does not vary: SSI is available to single persons with assets of $2,000 or less and to couples with assets of $3,000 or less. Social Security does not count a home or most personal belongings for purposes of meeting the asset test, but it does count bank accounts, cash, and other financial assets. For information on SSI requirements and on SSI rates in your state, contact your local Social Security office. For a fuller explanation of all Social Security programs, call 1-800-772-1213 to request the free booklet, "Understanding Social Security" (Publication No. 05-10024).

Food Stamps SSI recipients generally qualify for food stamps as well, which can be used only to buy food. For more information, call Social Security at 1-800-772-1213 to request the booklet, "Supplemental Security Income" (Publication 05-11000) and the fact sheet "Food Stamp Facts" (Publication 05-10101).

Medicaid Medicaid is a program jointly funded by the states and the federal government to pay health care expenses for low-income persons. If you receive Medicare and don't have enough income and assets to pay your Medicare premiums, your state's Medicaid program may pay your Medicare premiums and, in some cases, other out-of-pocket Medicare expenses such as deductibles and co-insurance. To find out whether you qualify for such assistance, contact your state or local welfare or Medicaid office.

When the Unexpected Occurs

No matter how carefully you plan your affairs during retirement, you are subject to one of life's immutable laws: stuff happens. Any number of unforeseen events during retirement can have a big impact on your financial well-being. This section discusses some of the financial implications of some relatively common crises that can upset the retirement apple cart.

An Unexpected Addition to Your Empty Nest

"Human beings are the only creatures on earth that allow their children to come back home."

Bill Cosby

Most retirees envision an empty nest during retirement. The kids are grown and gone off on their own, and retirement becomes a period of freedom, with responsibilities limited to yourself or you and your spouse. Unfortunately, this vision of retirement increasingly does not square with reality, as more adult children than ever are returning to the nest. Divorce and the economic dislocation it brings are sometimes the reason. Other times, children simply aren't able to find work that pays enough to finance an independent lifestyle, to repay college loans, or to meet other financial obligations.

Financial and family counselors offer some tips to keep the return of an adult child from disrupting your life or becoming a permanent burden. Among their suggestions:

- Agree to keep communication lines open, to discuss gripes or problems, and to try to reach agreements for solutions to problems. You have a right to know when your child will be home at night or whether he or she plans to be home for dinner. Your child has the right not to be grilled about precise activities away from the home.
- Make sure that the child shares in work around the house. You've already cleaned, cooked, and cared for your child once; you shouldn't have to do so again.
- Have a clear understanding of what behavior is expected and what activities are forbidden in your home. Each of you should understand that the other needs some privacy.
- Negotiate a financial deal. Your child should contribute some financial resources to cover the costs of running the household, from food to utilities. Your child should also pay for telephone calls that he makes. You may even find that a separate phone line is necessary.
- If the child is unemployed, make sure that a job search is clearly understood to be the child's main duty. If your offspring won't take job-hunting seriously, you may have to insist that she departs.

Sometimes the unexpected addition to your household comes from the opposite generational direction. You may find yourself responsible for the care or financial support of a parent who has outlived his or her own financial resources. This phenomenon is a product of increasing longevity, which has made the 85-and-older age group the fastest-growing segment of the U.S. population. If you become financially responsible for the care of a parent, you should investigate sources of government assistance mentioned earlier in this chapter.

Considerations for the Recently Widowed

You should never make quick financial decisions after your spouse has died. Grief and the mourning process are difficult enough to cope with, and you should avoid added stress and complications at such times. There may be some matters you'll have to decide quickly, such as filing for probate to handle your spouse's will, or deciding how to receive payment of any life insurance benefits. But do not make long-term financial or investment decisions until you are certain you are ready and have thought through the situation.

For example, an insurer may suggest that you use life insurance proceeds to buy an annuity. While that may ultimately be the course you want to follow, there is little to be gained—and potentially much to be lost—by rushing into such decisions. You may, after reflection, decide you'd rather invest the insurance proceeds in another fashion, perhaps to pay off your mortgage. While you wait for your life to get more settled, you can safely put the money into stable, interest-bearing investments such as money market funds, short-term Treasury bills, or short-term bank CDs. Then, after you've had time to assess your financial goals and your financial situation, you can invest the money in appropriate, longer-term assets such as stocks, bonds, or mutual funds that hold stocks or bonds.

Redefining Your Financial Goals After the death of your spouse, you should reassess your financial situation and your retirement goals. Start with an inventory of your income sources, your financial assets, and your spending to see what has changed.

Unless you signed away the rights to your spouse's pension, you'll be getting a survivor's benefit from any pension plan your spouse had at work. If your spouse had an IRA or a self-directed retirement account such as a 401(k) plan, you should roll over the proceeds directly into an IRA in your name. (Be sure that the rollover goes directly from the trustee of your spouse's retirement plan to the trustee of your IRA.

If the proceeds are sent to you, the trustee of your spouse's plan will withhold 20% of the amount for taxes, and you'll have to file for a refund, even if you've rolled the money into an IRA.) You'll generally be eligible for Medicare at age 65 based on your spouse's work record, even if you haven't worked enough outside the home to qualify. Also, if you're 60 or older, you are entitled to Social Security benefits based on your deceased spouse's work record.

Your income quite likely will change after your spouse is gone. For example, income from pensions and Social Security typically declines when a spouse dies. On the other hand, if you have received life insurance proceeds, you will be able to get more income from your investments by drawing on these additional funds. Your living expenses will decline, since it's not quite true that two can live as cheaply as one. But it's unlikely that your expenses will be cut in half. You may want to use the budgeting worksheets from Chapter 2 of this guide to get a new picture of your finances.

Finally, your plans and goals may well change after your spouse is gone. You may expect to do more or less traveling, to engage in different hobbies or recreational pursuits, or to relocate to be nearer your children. Such changes in your lifestyle may alter your financial needs. If you left most investing and financial management decisions to your spouse, budget some time to learn more about money matters. Even if you decide to hire a financial planner or use the services of a broker, you'll need to become informed about finances to make good decisions and to evaluate the recommendations of your adviser.

Divorce and Retirement

Along with all the emotional and family fallout from divorce, there are important financial implications for retirees. The cost of living is almost always higher for two people living separately than for two living together. Social Security and pension payments typically are affected by a divorce, and your needs for insurance change. The following are some key financial aspects of divorce that are of special interest to retirees.

Pensions and Divorce You generally are entitled to a share of your spouse's pension assets, including company pension and profit-sharing plans, 401(k) plans, IRAs, and Keogh plans for the self-employed. The split isn't necessarily 50–50, however. Once a court determines how a couple's assets are to be divided, it can issue a qualified domestic relations order (QDRO) to give a pension plan participant access to retirement assets that must be used to pay an ex-spouse or dependent children. Because women are more likely than men to rely on the pension benefits of a spouse, it's particularly important for women to understand the ramifications of divorce on pension benefits. An excellent source of information is the book *Your Pension Rights at Divorce: What Women Need to Know.* Look for it in your local library, or send a check or money order for $23.95 to Pension Rights Center, 918 16th St. N.W., Suite 704, Washington, D.C. 20006.

Social Security and Divorce You are probably entitled to payments based on your ex-spouse's Social Security earnings record if you were married for 10 years or longer, you have not remarried, and you and your ex-spouse are both 62 or older. Even if you've remarried, you may be eligible for benefits on your ex-spouse's account if your new spouse is receiving Social Security benefits and your benefits under the new spouse's account would be lower than those you're eligible for from the account of your ex-spouse.

Other Considerations Make sure to notify, in writing, any institution where you have joint savings or investments—a bank, mutual fund, or brokerage firm—that no jointly owned asset is to be sold unless you have signed the sales order. If you have a power-of-attorney giving your spouse authority to dispose of your assets, you'll want to destroy it and notify financial institutions not to honor copies of the power.

If you had life insurance to protect your spouse, you may no longer need life insurance after a divorce. You can use the cash value from the policy to add to your investments and remove the insurance premiums from your list of expenses. Finally, unless you expect the assets to be included in the divorce settlement, change the beneficiaries of insurance policies; bank, brokerage, and mutual fund accounts; your pension; IRAs; and your will.

Final Thoughts

Uncertainty is a given in life. The only thing you can be sure of is that conditions and circumstances will change. The scenarios discussed in this chapter are, of course, only a few of the special circumstances that a retired investor may confront; it is impossible to prepare for every eventuality. Nonetheless, you may find it easier to roll with the punches that come your way if you have done some thinking in advance about how to deal with emergencies.

Conclusion

After a lifetime of work, it would be nice if the retiree could simply sail away into the sunset, without a care in the world. The reality is that most retirees will be confronted with a variety of challenges, including adapting to a new set of activities, adjusting relationships with family, friends, and former colleagues, and determining how to finance a potentially lengthy period in the face of all sorts of uncertainties.

"You are responsible for your own financial matters. I mean, it's your life and you should keep track of it."

California

While investing well before you retire is certainly a critical determinant of your retirement success, investing well *during* retirement will also be crucial in meeting its financial challenges. It is the rare individual who can live comfortably during retirement solely on the income from Social Security or pensions. Investing well requires some forethought and, frankly, some work. But one need not have a vast, specialized knowledge to invest successfully during retirement. Most retired investors will find they can manage well by following these basic guidelines, which capture the major points of this guide.

Be Knowledgeable

The retired investor needs to have some basic familiarity with the workings of the economy and the financial markets and to keep abreast of changes in the economic and financial environment. You also need to understand the nuances of your benefits under Social Security and Medicare to maximize your income and minimize health care costs. You should address basic estate-planning issues to assist your loved ones and to make sure that your assets are distributed according to your wishes after your death.

As an investor, be ever mindful of the eternal trade-off between risk and reward. There is no magic investment formula that provides high returns and low risk. You should understand how your investments have performed historically—i.e., What sort of returns have been chalked up in "good" and "bad" markets? How have they held up under unfavorable markets?—and make appropriate changes in your asset allocation as market conditions and your personal financial circumstances change. When considering an investment in a mutual fund, evaluate the fund's performance and risks in light of its investment objectives and policies. In the final analysis, you'll generally make sound fund selections if you focus on a mutual fund's continuity of management, the reputation of its sponsor, and its costs.

Be Realistic

In developing your financial plan, use realistic assumptions for returns from your investments. The inordinately high returns on all three asset classes over the past 12 to 15 years are not likely to persist in the decade ahead. Do not let impatience or fear rule your investment decisions. Remember that financial markets move in cycles, and that you should expect downturns as well as upturns. During periods of low returns, avoid the temptation to compensate by taking on too much risk in your investment portfolio.

Be Prepared

In developing and periodically evaluating your financial plans, play the "What if" game. Consider how you—and your spouse—would deal with various scenarios. What if investment returns prove to be lower or higher than you expected? What if inflation is higher than anticipated in your spending plan? What happens financially if you or your spouse becomes incapacitated or dies? You can't plan for every possibility, but thinking about various scenarios may pinpoint weaknesses in your financial plans or estate plans that you should correct.

Be Steadfast

Once you have developed a basic financial plan for retirement and your investments, stay the course through the inevitable fluctuations of financial markets. Trying to time the movements of the markets is extremely difficult and most often leads to subpar results. The temptation to make big changes in your asset allocations is strongest during or after downturns in financial markets, which are usually the worst times to shift your money around.

Be Vigilant

Periodically revisit your financial plan so that you can check the assumptions you made. If you estimated conservatively, you may find that your income is higher and your expenses lower than anticipated, enabling you to give yourself a "raise." Or you may not have anticipated some problem, and your projections may have been too optimistic. By conducting regular financial check-ups, you can spot problems early enough to correct them without taking draconian measures.

"Old age isn't too bad when you consider the alternatives."

Maurice Chevalier

Be Balanced

Invest in a combination of stocks, bonds, and short-term reserves. Such a mixture offers you the ability to generate current income for your retirement needs, to achieve some growth over time in your income, and to protect yourself against the vagaries of the financial markets. If you have sufficient assets and expertise, you can assemble a diversified, balanced portfolio by investing in individual securities. You can also hold a balanced mix of assets through mutual funds or even through a single balanced fund with the mix of assets that fits your needs. As you move through the stages of retirement, you may well wish to alter the proportions of stocks, bonds, and reserves in your portfolio. But it is the rare investor who can safely reach his or her investing objectives by sticking with one type of asset. Nearly all investors—even those well into their retirement years—should retain some representation in all three asset classes.

Be Diversified

Diversification—spreading your eggs among several baskets—is common sense; it's also uncommonly *good* sense. Whatever the investment balance you choose, spread your money among a large number of stocks and bonds. The easiest, and often the least expensive, method of achieving diversification is to invest in mutual funds. A single mutual fund portfolio can provide a level of diversification that would be hard to match with investments in individual securities.

Be Risk Aware, Not Risk Averse

You should, of course, carefully evaluate the potential risks of every investment before making the investment. The risks should be weighed in light of your personal financial situation and your ability to tolerate risk. The biggest risk is that your retirement assets will not be sufficient to meet your financial goals. Hence, you need to consider not only the risk that an investment's price will fluctuate, but also the risk that its returns will not keep up with inflation and the risk that the income it produces will fluctuate. By remembering that there is more than one type of risk, you will avoid concentrating all or nearly all of your assets in supposedly "risk-free" investments. An investment that provides stability of principal—such as a money market fund or bank CD—most certainly does not provide stability of income, a crucial consideration for an investor relying on the income to meet living expenses.

Be Cost Conscious

Cost, along with risk and return, is a crucial consideration for investors. Never forget that sales commissions, operating expenses, and investment management fees come out of your pocket, in one form or another. For mutual fund investors, sales loads and annual management and administrative expenses paid by investors reduce, dollar for dollar, the gross returns the funds earn. Thus, *other factors held equal,* the investment program with the lowest cost will provide the highest return.

If investment returns in coming years are likely to be more modest than returns of the recent past (an assumption that seems reasonable) the costs of investing can be the difference between success and failure. The difference between a high-cost fund with an annual expense ratio of 2.0% and a low-cost fund with an annual expense ratio of 0.5% may not have caught your attention during the 1987–96 decade, when stocks returned an average of 15.3% and bonds provided annual returns averaging 9.4%. But if annual returns are 7% or 8%, the cost differential is far more meaningful. A 2% expense ratio consumes one-seventh of your return when stocks are providing a 14% annual return; it consumes one-fourth of an 8% return.

Be Skeptical

Willie Sutton said that he robbed banks because "that's where the money is." For the same reason, confidence artists and investment scamsters target retired investors, who are managing substantial assets accumulated through a lifetime of work and thrift. Never invest in anything you do not understand and have not carefully analyzed. And never, ever entrust money to someone who insists that you must invest now "or miss a golden opportunity."

Similarly, if your investment returns are falling short of expectations, avoid the temptation to leap into more speculative investments in search of a big score. As Mark Twain said, "There are two times in a man's life when he should not speculate: when he can't afford it, and when he can." Avoid these common mistakes: (1) making investment decisions based on crowd psychology or the "mood of the markets"; (2) following the lead of market gurus; or (3) giving in to the allure of market timing. When selecting an investment, do not be dazzled by past returns. They indicate only how an investment performed yesterday and have virtually no value in predicting how it will perform tomorrow. Be skeptical of any financial advice, including the advice in this guide. Accept only the advice that, after careful consideration, makes sense to you and fits your financial situation.

Despite the many challenges of retirement, most retirees find this period of life enjoyable and satisfying. Those who successfully handle the financial aspects of retirement tend to have planned the voyage instead of allowing the tides and currents to sweep them along. Plan your voyage through retirement, chart your course, and then stay the course, whether the seas be calm or stormy.

Glossary

A

active investing An investment approach that seeks to exceed the returns of the financial markets. Active managers rely on research, market forecasts, and their own judgment and experience in making investment decisions.

actuarial equivalence A situation when two annuity payout options have the same actuarial value. For example, a lifetime monthly benefit of $67.60 starting at age 60 has an actuarial equivalence to a monthly benefit of $100 beginning at age 65. The value of annuity payout options varies depending on the assumed interest rate and life expectancy of the annuitant.

annuitant A person covered by an annuity contract.

annuity In general, a series of payments continuing until death. A commercial annuity is a contract issued by an insurance company that provides some level of payments for the life of the annuitant (or for an agreed-upon term of years). Fixed annuities guarantee a particular rate of interest for a certain period, after which the guaranteed rate is reset. Variable annuities permit you to allocate your money among a group of mutual funds with different investment objectives. *See also single-life annuity* and *joint-and-survivor annuity.*

annuity payout option A pension plan benefit that is paid in the form of a monthly distribution for life.

asset allocation The process of deciding how your investment dollars will be apportioned among various classes of financial assets, such as stocks, bonds, and short-term reserves, or among such "hard" assets as real estate, commodities, precious metals, and collectibles.

asset allocation fund A type of "balanced" mutual fund whose investment adviser may alter the fund's ratio of stocks, bonds, or cash reserves in an attempt to find the best balance between risk and potential returns.

asset classes Major categories of financial assets, or securities. The three primary classes are common stocks, bonds, and short-term cash reserves.

automatic investment plan An arrangement that permits regular investments in a mutual fund through payroll deductions, automatic transfers from a checking account, or automatic exchanges from another mutual fund.

automatic reinvestment An arrangement whereby distributions of mutual fund dividends or capital gains are used to purchase additional shares of a fund.

automatic withdrawal plan *See withdrawal plan.*

B

back-end load A sales commission paid when mutual fund shares are sold. May also be called a redemption fee or a contingent deferred sales charge. Some funds gradually phase out back-end loads over several years.

beneficiary The person designated to receive the proceeds of a pension, retirement account, annuity contract, or insurance policy in the event of the holder's death.

bequest Property left to an heir under the terms of a will.

bonds A form of IOU issued by corporations, governments, or government agencies. The issuer makes regular interest payments on the bond and promises to pay back, or redeem, the face value of the bond at a specified point in the future, called the maturity date. Bonds may be issued for terms of up to 30 years or sometimes even longer.

C

capital gain/loss The difference between the sales price of a capital asset, such as a stock, bond, or mutual fund share, and the cost basis of the asset. If the sales price is higher than the cost basis, there is a capital gain. If the sales price is lower than the cost basis, there is a capital loss.

capital gains distribution Payment to mutual fund shareholders of any gains realized during the year on securities that have been sold at a profit. Capital gains are distributed on a net basis, after any capital losses for the year are subtracted. When losses exceed gains for the year, the difference may be carried forward and subtracted from future gains. Capital gains distributions are usually made once a year.

certificate of deposit (CD) An insured, interest-bearing deposit at a bank, which requires the depositor to keep the money invested for a specific period of time.

compounding The interest or earnings on the principal and reinvested earnings of an investment. As Benjamin Franklin put it: "The money that money makes, makes money."

contingent deferred sales charge *See back-end load.*

credit quality A measure of a bond issuer's ability to repay interest and principal in a timely manner.

credit rating A published ranking, based on a careful financial analysis, of a creditor's ability to pay interest or principal owed on a debt.

credit risk The risk of losing money because of a borrower's inability or unwillingness to pay interest or principal owed on a debt.

custodian A bank, trust company, or other organization responsible for safeguarding financial assets.

D

defined benefit plan A retirement plan that guarantees a certain benefit, usually based on the number of years of service and on the average salary in the period before retirement. Employers bear the investment risk with defined benefit plans. In most cases, benefits are guaranteed (to a limit of $2,761.36 per month in 1997) by the federal Pension Benefit Guaranty Corp.

defined contribution plan A retirement plan offering a benefit that depends on the amount of contributions made by the employer and the employee and on the investment returns earned by those contributions. Employees bear the investment risk with defined contribution plans. *See also 401(k) plan* and *403(b) plan.*

direct transfer Moving tax-deferred retirement plan money from one plan or custodian directly to another. A transfer is not a withdrawal and therefore incurs no taxes or penalties.

diversification Spreading one's money among different classes of financial assets and among the securities of many issuers.

dividend distribution Payment to mutual fund shareholders of income from interest or dividends generated by the fund's investments. Dividends may be paid on a monthly, quarterly, semiannual, or annual basis.

dollar-cost averaging Investing equal amounts of money at regular intervals on an ongoing basis. This technique reduces risk of loss from a sudden market downturn and ensures that the investor acquires more shares during periods when prices are lower and fewer shares when prices are higher.

duration A measure of the sensitivity of bond or bond fund prices to changes in interest rates. For example, if a bond fund has an average duration of two years, its price will fall about 2% when interest rates rise by one percentage point. Conversely, the bond fund's price will rise about 2% when interest rates fall by one percentage point.

E

early withdrawal penalty A 10% penalty (in addition to ordinary income taxes owed) on money withdrawn from a tax-advantaged retirement plan before the participant reaches age 59½. The penalty does not apply in some special circumstances. Also a penalty banks charge for early redemption of a ***certificate of deposit.***

estate planning The preparation of a plan, and any related documents, to carry out your wishes as to the administration and disposition of your property before or after your death. Common elements of an estate plan include a last will, a power of attorney, and trusts.

estimated tax Tax a person is required to pay on income that is not subject to withholding tax, including investment income, alimony, rent, and capital gains.

exchange privilege The right to exchange shares in one fund for shares in another within the same fund family, typically at no charge or for a nominal fee.

expense ratio The percentage of a fund's average net assets used to pay fund expenses. The expense ratio takes into account management fees, administrative fees, and any 12b-1 marketing fees.

F

401(k) plan A defined contribution plan that allows employees to contribute part of their salary before it is taxed. Many plans offer a variety of investment options, including stocks, bonds, short-term reserves, and company stock.

403(b) plan A type of tax-sheltered annuity available to employees of the government and nonprofit organizations. Employees can make pretax contributions up to an annuity limit (generally $9,500 in 1997).

fee table A table in the front of a mutual fund's prospectus illustrating the expenses and fees a shareholder will incur.

fixed-income securities Investments, such as bonds, that have a fixed payment schedule. While the level of income offered by these securities is predetermined and usually stable, their prices may fluctuate.

forward averaging A method of calculating taxes on a lump-sum distribution from a qualified retirement plan that enables a person to pay less than his or her current tax rate.

front-end load A sales commission, or load, paid when shares of a mutual fund are purchased.

fund family A group of mutual funds sponsored by the same organization, often offering exchange privileges between funds and combined account statements for multiple funds.

I

income risk The possibility that income from a mutual fund or other investment will decline, either as a fund's assets are reinvested or when a fixed-income investment matures and is replaced with a lower-yielding investment.

individual retirement account (IRA) A tax-advantaged retirement account for workers and their spouses. Contributions to a "traditional" IRA may be fully or partially deductible up to certain limits for those who participate in employer-sponsored retirement plans. For those who do not qualify for IRA deductions, nondeductible contributions are permitted. In each instance, gains are taxable upon withdrawal. With a Roth IRA, only nondeductible contributions are allowed and income limits apply. The entire account—including all gains—can be withdrawn tax-free under certain circumstances.

inflation A general rise in the prices of goods and services. Measures of inflation include the Consumer Price Index and the Producer Price Index.

interest-rate risk The risk that a security or mutual fund will decline in price because of changes in interest rates.

investment adviser An individual or organization that manages a portfolio and makes day-to-day investment decisions regarding the purchase or sale of securities.

investment horizon The length of time one expects to keep a sum of money invested. A 62-year-old who is just starting retirement may have an investment horizon of 30 years or more.

investment objective A mutual fund's performance goal, such as long-term capital appreciation, high current income, or tax-exempt income.

J

joint-and-survivor annuity An annuity covering two people and paying benefits until both have died. A 100% joint-and-survivor annuity pays the same benefit to both annuitants. A 50% joint-and-survivor annuity pays the surviving annuitant only half of the amount paid to the first annuitant.

L

life expectancy The age to which an average person is expected to live, as calculated by actuaries. Life expectancy is affected by many factors, including current age, sex, heredity, and health characteristics.

living trust A trust established when you are alive, enabling you to control the assets that you contribute to the trust. Also called an *inter vivos* trust.

living will A document in which a person specifies the kind of medical care he or she wants—or does not want—in the event of terminal illness or incapacity.

load fund A mutual fund that charges a sales commission, or load.

low-load fund A mutual fund that charges a sales commission equal to 3% or less of the amount invested.

lump-sum distribution A payment that represents an employee's interest in a qualified retirement plan. The payment must be prompted by retirement (or other separation from service), death, disability, or attainment of age 59½, and must be made within a single tax year. Lump-sum distributions are eligible for ***rollover*** into another qualified plan or for ***forward averaging.***

M

management fee The fee paid by a mutual fund to its investment adviser.

manager risk The possibility that a fund's investment adviser will do a poor job of selecting securities for the fund.

market risk The possibility that an investment will fall in value because of a general decline in financial markets.

marital deduction A provision of federal estate tax law that allows one spouse to transfer at death an unlimited amount of property to another spouse without incurring estate tax.

Medicaid A program that pays for medical care for the poor. Medicaid is funded jointly by states and the federal government.

Medicare The federal program that pays for health care for people age 65 or older. It is supported by a combination of payroll taxes and premiums charged to beneficiaries of the program.

mutual fund An open-end investment company that pools money from individuals and uses it to buy securities such as stocks, bonds, and money market instruments. Mutual funds issue and redeem shares on a daily basis at net asset value, minus any applicable sales commissions.

N

net asset value (NAV) The market value of a mutual fund's total assets, less its liabilities, divided by the number of shares outstanding.

net worth The total value of an individual's assets, less the value of any outstanding debts.

no-load fund A mutual fund that charges no sales commission, or load.

nominal return The return on an investment before adjustment for inflation. ***See real return.***

nonqualified plan A retirement plan that does not meet the IRS requirements for favorable tax treatment.

normal retirement age The age at which a participant in Social Security or a private pension plan is eligible for full retirement benefits.

O

offering price The purchase price of a mutual fund share, determined by adding any applicable sales charge to the fund's net asset value (NAV) per share. Also known as *ask price.* ***See also redemption price.***

P

passive investing An investment approach that seeks to mimic the return and risk characteristics of a discrete market segment, or index, by holding all the securities that compose the market segment or a statistically representative sample. ***See also active investing.***

pension plan A retirement plan under which an employer provides benefits or contributions toward retirement benefits for employees who meet certain criteria.

portfolio All the securities that are held by a mutual fund; or the total investment holdings of an individual.

portfolio manager ***See investment adviser.***

portfolio transaction costs The costs associated with buying and selling securities, including commissions on stocks, dealer markups on bonds, bid–ask spreads, and any other miscellaneous expenses.

power of attorney A document that grants someone the authority to perform certain acts on behalf of the individual who signs the document. The power of attorney may be limited or full.

principal The amount of your own money you put into an investment.

prospectus A legal document providing pertinent information about a mutual fund, including discussions of the fund's investment objectives and policies, risks, costs, past performance, and other information useful to prospective investors.

Q

qualified plan A retirement plan approved by the IRS and eligible for favorable tax treatment. Employer contributions are deductible as business expenses, and earnings on plan assets are not taxed until they are distributed, or withdrawn.

R

real return Investment return, adjusted for inflation. For example, if the nominal investment return for a particular period is 8% and inflation is 3%, the real return is 5%.

redemption fee ***See back-end load.***

redemption price *Also bid* or *sell price.* The price at which a mutual fund's shares can be redeemed, determined by deducting any applicable sales charge from the net asset value (NAV) per share. ***See also offering price.***

required minimum distribution The amount that must be withdrawn each year from all your retirement plans once you reach age 70½. Withdrawals can be made based on your life expectancy or on the joint life expectancy of you and your primary beneficiary.

reverse mortgage An arrangement in which a homeowner borrows against the equity in the home and receives regular monthly payments from the lender for as long as the homeowner lives in the residence.

risk tolerance An investor's personal ability or willingness to withstand declines in the prices of investments.

rollover Moving all or part of the balance of a tax-deferred retirement plan into an IRA or other eligible plan, thus avoiding any current tax liability.

Roth IRA *See individual retirement account.*

S

Securities and Exchange Commission The federal government agency that regulates mutual funds, registered investment advisers, the stock and bond markets, and securities broker–dealers.

short-term reserves Investments in short-term, interest-bearing bank deposits, money market instruments, and U.S. Treasury bills or notes.

single-life annuity An annuity covering one person. There are two types of single-life annuities. A straight life annuity provides payments until death. A life annuity with a guaranteed period provides payments until death or continues payments to a beneficiary for a guaranteed term, such as 10 years.

statement of additional information A separate document that supplements a mutual fund's prospectus. It contains more detailed information about fund policies, operations, and investment risks, and lists officers and directors of the fund and their compensation. Also known as *Part B* of the prospectus. Available on request from the mutual fund sponsor.

stocks Securities that represent part ownership, or equity, in a corporation. Each share of stock is a claim on its proportionate stake in the corporation's assets and profits, some of which may be paid out as dividends.

T

12b-1 fee An annual fee some mutual funds charge to pay for marketing and distribution activities.

tax-deferred retirement plan Any retirement plan in which earnings are not currently taxable.

tax-exempt bond A bond whose interest payments are not subject to income tax. Bonds issued by municipal, county, and state governments and agencies typically are federally tax-exempt and may also be exempt from state or local income taxes. Also known as a *municipal bond.*

total return The percentage change, over a particular period, in the value of an investment, including both any income produced by the investment and any change in its market value.

trust A legal arrangement under which a fiduciary, or trustee, holds title to assets (investments, real estate, etc.) for the benefit of another person or persons.

turnover rate A measure of a mutual fund's trading activity. Turnover is calculated by taking the lesser of the fund's total purchases or total sales of securities (not counting securities with maturities under one year) and dividing by the average monthly assets. A turnover rate of 50% means that during a year, a fund has sold and replaced securities with a value equal to 50% of the fund's average net assets.

U

unified tax credit A federal tax credit that may be applied against the gift tax, the estate tax and, under certain limited circumstances, the generation-skipping transfer tax. Each individual is entitled to a credit sufficient to shield $600,000 in assets from estate tax in 1997, gradually increasing to $1 million in 2006.

V

volatility The fluctuations in market value of a mutual fund or other security. The greater a fund's volatility, the wider the fluctuations between its high and low prices.

W

withdrawal Taking money out of a tax-advantaged retirement plan, which makes it subject to tax and, if you're under age 59½, to possible penalty.

withdrawal plan A method of gradually converting one's mutual fund balance into income by arranging for regular (usually monthly) redemptions of a preset dollar amount. Also known as a *systematic withdrawal plan.*

Y

yield The annualized rate at which an investment earns income, expressed as a percentage of the investment's current price.

Worksheets

Appendix A

Net Worth Worksheet

See Chapter 2 for more information.

Assets	Current Value
Short-Term Reserves	
Checking account	$ ________
Savings account	________
Money market mutual funds	________
Certificates of deposit	________
U.S. Treasury bills	________
Cash value of life insurance	________
Taxable Accounts	
Stocks	________
Bonds	________
Stock mutual funds	________
Bond mutual funds	________
Tax-Exempt Accounts	
Municipal bonds	________
Municipal bond mutual funds	________
Tax-Deferred Investments	
IRA/Keogh accounts	________
Employer savings plan (e.g., 401(k), 403(b), profit-sharing)	________
Pension (lump-sum value)	________
Accumulated value of annuity (fixed or variable)	________
Personal Property	
Principal home	________
Vacation home	________
Rental property	________

Assets *(continued)*	Current Value
Personal Property (continued)	
Partnership or business ownership	$ ________
Cars, trucks, boats	________
Home furnishings	________
Art, antiques, coins, collectibles	________
Jewelry, furs	________
Other assets	________
TOTAL ASSETS	$ ________

Liabilities	
Current	
Credit card balances	$ ________
Margin loans on securities	________
Estimated income tax owed	________
Other outstanding bills	________
Long-Term	
Home mortgage balance	________
Home equity loan	________
Mortgage on rental property	________
Car loans	________
Tuition loans	________
Life insurance policy loan	________
Other long-term debt	________
TOTAL LIABILITIES	$ ________
NET WORTH (Assets – Liabilities)	$ ________

Budget Worksheet

See Chapter 2 for more information.

Your Projected Expenses	Monthly Amount	× 12	Annual Amount
Housing			
Mortgage/rent payment	$ _______		$ _______
Utilities			
Heat	_______		_______
Electricity	_______		_______
Sewer	_______		_______
Trash removal	_______		_______
Water	_______		_______
Telephone	_______		_______
Cable television	_______		_______
Property taxes	_______		_______
Homeowners'/renters' insurance	_______		_______
Maintenance/repairs	_______		_______
Association/management fees	_______		_______
Furniture/appliances	_______		_______
Household incidental items	_______		_______
Transportation			
Auto expenditures			
Auto loan	_______		_______
Auto insurance	_______		_______
License/registration fees	_______		_______
Maintenance	_______		_______
Gasoline	_______		_______
Public transportation	_______		_______
Food			
Groceries and beverages	_______		_______
Dining out	_______		_______
Health Care and Personal			
Health care			
Insurance			
Health	_______		_______
Life	_______		_______
Disability	_______		_______
Medicare Part B	_______		_______
Medigap	_______		_______
Long-term care	_______		_______
Out-of-pocket medical	_______		_______
Out-of-pocket dental	_______		_______

Budget Worksheet *(continued)*

Your Projected Expenses	Monthly Amount	× 12	Annual Amount
Health care *(continued)*			
Out-of-pocket vision	$ ______		$ ______
Prescriptions	______		______
Other	______		______
Personal care			
Clothing	______		______
Cosmetics/toiletries	______		______
Barber/beauty care	______		______
Dry cleaning	______		______
Other Expenditures			
Entertainment			
Club dues	______		______
Movies	______		______
Activities/admission fees	______		______
Hobbies	______		______
Subscriptions	______		______
Travel/vacation			
Airfare	______		______
Train	______		______
Hotel/motel	______		______
Other	______		______
Taxes			
Personal property taxes	______		______
Other taxes	______		______
Other debt			
Credit card debt	______		______
Home equity loan	______		______
Other	______		______
Gifts			
Family/friends	______		______
Charitable contributions	______		______
Alimony	______		______
Dependent care	______		______
Education	______		______
Professional dues	______		______
Pet care	______		______
Other ______	______		______
Other ______	______		______
Other ______	______		______
TOTAL PROJECTED EXPENSES	$ ______		$ ______

Income Worksheet

See Chapter 2 for more information.

Your Projected Income	Monthly Amount	× 12	Annual Amount
Social Security			
You	$ ______		$ ______
Your spouse	______		______
Wages			
You	______		______
Your spouse	______		______
Pension			
You	______		______
Your spouse	______		______
Other Income			
Income from your home	______		______
Rental income	______		______
Trust income	______		______
Dividend income	______		______
Interest	______		______
Annuities	______		______
Royalties	______		______
Veterans' benefits	______		______
Other income	______		______
TOTAL INCOME	$ ______		$ ______

Will I Have Enough to Meet My Retirement Spending Plans?

See Chapter 8 for complete instructions.

	Alice and Ralph	Your Situation
Income Summary		
1. Social Security	$1,250	
2. Pension	800	
3. Other income (e.g., rental payments, part-time job)	425	
4. Total income (Line 1 + Line 2 + Line 3)	2,475	
Your Retirement Assumptions		
5. Investment return	7%	
6. Retirement period (in years)	30	
Withdrawal Factors		
7. Level income factor (Table 8–5)	0	
8. Rising income factor (Table 8–5)	0.0489	
How Much Can You Withdraw from Your Investments?		
9. Retirement lump-sum savings	150,000	
10. Level income, annual (Line 9 × Line 7)	0	
11. Level income, monthly (Line 10 ÷ 12)	0	
12. Rising income, annual (Line 9 × Line 8)	7,330	
13. Rising income, monthly (Line 8 ÷ 12)	610	
The Reality Check		
14. Total monthly retirement income (Line 4 + Line 11 or Line 13)	3,085	
15. Your monthly retirement budget	3,000	
16. Monthly surplus (shortfall)	$ 85	

Note: Figures in our example are rounded and assume a 4% annual rate of inflation.

Personal Records and Financial Summary

Appendix **B**

Personal Information

Full name: ______________________ ______________________
Husband *Wife*

Maiden name: ______________________
Wife

Social Security No.: ______________________ ______________________
Husband *Wife*

Residence Address: ______________________

Previous Address: ______________________

Place/Date of Birth: ______________________ ______________________
Husband *Wife*

Marital Status: (single/married/divorced/widowed) ______________ ______________
Husband *Wife*

Children:

Name ______________________ Name ______________________

DOB __________ SS# __________ DOB __________ SS# __________

Name ______________________ Name ______________________

DOB __________ SS# __________ DOB __________ SS# __________

Parents:

Father's Name ______________________ ______________________
Husband *Wife*

Mother's Name ______________________ ______________________
Husband *Wife*

Veteran:

Husband
Branch of Service ______________________

Rank/Serial No. ______________________

Date of Discharge ______________________

Wife
Branch of Service ______________________

Rank/Serial No. ______________________

Date of Discharge ______________________

Education:

	School	Degree	Year
Husband			
Wife			

Professional Contacts

Attorney Name: ______________ Telephone: ______________
Address: ______________________________

Accountant Name: ______________ Telephone: ______________
Address: ______________________________

Insurance agent Name: ______________ Telephone: ______________
Address: ______________________________

Bank officer Name: ______________ Telephone: ______________
Address: ______________________________

Financial adviser Name: ______________ Telephone: ______________
Address: ______________________________

Stockbroker Name: ______________ Telephone: ______________
Address: ______________________________

Physician Name: ______________ Telephone: ______________
Address: ______________________________

Clergy Name: ______________ Telephone: ______________
Address: ______________________________

Other __________ Name: ______________ Telephone: ______________
Address: ______________________________

Other __________ Name: ______________ Telephone: ______________
Address: ______________________________

Location of Important Documents	
Automobile titles	________________
Bank records/account statements	________________
Birth certificates	________________
Burial plot deeds	________________
Citizenship papers/passports	________________
Divorce papers	________________
Insurance policies	________________
Living will	________________
Marriage certificate	________________
Medical insurance records	________________
Medicare cards	________________
Military discharge papers	________________
Mutual fund/stock/bond certificates	________________
Power-of-attorney documents	________________
Rental property leases	________________
Retirement documents	________________
Social Security cards	________________
Tax returns/receipts/canceled checks	________________
Title/deeds/mortgage agreements	________________
Trust agreements	________________
Will	________________
Other ____________	________________
Other ____________	________________
Other ____________	________________

Insurance Policies (Life, Health, Auto, Home)

Insurance company ______________________________

Policy type ____________________ Policy number ____________________

Amount insured ____________________ Beneficiary ____________________

Covers (who/what) ______________________________

Insurance company ______________________________

Policy type ____________________ Policy number ____________________

Amount insured ____________________ Beneficiary ____________________

Covers (who/what) ______________________________

Insurance company ______________________________

Policy type ____________________ Policy number ____________________

Amount insured ____________________ Beneficiary ____________________

Covers (who/what) ______________________________

Insurance company ______________________________

Policy type ____________________ Policy number ____________________

Amount insured ____________________ Beneficiary ____________________

Covers (who/what) ______________________________

Real Estate

Type ______________________________

Location ______________________________

Purchase date ____________________ Purchase price ____________________

Type ______________________________

Location ______________________________

Purchase date ____________________ Purchase price ____________________

Type ______________________________

Location ______________________________

Purchase date ____________________ Purchase price ____________________

Safe-Deposit Boxes

Owner(s) of assets ______________________________

Name and address of bank ______________________________

____

Box number ______________ Location of keys ______________

Power-of-attorney ______________________________

Contents ______________________________

____

Owner(s) of assets ______________________________

Name and address of bank ______________________________

____

Box number ______________ Location of keys ______________

Power-of-attorney ______________________________

Contents ______________________________

____

Bank Records (CDs, Checking, Savings)

Name of institution ______________ Account type ______________

Account owner(s) ______________________________

Account number ______________ Maturity date (if CD) ______________

Name of institution ______________ Account type ______________

Account owner(s) ______________________________

Account number ______________ Maturity date (if CD) ______________

Name of institution ______________ Account type ______________

Account owner(s) ______________________________

Account number ______________ Maturity date (if CD) ______________

Name of institution ______________ Account type ______________

Account owner(s) ______________________________

Account number ______________ Maturity date (if CD) ______________

Mutual Fund Investments

Name of company ______________________________
Account owner(s) (individual/joint) ______________________________
Fund name ______________________ Account number ______________________

Name of company ______________________________
Account owner(s) (individual/joint) ______________________________
Fund name ______________________ Account number ______________________

Name of company ______________________________
Account owner(s) (individual/joint) ______________________________
Fund name ______________________ Account number ______________________

Name of company ______________________________
Account owner(s) (individual/joint) ______________________________
Fund name ______________________ Account number ______________________

Name of company ______________________________
Account owner(s) (individual/joint) ______________________________
Fund name ______________________ Account number ______________________

Name of company ______________________________
Account owner(s) (individual/joint) ______________________________
Fund name ______________________ Account number ______________________

Name of company ______________________________
Account owner(s) (individual/joint) ______________________________
Fund name ______________________ Account number ______________________

Name of company ______________________________
Account owner(s) (individual/joint) ______________________________
Fund name ______________________ Account number ______________________

Name of company ______________________________
Account owner(s) (individual/joint) ______________________________
Fund name ______________________ Account number ______________________

Individual Stocks

Brokerage firm ____________________

Brokerage account number (if applicable) ____________________

Number of shares__________ Purchase date__________ Purchase price __________

Brokerage firm ____________________

Brokerage account number (if applicable) ____________________

Number of shares__________ Purchase date__________ Purchase price __________

Brokerage firm ____________________

Brokerage account number (if applicable) ____________________

Number of shares__________ Purchase date__________ Purchase price __________

Brokerage firm ____________________

Brokerage account number (if applicable) ____________________

Number of shares__________ Purchase date__________ Purchase price __________

Individual Bonds (Corporate, Municipal, Treasury)

Issuer ____________________ Number of bonds __________

Purchase date__________ Purchase price __________ Maturity date __________

Issuer ____________________ Number of bonds __________

Purchase date__________ Purchase price __________ Maturity date __________

Issuer ____________________ Number of bonds __________

Purchase date__________ Purchase price __________ Maturity date __________

Issuer ____________________ Number of bonds __________

Purchase date__________ Purchase price __________ Maturity date __________

Issuer ____________________ Number of bonds __________

Purchase date__________ Purchase price __________ Maturity date __________

Issuer ____________________ Number of bonds __________

Purchase date__________ Purchase price __________ Maturity date __________

Retirement Accounts [IRA, Self-Directed IRA, 401(k), Keogh Plans: Profit Sharing, Money Purchase Pension]

Name of company ______________________________

Trustee ______________________ Plan type ______________________

Account owner ______________________ Account number ______________________

Beneficiary ______________________________

Name of company ______________________________

Trustee ______________________ Plan type ______________________

Account owner ______________________ Account number ______________________

Beneficiary ______________________________

Name of company ______________________________

Trustee ______________________ Plan type ______________________

Account owner ______________________ Account number ______________________

Beneficiary ______________________________

Name of company ______________________________

Trustee ______________________ Plan type ______________________

Account owner ______________________ Account number ______________________

Beneficiary ______________________________

Name of company ______________________________

Trustee ______________________ Plan type ______________________

Account owner ______________________ Account number ______________________

Beneficiary ______________________________

Name of company ______________________________

Trustee ______________________ Plan type ______________________

Account owner ______________________ Account number ______________________

Beneficiary ______________________________

Index